The Theory and Interpretation
of NARRATIVE Series

Invisible
AUTHOR

LAST ESSAYS

Christine Brooke-Rose

THE OHIO STATE UNIVERSITY PRESS
Columbus

COPYRIGHT © 2002 BY THE OHIO STATE UNIVERSITY
All rights reserved.

Library of Congress Cataloguing-in-Publication Data

Brooke-Rose, Christine, 1923–
    Invisible author : last essays / by Christine Brooke-Rose.
    p. cm.—(The theory and interpretation of narrative series)
    Includes bibliographical references and index.
    ISBN 0-8142-0893-2 (cloth: alk. cloth)
    1. Brooke-Rose, Christine, 1923—Authorship. 2. Brooke-Rose,
    Christine, 1923—Interviews. 3. Authors, English—20th
    century—Interviews. I. Title. II. Series
    PR6003.R412 Z465 2002
    823'.914—dc21
                                2001006333

Cover and text design by Jennifer Shoffey Carr
Type set in Adobe Sabon by Jennifer Shoffey Carr
Printed by Thomson-Shore, Inc.

The paper used in this publication meets the mimimum requirement of the American National Standard for Information Sciences—Permanence of Paper for Printed Library Materials. ANSI Z39.48-1992

9 8 7 6 5 4 3 2 1

Je veux . . . que la mort me treuve plantant mes choulx, mais nonchalant d'elle, et encores plus de mon jardin imparfaict.

—MONTAIGNE, *Essais,* Book 1, Chapter 19

ConTENTS

1	Invisible Author	1
2	Splitlitcrit	20
3	A Writer's Constraints	36
4	Remaking	53
5	Is Self-Reflexivity Mere?	63
6	Interlude: Exsul	109
7	The Author Is Dead Long Live the Author	130
8	Two Codas	156
9	Interview by Lorna Sage: Subscript	169
	NOTES	181
	REFERENCES	187
	INDEX	195

1
Invisible AUTHOR

HAVE YOU EVER TRIED to do something very difficult as well as you can, over a long period, and found that nobody notices? That's what I've been doing for over thirty years.

In many ways I've been glad, because it has allowed me to do what I wanted, with very little compromise, and I've had just the amount of success needed to continue. More would have been fatal, for I've always valued peace above all and could never have coped with real hype. But now that I have stopped, I have been wondering: why do both praise and blame often seem so irrelevant to what authors are actually doing?

By "very difficult" I don't mean difficult for the reader to read but difficult for the author to write. In theory, at any rate, the end result of the specific constraints I shall be discussing should be invisible as such; in practice (otherwise the author wouldn't do it) it does alter the text read by the reader, who feels it as unfamiliar and for that reason alone drops it, dismisses it, the pleasure of recognition being generally stronger than the pleasure or puzzlement of discovery.

Of course the notion of difficulty, once so dear to the Moderns, is itself highly variable, but in addition it has now become unfashionable. It is still accepted for the sciences (intellectual) and for sport (physical), both highly élitist, requiring long training and huge effort, so that even popularizations are accepted as not giving real access, only an illusion of it. However, the humanities, especially literature, seem sometimes to have survived only by increasingly allowing that illusion to pass for reality. More and more blur became more and more accepted as the norm.

The Structuralist attempt in the fifties and sixties to counter this already sliding blur by creating a "science" of literature was a catastrophe, though it taught many of us a greater rigor of thought. But it brought its own jargonesque obscurity.[1] Then, when Structuralism was over, it was the sliding blur that won and pervades.

So I decided to edit this book, as a writer but also as a long practicing critic, theorist, and teacher, in order to analyze this seemingly new irrelevance of criticism. I do so in the name of all fiction writers, but use for practical reasons my own work by way of example, partly because it is particularly apposite to the problem, partly because I know it best and have it by me, but mostly because I am now too infirm to do a full scholarly job on other authors and their misrepresenters. I can appreciate the problem because my topics were usually attention-catching, so that I did catch plenty, but not for my actual, though modest, contribution. And it is this ignored aspect that has remained salient for me, not so much as writer (who is content to say "go, little book," etc.) but more as critic, because it raises several much more important theoretical points that underlie all that I shall later have to say.

The difficult thing I've been doing, on and off, for thirty-six years, has a technical name: a lipogram, though I prefer the word *constraint.* I didn't learn the technical name until well after I'd developed it. A lipogram (from Greek *leipein,* remove, + *gramma,* letter) is a self-imposed omission, and presumably the term can be extended to cover more than a letter, since *gramma* also means "writing." My main lipogram, in this slightly extended sense, begun in 1961–62 (*Out* 1964) and developed in most of my novels since, is a refusal of the narrative past tense, replaced by a simultaneous present tense. This has now percolated through, and is quite frequently but conventionally used as part of the speech system (i.e., with its pronouns). I use the present tense in a specific, paradoxical way I owe to the French writer Alain Robbe-Grillet, and I shall be dealing with this later. I lead up to it gradually and come to it in chapter 7, where I analyze this particular feature: its history, its grammatical mechanism, and my development of it. In theory, however, it is not necessary to understand all this background (after all, I didn't) to notice the narrative method, which creates my individual tone. I have had very high-quality treatment from my critics, both reviewers and academics. Yet for thirty-six years now not a single one has been able or willing to formulate this one feature, my narrative technique, accurately. Nor, for that matter, could I, nor did Robbe-Grillet himself, nor did the best and most rigorous narratologist Gérard

Genette (1972) on Robbe-Grillet, though he deals with him otherwise enlighteningly. Hence this book, which indeed could be called *The Loneliness of the Long-Distance Experimenter*, except that I'm never lonely.

That's for my main lipogram. I have also added punctual ones, which are as difficult for the writer but easier to discuss, once known, such as no verb *to be* in one novel, no verb *to have* in another, or only the future and other "nonrealized" tenses in yet another, and no pronouns in two more. These are much closer to what is usually called a lipogram, and I shall be analyzing my reasons and usage during some of the following chapters as well as the whole problem of "visibility/invisibility" raised by the lipogram in the first place. It is this specific feature alone that is the topic of this book, not my delightful fans and truly supporting critics, although I shall devote the second chapter to the general critical background that has produced this "invisibility."[2]

The term *lipogram* sprang into fashion with the most famous modern example, Georges Perec's *La Disparition* (1969), written entirely without the letter *e*, an almost impossible feat in French;[3] requiring, moreover, occasional contortions, such as putting a needed word in English, or in Latin. The novel also tells of a fictional character's disappearance, paralleling that of the character *e*.

Perec's appeared in 1969, just a few months after my own novel *Between* (1968, so there is no possible influence either way), in which, having already developed my main and continuous lipogram begun in *Out* and *Such* (1966), I also add the punctual one of omitting the verb *to be*. I shall return to the reasons in a later chapter, as well as to other lipograms, which are all grammatical, not alphabetical—and grammar is a far more complex system than the alphabet. My point here is only the noticing. Perec told of his lipogram and got lots of attention, then and ever since, just as Eliot printed footnotes to *The Waste Land* and Joyce was careful to leave keys that soon overcame both the horror at "obscenity" and the mystification about meaning, keys that initiated and continue to feed the immense Joyce industry. I said nothing and was more than spared the industry: no one noticed.

That in fact is not quite true: I did tell one person in France, Hélène Cixous, who at the time (1968, but before the publication of *Between*) had written to me in London and asked me to explain my novels, since she was writing an article on me for *Le Monde*. I did so. My surprise was great when the article came out, a weirdly posh rehash of my letter but discussing only *Out* and *Such* so that the absence of *to be* appeared to apply to them. I didn't mind—it was not my main lipogrammic technique (which I had not mentioned), only a punctual one, and indeed I had forgotten all about it until I saw the mistake picked up in a student thesis. I only cite this as an example of what George Steiner (1972) a little later called the apparent difficulty that comes from the critic not doing his homework. Cixous was busy at the time founding, with a few colleagues, the new left-wing University of Vincennes (Paris VIII), which she had invited me to join, so that I was in Paris in December when the article came out. Still, in this case, she had initiated the request, and even with the best intentions of a good turn, it was more than not doing one's homework, it was simply not reading. It is also an example, not at all typical of Cixous, of the trend that has arisen in the last twenty years or so of simply asking the author—but I'll return to that in chapter 2.

Of course one can hardly expect a lipogram—the absence of something—to be noticed (unless mentioned) in the way, say, an extravagant or a pornographic style attracts notice. Nor did I expect it, for my reasons were my own, part of the writing, explored in chapter 3, and not attention-getting. My point is that the only person I did mention it to wasn't interested. And this continued to be the case, not only with my narrative lipogram or constraint but with all other more punctual constraints I used, both earlier and later, mentioned or unmentioned. If mentioned (e.g., in the blurb, or an interview), the fact might be repeated as mere fact or ignored. Either way, it aroused not a glimmer of curiosity.[4] This indifference raises several general points, old ones, of the sort that come in and out of fashion.

The first point is the common experience, repeated many times, that while any experiment with the language or the conventions of the novel is at first automatically overlooked, this applies much more consistently and durably to a woman experimenter than to a man. A man experimenter, once he does attract attention, is innovative, bold, original, and so on, in articles that show a knowledge of development from precedents; a woman experimenter is just, well, an experimenter, the term often slightly pejorative, without further exploration. Indeed, any noticed or imagined development from precedents is mentioned only for dismissal as imitation. Sacred cows are mysteriously needed but must be male. Any female who left "keys" would be laughed out of court or ignored, as I shall be, no doubt (see second point below). I have long accepted all this, for reasons profoundly buried in the literary male unconscious, which I analyzed in an essay called "Illiterations," contributed to a collection on that very topic (Friedman and Fuchs 1989, repr. in Brooke-Rose, *Stories, Theories,* 1991), and I have nothing further to add on the topic.

The second point raised is the current double paradox, that despite the long taboo on author intention (reanalyzed in chapter 2), writers are constantly invited to talk about their work (first paradox), though the taboo survives in that they are not supposed to *write* about it (second paradox). As this is my last publication, consisting wholly (apart from this introductory chapter, a short chapter 8 as *coda,* and the final interview) of lectures I was invited to give about my work—or "what I am trying to do"—lectures that were all published, I shall happily ignore that contradiction. In other words, I will break the rules, since reviewers break the most fundamental rule constantly by merely repeating the blurb rather than reading. I shall try to differentiate the evaluative aspect of criticism, which an author clearly cannot undertake, from the technical aspect and its history, which, as professional critic, I have never ceased to apply to myself, though privately.

The third point raised is that of the author's presence and tone. In the early fifties there was a revolt of young English writers against the "Apocalyptic" poets who followed Dylan Thomas and the manderin Modernist style and its classical allusions. It was the tail end of a movement that started much earlier in the century, against the author's "authority" in the novel (see chapter 7). I well remember how Kingsley Amis, then one of these new young writers, both novelist and poet, gave a radio talk in which he emphasized that the poet shouldn't be seen "doing his stuff," meaning , at the time, showing his learning with allusions, clever world-play, and so on.[5] This was the beginning of "The Movement," and no doubt a healthy anti-mandarin reaction, but of course it doesn't represent a general rule, otherwise we shouldn't have had Shakespeare, or Donne, or Milton, or Pope. By the sixties and seventies the so-called Postmodern novelists had started their "look-at-me" tricks in America, with later reactions against that. I have written elsewhere about these (1981, 1991) and here will only stress the irony of my lipogrammic "invisibility", which agrees with that so-called rule, having on the contrary stamped me as only too visibly "doing my stuff," though few can say quite what it is.

The fourth point raised, or at least touched on unwittingly—of which the third represents only a superficial symptom—is another age-old dispute between form and content, so old that nobody wants to discuss it anymore. Indeed, the very order of the words usually reveals the higher value placed on content. In the English "form and content," form comes first with I. A. Richards in the twenties and then with the New Criticism, both out of fashion, but in the later "story and technique" (often called "mere" despite its link to Greek *techne,* which meant skill, art), it comes second. On the Continent, form traditionally comes second, even when the emphasis is (briefly) on form, so strong is the swiftly recurring preference for content: *le fond/la forme, histoire/discours, énoncé/énonciation, signifié/signifiant,* Realism/Formalism, and so on. Genette's *Discours du récit* (1972, see chapter 3) is a rare exception.

This preference for content seems relatively modern. Right through classical, medieval, and Renaissance times, there were always rhetorics, both descriptive and prescriptive "technical" treatments of how to write. Both Chaucer and Shakespeare mocked them but used them. There were disputes on rhyme and other such topics, and Pope enjoyed miming, in his verse, the overuse of open vowels or expletives or "a needless Alexandrine" (*An Essay on Criticism* 1709). Perhaps Shelley's defense of poets as "unacknowledged legislators"—not of a work, but of mankind—initiated this change (*Defence of Poetry,* 1821, publ. 1840). Or perhaps Hegel did, with his treatment of Formalism as mere decoration in the preface to *The Phenomenology of Mind* (1807), the more important term for him being Realism. I shall briefly return to this in chapter 3.

Perhaps, too, there is an element of superstition in the dislike of "technique," a strong sense of not wanting to find out how the magician performs his illusions: the poet mustn't be seen "doing his stuff." But as this is clearly not so with the other arts (such as the endless analyses of special effects in film), the technical reluctance seems in practice to be reserved for literature, where it has long been unpopular, "pretentious" (as Sarraute observed in 1947, repr. in Sarraute 1956), indeed impossible, to discuss any technical aspect of writing. This is presumably because words have referents, as color, shape, and sound do not, so that the other arts break through earlier, when innovative (partly because it's easier to enjoy color, shape and sound and even to fake understanding), whereas referents "take over," leading straight to "significance," the story, the characters, their psychology, the underlying philosophy—in other words the content—which must be understood in order to summarize.

It's true that in the U.S., and much later in England (though not at all in Europe), writing could be taught but had to be distinguished from "mere" writing with the word *creative*. I'm not sure whether the many schools of creative writing teach "technique" or only "topics," but I am sure that when I taught one such course in America, narratological detail was enthusiastically responded to. There are now Ph.D.s in creative writing. Presumably these schools deal with technique, as do art schools and schools of music. So the pendulum may slowly be swinging back, for a while at least.

༺༻

I don't know how it came about, but as far back as I can remember I have always been passionately interested in form, by which I then meant language. I had chosen the medieval course in Oxford just after the war because I thought the word *philology* meant "linguistics." I suffered, but learned a lot. Back in London doing a doctorate, I chased *Linguistics* in the British Museum catalogue and fell upon Saussure, *Cours de linguistique générale* (1915). This was in 1950, before the French fuss about him and about Structuralist linguistics generally, then ignored by philologists, as was a growing discipline called Stylistics, where I also discovered the early French analyses of *style indirect libre* (free indirect discourse), which was to play such a part in the quarrels about the "author's voice" (see chapters 3 and 7). But I wasn't yet a practitioner. Both Structuralist Linguistics and Stylistics were to die anyway, but at least I got away from pure phonology and medieval dialects. What I was after was literary form.

Perhaps the very words *form* and *content* had already become too vague. In what eventually became my very first critical work (an adaptation of my thesis), I avoided them and chose two simple adverbs, nominalized as the "how" and the "what," which seemed innocuous. Even then I put the how first.

Why? Because I was in fact analyzing the how of metaphor, which cuts right across the what (meaning, value) or the why (why is love called a fire, that is, the mental links between the two terms). The thesis was about metaphor in medieval French and English lyrics and romances. I had been fascinated by my observations that metaphors in Old English (Anglo-Saxon) poetry were mostly kennings, that is, two nouns juxtaposed in an implied genitive relation (e.g., "whale-path" for sea), whereas metaphors in the fourteenth-century alliterative revival contemporary with the more Frenchified Chaucer were, like him, influenced by a far wider grammatical choice, not only of nouns but also of verbs (the walls wade in the water) and other parts of speech.⁶

So I undertook a grammatical analysis, discovering many types of change never spoken of in traditional definitions, and notably the very different relationships that nouns can have to their proper term while verbs have none—or at least the proper term doesn't matter, the main relationship being with their subject, direct or indirect object (or two of these or all three), which are changed into something else. In the classic example, "the ship ploughs the waves" (discussed already then by Hugh Kenner 1951, 87, and Donald Davie 1955, 41, for how many terms are involved, four or six), the proper term is "cuts through," but what matters is that the ship implicitly becomes a plough and the sea a field. Clearly the invasion of French and later Italian poetry had altered and widened native perceptions, but via the poetry and its grammar, not via the rhetorics. When I finished the thesis in 1954, Secker and Warburg got interested in publishing my analysis and commissioned a book. But I had to drop all the medieval poets and all the comparative aspect (i.e., half the main point, the invasion of a language, the other main point being theoretical, showing the how). So I did all my analyses all over again on fifteen English poets from Chaucer to Dylan Thomas, keeping only Chaucer's *Troylus and Criseyde*. But the repeated analysis enabled me to refine my methods. Moreover, I had an aging but extraordinarily brilliant editor, Roger Senhouse (a Bloomsbury survivor, who died a decade later), and naively thought I would always receive such critical counseling. Indeed, the slow but steady decline in the quality of the publisher's role may be linked to my early remark about the humanities and the general decline of reading as an activity.

The book, *A Grammar of Metaphor*, came out four years later, in 1958, and though by then I had published my first novel, also with Secker and Warburg, this was my first critical work, and it received unexpected attention—a top article in the *Sunday Times* by Raymond Mortimer (another Bloomsbury survivor)—which gave me my first launch on the literary scene.

Mortimer appreciated that no one had done this before. My supervisor had originally asked for an introductory chapter presenting what everyone else had said about metaphor. So, starting with the Greeks, through the Roman and medieval rhetoricians all the way to modern thinkers, I found to my amazement that no one discussed metaphor grammatically, except Geoffrey of Vinsauf,⁷ a thirteenth-century rhetorician, who classified metaphors as nouns or verbs, with a clear preference for verbs (using lovely examples in Latin, such as the air unclasps the clouds), on the grounds that "it is easier to understand a metaphor when it is transferred from thing to man, unless the metaphor is very obvious" (Faral 1924, 287–88). So Roman rhetoric was still lurking there.

Apart from Geoffrey, the constant viewpoint was always one of content: why is A called B? I simplify: 1) it could represent a passage from genus to species or vice versa, or from species to species (as in Aristotle, in his *Poetics,* who seems to exclude the fourth possibility, genus to genus, and replaces it with *analogy* [see Brooke-Rose 1958b, for this lack of logic], and he admits in *Rhetoric* that *analogy* covers all metaphors); 2) from inanimate to animate or vice versa, equally four ways, Roman and medieval rhetorics, so that Geoffrey's "easier" refers to the notion of "animating," itself echoing Aristotle in his description of metaphor as actualizing [see below], but by then reduced to one of four categories and, like Aristotle, making no grammatical distinction; 3) from one domain of thought or activity (e.g., jewelry) to another (beginning in the Renaissance, with a reprise in nineteenth-century French and German criticism and lasting into the twentieth), which I called "analysis by dominant trait." At its worst, this could (and did) easily decline into the type of study that proves from their metaphors that the Greeks were a maritime people.

These early analyses attempted to structure content and could be very meticulous. Aristotle discovers different transfers, such as metonymy (matter for object) and synecdoche (part for whole). But clearly a metaphor can also be a metonymy or a synecdoche or a hyperbole, as Fouquelin saw in the sixteenth century (1557), and in the *Rhetoric* (3.11.15) Aristotle admits this.

For Aristotle it was less a question of "form and content" than (in physical terms) matter and form, with form almost equivalent to our content. For I soon discovered that what is translated as "form" in Aristotle had various meanings, from "shape" (*morphe*) to vehicle support (*oxema*) to *logos* and all the way to Plato's Idea or *eidos,* and that the long dispute about "pure" Forms (in practice ideas, abstractions) had been going on for some time and still hovered now in the constant blurring of each into the other: for example, the Russian "Formalists" had called the "content" of a story *(fabula)* and the form *sjužet* (subject), which to me meant "theme" (i.e., content). I also discovered that nearly all genre-names, classical and modern, originally referred to what I would call "form" but soon lost that sense, shifting to what I would call "content" (e.g., *myth* originally meant "word discourse," as did *epic* = word, or what is expressed in words). *Drama* meant performance, *tragedy* came from "goat" + "ode" or "song," *comedy* from feast + ode, *fable* from *fari,* to speak, etc.[8]

So my insistence on "form and content" was no doubt metaphysically and philosopically naive, though the lesson was deeply instructive. And for my immediate purpose I persisted. I knew by then that a content analysis could make no clear distinction between metaphor and comparison or even simile (long comparison), both very different in syntax and effect. Indeed the Poundian word *image* in the criticism of the time had come to include not only metaphors and comparisons but symbols, as well as any (literal) visual picture evoked—a wild moor, a pylon, a street—so that it was only necessary to use the definite article or the demonstrative pronoun (= "you know what I mean") in, say, "the dead tree," "this red rock" (Eliot) to make them somehow vaguely symbolic of something else. The blur had begun already.

Whereas grammar—ah, grammar! If the mere use of a definite article or a demonstrative pronoun could alter a word's connotation, what could a copula do, or a verb of making, whereby a third party (love, God, misery) could transform a meaning before our eyes like a pumpkin, or parallel syntax (as in the Bible) that merely implies equivalence between two stated entities?[9] Thus, I could (rightly or wrongly) come to fairly surprising conclusions about each of the fifteen poets I had analyzed, category by category, that showed not only that the copula to link A and B allowed highly original metaphors and sounded bathetic with the banal, but also that Shakespeare and Donne used it most and most boldly, compared to, say, Chaucer's predilection for the genitive or the more syllogistic "pointing formulae"—and I could speculate why.

I say "rightly or wrongly" because, although the book sold steadily and, as I heard with gratitude from private testimony, was used by many teachers, it could not, on its female own, break through as a method. It appeared a year after Noam Chomsky's *Syntactic Structures* (1957), which I naturally hadn't read (my book took a year to come out) and which created a completely different and very exciting way of looking at grammar. I had used traditional grammatical categories, of surface structures only, and innocently thought, for instance, that I had invented the term *noun phrase* (observing that a metaphor often refers back to a complex phrase rather than to one noun). For years I hoped that Generative

Grammarians would take up my method and do it better. But no one did. And by the time metaphor as subject came back into fashion in the seventies, everyone, even the Structuralists who were supposedly such Formalists, had all gone back to the what and the why, the philosophy of it, and the nature of the mental transfer, as in Aristotle's analysis by content: metonymy, synecdoche, metaphor.

Even Paul Ricoeur, who in *La Métaphore vive* (1985) brings out the link that so excited me as a student between Aristotle's description of metaphor as "setting things before the eyes . . . in actuality" (*Rhetoric* 3.10) and the much vaster question of time in narrative tragedy and comedy imitating men in action (*Poetics* 1448a24), seems more interested in content: the visual element ("before the eyes"), the alien element (*allotrios*), and above all in the *pairing* (his italics, p. 31) of species/genre, etc.; in other words the notion of substitution. When he does mention words (*lexis*), it is only to pick *onoma* (noun) from Aristotle's mere enumeration of possibilities.

೦෨

Imagine then my consternation forty years ago when, shortly after the publication of *A Grammar of Metaphor* in 1958—having turned from poetry to the novel and even having published a couple—dissatisfied with my superficial social satire and the ease of it all, I plunged into two contemporary French writers who had been attracting much attention as formal experimenters: Nathalie Sarraute's *L'Ère du soupçon* (1956) and her novels to date, as well as the novels of Robbe-Grillet and his contemporary essays (later collected in *Pour un nouveau roman,* 1963).

In practice, despite Sarraute's claimed interest in technique, which she prefers to call method, and her superb reversal of the Formalist/Realist opposition (see chapter 3), she discusses every problem she mentions, and every author, purely in terms of content. That may result from her curious way of exposing the problems as summary of critical thought, as if she were inside another, more traditional critic's mind: "The time was well past when Proust had boldly believed that by urging his impression on us . . . [he could] try to reach the ultimate deep where lie truth, the real universe. . . . Modern man, having become a soulless body tossed about by hostile forces, was nothing. . . . And . . . Kafka, whose message combined so felicitously with that of the Americans, showed what still unexplored regions could open up for the writer" ("From Dostoevsky to Kafka," originally published in 1947). Was this parody? Here was someone clearly pleading for form yet stuck in content, however grandly, and representing traditional criticism, moreover, in free indirect discourse (for which see chapter 3 and, more analytically, chapter 7).

But even when this kind of critical summary is disentangled from her own more direct views in the critical present tense Sarraute never seems to pass from abstract feelings to what I call the how. She describes the arrival of Camus's *The Outsider* (1942) and the great hopes it aroused without once referring to its most outstanding grammatical feature (the present perfect, in fact already used by Céline in 1932; see chapter 7). Instead, she talks of *Homo absurdus* and the outside/inside paradox (inside but with no psychology), and other "still more disturbing" features, which take her back to Dostoyevsky, ending with a quote from Katherine Mansfield about "[his] terrible desire to establish contact." Yes, but how? I read in vain. Camus's Meursault "does occasionally discover, within himself, a few of the sentiments that classical analysis, albeit with a certain timorous fluster, succeeded in uncovering. . . . The very style [?] in which he expresses himself makes him, rather than the rival of Steinbeck's bellowing hero, the heir to *The Princess of Clèves* and *Adolph*. As the Abbé Brémond would say. . . . "[10] But here we must be back in ironic summary of ultra-traditional prewar criticism. Or are we? In a later chapter on conversation and subconversation (the technique she made so very much her own), Sarraute can only talk of "subtle, barely perceptible, fleeting, contradictory, evanescent movements . . . timid appeals," and so on, without once analyzing how in fact she creates, or as she would prefer to say, captures these. That was "not done."

With Robbe-Grillet it was much the same, although more direct—against "les mythes de la profondeur," anthropomorphic metaphors, social realism—with one important difference: he condemns the past tense as *the* mark of the traditional novel, and so, implicitly, defends his own use of the present tense. But this as such was not all that new. What he never mentions, even in his essays recently collected in *Le Voyageur* (2001), is his own, unique use of the present tense. It's as if he couldn't (or wouldn't?) quite formulate his own precise experiment. Many experimental authors can't, even when they try. On this precise point, I couldn't myself until quite recently, for my last lecture (see chapter 7, where I discuss the present tense and Robbe-Grillet in much more detail).

It was as if, at the time, these two authors, who, with Samuel Beckett and Michel Butor and quite a few others, did most to change the language of the novel, were nevertheless still so steeped in the critical attitudes of the time that even they couldn't describe clearly just what they were doing. I mention only those two because they most directly influenced me, in different ways, Sarraute more in her chapter on "the age of suspicion" (suspicion of fiction and the demand for "le petit fait vrai"), Robbe-Grillet more technically. But it was my first big lesson in the deep-down modern preference for content over form, the what over the how, even at a time of technical innovation.

France had not been through the New Criticism and its close reading (which in any case concerned only poetry) and learned of it only later through Roman Jakobson's Structuralist version of it, and at first only through his famous analysis, with Claude Lévi-Strauss in 1962, of a Baudelaire sonnet. The Chicago school produced Wayne C. Booth, who did attend to the novel very well, in *The Rhetoric of Fiction* (1961), another landmark book for me. But meanwhile La Nouvelle Critique had started (contemporary with Sarraute's book as published in 1956). And by the time I went to live in Paris in 1968, to find I had to teach Structuralism to first-year students, I also learned one surprising thing about the so-called Formalism of Structuralism (for which it was attacked in England): that it was mostly a new way to analyze content, to "structure" it: e.g., the transfer of an object O (the princess) from one place (her parents' palace) to another (the villain's, etc.); so are actions seen as functions of narrative, almost independently of any text. Several French Structuralists, for example, when presenting their abstract narrative models, referred to no text, or, if they did apply it to a text, used a short synopsis and could get it all wrong.[11]

I relearned, for fiction, about different levels in Formalism, and that content can also be formalized. Content such as plot or "functions" can be structured, which helps us better to understand not only a particular narrative, but also narrative in general. Structure can be as invisible as my constraints. It can also be too visible, as in what Northrop Frye (1957) called naive romances (which show their structure more clearly) and their modern equivalents. We have all by now learned to discern structure in that sense; indeed it was already taught last century by Bradley with regard to Shakespeare's tragedies, and ultimately goes back to Aristotle.

What is also visible, but more and more ignored (invisible?) is the language in which these structures are clothed, the actual words, the metaphors (which "set things before the eyes in action," said Aristotle in the *Rhetoric*, spurring on my love of verbs), the grammar, the tenses; or, inversely, the dysfunctional clichés. In poetry we have learned to analyze them, if sometimes (a) *too mechanically,* as in the traditional French *explication de texte,* which could amount to counting parts of speech, and to which Jakobson's method came to be unfairly assimilated, or (b) *too ideologically guided,* as in the New Criticism, with its elitism and its imposed need to find "organic unity" in all paradox and contradiction. And yet, in the novel, and perhaps in reaction to the above, these aspects are precisely what had become almost invisible; all the more so, of course, in the case of lipograms, which are non-uses. But I chose "Invisible Author" as the title for the book and for this introductory chapter, rather than "Invisible Writer," with its hint of invisible ink and secret codes, because such non-uses are also intimately tied up with the whole question of the so-called death of the author and the author's authority, which I shall be picking up throughout, leading to a full treatment in chapter 7.

By "full" treatment, I mean limited to literary and linguistic treatment. For practical reasons, I cannot take aboard either the "living present" of the present tense pursued by Heidegger and Derrida, with its inscribed absence—a problem that goes all the way back to the Greeks; nor the epistemological problems of "truth" versus "representation" and rhetoric that arose in both philopsy and history during the last thirty years of the twentieth century, even though they afford many parallels with the theme of the death of the author: e.g., Foucault's "archeology" of knowledge as opposed to archive theory, or, in Ricoeur's words on him, the notion of "statements without stater" (*énoncés sans énonciateur,* Ricoeur 2000, 256), Michel de Certeau's "Dans l'oeuvre de Foucault, 'Qui parle et d'où?'" (1973, 161) and Roland Barthes's first attack on the illusions of nineteenth-century Realism in "Le Discours de l'histoire" (1967) and "L'effet du réel" (1968), all the way to Hayden White's *Metahistory, Tropics of Discourse, The Content of Form,* and Ricoeur's monumental *Le Mémoire, l'histoire, l'oubli.*[12]

To have done so would have overloaded this short book, which represents only one writer's modest experience, in a few collected lectures on my work. I have moreover never been concerned with the philosophical paradox of factual truth versus rhetoric in my fictions, only with the linguistic paradox of the technically speakerless Narrative Sentence, freed from the speakerless state by the use of Speech Modes to narrate as "I" (fairly common) or (very uncommon) remaining speakerless. It is this conundrum I shall be dealing with in chapter 7.

Of course any attachment to form that excludes all else is totally withering. But if form alone is withering, the moment a critic deals primarily with content, taking form for granted as a mere window on the "reality" of a novel, there will emerge very little difference between the writers discussed (two black novels for instance), whereas if you approach them through the textual structures you will automatically get at the content and a good deal more besides. Naturally much the same applies to purely formal analysis: for Structuralists, all narratives sounded the same. Both content summary and structural analysis are extractions. The most enriching criticism mingles form and content constantly, but it is the most difficult to achieve.

Content is much easier to summarize, form much easier to ignore, so that even well-known critics who plead again today for more "theory" (booted out of fashion for two decades), for more "signifier," less "signified," or whatever terms they use, in practice fall back on content in their own criticism. Or else *theory* is taken to mean not narrative theory but psychoanalytical theory, or Marxist (etc.)—in other words, content again.

And if the two don't get thus blurred, they get totally separated, especially on the Continent (say, in Italy, Germany, France), where there may be a tough opening chapter on general theory, citing everyone in view, but then when it comes to dealing with the fictional texts in question, there's a collapse into content summary, without ever linking the two parts. Indeed, theory sometimes seems erected against having to read. France still has separate classes for *travaux pratiques* and *travaux théoriques,* rather like their driving test, in which *le Code* is first learned by heart in multiple-choice questions under hundreds of pictures, then, with all this quite unabsorbed into the body movements, one receives driving lessons. France has the highest accident rate in Europe.

The worst example I found of separation of form and content with a withering exclusion of form was a French doctoral thesis in the eighties, about an English poet. I had been asked very insistently to serve on the jury by the unknown candidate (a uniquely French situation), met at the Anglicist Congress, because he so admired my *Grammar of Metaphor.* To my horror, it was a thesis in statistics, and the other four members of the jury were statisticians, all extremely enthusiastic, who didn't know the poet in question. It was full of graphs showing, say, the increase in the poet's use of adjectives towards the end of his life, and other much more complicated "facts," all made meaningless because all the words counted had been totally extracted from their context. When, in the final section, he at last dealt with metaphor, he was obliged, significantly, to drop his statistical method, since a metaphor interacts with other words in the same sentence, and can't be "extracted," except as mere occurence in a simple count. He relied entirely on my book. He aped my method, but almost every example was a grammatical misreading, because he wasn't trained in close analysis. "Vous êtes bien sévère, Madame," said the innocent statisticians. Despite my dissent (mild, because I knew it was useless), the thesis got the topmost result. I left the champagne party early, hugging my two heavy tomes of thesis, and deposited them in the first bin I could find, on a bridge on the way back to the Rive Gauche.

༄

I said at the beginning that my topics were usually attention-catching enough to catch some, though my formal contribution tended to be ignored. In fact, thinking it over, I even doubt this. I can't check it (I speak only of reviews, and mine are archived in Texas).[13] But I have a distinct memory of puzzlement and of my works being unanalytically labeled "the *nouveau roman* in English"; this was true of *Out,* but the SF and race-inversion theme wouldn't have interested Robbe-Grillet. He condemned metaphor for one. And by the next novel, *Such,* the narrative method I learned from him had already become a style individual to me, and it has been my most pervasive constraint ever since (dealt with in chapter 7).

For although I was of course labeled "experimental" without further detail, my topics were seldom signaled as original (which they were, if *original* is taken to mean not tackled before or since), indeed were seldom grasped. So, before passing to my five lectures, I shall assume nobody has ever heard of me and briefly describe the topic of my novels from *Out* (my first "experimental" novel, i.e., leaving aside my first four novels) to *Subscript* (1999), when I stopped. I spend a little longer on those I won't be dealing with later. The first two, for example.

In *Out,* I completely reverse the race situation, inventing a world, without explanation, in which the blacks rule and the whites are discriminated against and are unreliable, sick of a mysterious radiation illness the others were immune to; indeed any color is better than white: brown, beige, even dark pinkly cardiac. The irrationality of racism is laid bare, as is the sense of exclusion both race and sickness produce. I'm inside a mind, that of an old white man looking for work, though his wife has a menial job up at the big house belonging to Mrs. Mgulu. I simply register all he sees, hears, and thinks, in a pronounless present tense. Perhaps it was the unfamiliar technique that prevented reviewers from discerning the originality: for the race reversal was mostly ignored, and only the old white man's deteriorating state reported on as if *Out* were a novel about psychic breakdown.[14] This continues today, in reference books that purport to give content summaries but perpetuate the error. In other words, I received neither form nor content criticism but label-clichés.

In *Such,* I tell of a man who dies and returns to life, and his adventures in that metapsychological space of death are told in terms of astrophysical space, a metaphoric constraint. As in most of my novels since *Out,* I am inside his mind in an instantaneous present tense and don't have to give realistic reasons he wouldn't know or understand. He could have had a heart massage or be a more mythical resurrection figure (his space girl and fellow traveler calls him Lazarus), I merely put down each happening, with scenes from his real life becoming more frequent and longer as he slowly returns, seeing everyone as a radio telescope sees the stars, with red shifts and such becoming metaphors for the distances between people.[15]

In *Between,* with its *to be* constraint (which I'll come to in more detail in chapter 3), I'm inside a simultaneous interpreter who is never in one place, always in planes and hotel rooms and among slogans and instructions in ten different languages that her bilingualism is insufficient to cope with.

Thru (1975), though my favorite, is the novel that even my fans get most wrong, not noticing, because it really is typographically quite hard to read, explanations that are clearly given. It's a novel about the textuality of a text, the fictionality of fiction (see chapter 5 for a close reading of the first twenty pages).

Amalgamemnon (1984) was purposely wholly discursive again, without typographical games, if many metaphoric ones. It was said to be "about" a teacher made redundant, though that was hardly the point. It's written wholly in nonrealized tenses, such as the future. I'll be discussing it in more detail in chapter 3, together with *Between.*

My next two novels were science fictions, *Xorandor* (1986) and *Verbivore* (1990), and here at last originality was recognized, at least with

Xorandor. As far as my fairly wide reading in SF goes, nobody has, or had then, thought of an extraterrestrial as a computer-rock belonging to a silicon civilization, feeding on both nuclear waste and intercepted information, found in Cornwall by two children who dictate their adventure into a pocket computer. In other words, the narrative is wholly in dialogue, perhaps easier to follow than the new type of narrative I had been exploring since *Out.* As I had no idea how English kids talk today, I invented a slang based on electronic and computer words (e.g., diodic for super), but this didn't seem to create a barrier.

The sequel, *Verbivore,* was, I think, sent off to the publisher too fast after finish.[16] By the time it came out, I saw that I had missed an opportunity to develop and explore a splendid idea (creatures feeding on our broadcast words and getting so overloaded they demolish all our systems) by working it out more scientifically and above all by a better how for a very good what. No one said so, however (except the *New Scientist,* on the science, quite rightly). So good technique is a barrier to grasping original subject matter, but so is the same technique when it is not well used.

Then came *Textermination* (1991), which is "about" fictional characters praying to the Implied Reader for existence, at a Convention of Prayer for Being, in San Francisco. Because of the unfamiliarity of many of these characters, I made a few explanatory concessions in my (nevertheless still lipogrammic) narrative method (since my characters mostly came out of traditional narratives), but I felt free to invent literary high jinks with fictional levels, including "real" fictional characters, the hosts running the convention. I don't think any contemporary writer has imagined anything quite so unusual, yet once again it hardly pierced through the reviewing world. It's true that an extra constraint was, through much reading and research, one of content: to make it impossible, on both theoritical and realistic grounds, for any one actual reader (even myself later!) to recognize every character. The implied reader is pure theory. Realistically, none of us has read everything, and none of us knows everyone in the swirling mill of huge international conferences.

So an original idea (content) in slightly more traditional narrative (form) also failed to be appreciated. My fans (who loved it) are all academic, either teachers or students. Yet curiously enough, even here, two professors of literature who much admired the book nevertheless complained, privately, that they couldn't recognize all the fictional characters. So I was pleased, since that was the point. And probably the barrier too.

My next novel, *Remake* (1996), was autobiographical, and I'll be describing the constraints I used for it in chapter 4. The following novel, *Next* (1998), was my least original in terms of subject matter (street-sleepers), but at least I can't, from *Out* onwards, be accused of writing about bourgeois tizzies or ivory-towerish topics. Here it is probably the how that once again created a barrier: I wrote from inside the mind of each character, without marked transition, only content showing that we're in a different mind. I also used different levels of "Estuarian" accent (as Cockney is now called), phonetically transcribed, for each character, to stress the distances between them. But this demands an unfamiliar visual effort, whereas we all decipher different accents automatically when heard orally through actors or in life (another double standard between oral and written). If the text as such "has to be read slowly," as one friend complained, any other formal points of interest seem to lose all value.

My last novel, *Subscript* (1999), is a paleontological (prehistoric) novel but not, like William Golding's splendid *The Inheritors* (1955), concentrated on one moment (the Neanderthal/Cro-Magnon moment). *Subscript* starts four billion years ago inside a prebiotic chemical activity that becomes a prokaryote cell, then a eukaryote cell, then a multicellular organism, as if these organisms had consciousness of a sort. Each chapter takes us in leaps through evolution. I'll return to this novel in chapters 7 and 9.

Meanwhile, I shall continue on the curious situation in contemporary criticism, trying to analyze it technically and historically, before dealing with my own experiments, their limitations and their advantages.

2

SplitlitCRIT*

I SHALL START WITH a personal anecdote. I have a delightful cleaning lady, wholly illiterate, who was pushing her children through an education. In 1993 I was helping her daughter to prepare the English oral exam for her baccalaureate, a school-ending exam at the university entrance level. There were five set texts, three in prose and two poems, by Frost and by Ferlinghetti. The exam was to last ten minutes, during which the candidate had to read one of the allotted texts aloud, translate it, and comment. Clearly that left little time for comment. To my horror, the girl had been told to learn by heart not only the translations but the overlong commentaries dictated by the teacher. Of the five texts I shall describe only the Frost poem, but the method applied to all. The sixteen-line poem, very well known, was "The Gift Outright," which I give below, to share the shock I received:

> The land was ours before we were the land's,
> She was our land more than a hundred years
> Before we were her people. She was ours
> In Massachussetts, in Virginia,
> But we were England's, still colonials,
> Possessing what we still were unpossessed by,

---

* Given as lecture to a Conference on Narrative at the University of Utah, Salt Lake City, 1995; printed in *Narrative* 4, no. 1 (January 1996). In all subsequent chapters lectures will be slightly revised (omission of formal openings, of repetitions, or regrouping these to one lecture, etc.).

> Possessed by what we now no more possessed.
> Something we were withholding made us weak
> Until we found out that it was ourselves
> We were withholding from our land of living,
> And forthwith found salvation in surrender.
> Such as we were we gave ourselves outright
> (The deed of gift was many deeds of war)
> To the land vaguely realizing westward,
> But still unstoried, artless, unenhanced,
> Such as she was, such as she would become. (Frost 1951)*

In forty-five seconds I did my usual stuff to show how the poem functions, noting, for instance, the sequence of possessives in the first five lines (*ours, the land's, our, her, ours, England's*), as well as *she* for the possessed land, opposed not only to *we* but also to *what* for the as-yet-unpossessed land, which nevertheless becomes *she* after "the gift outright" of *ourselves,* the words *possessing, unpossessed, possessed, possessed* cluttered in the sixth and seventh lines, and so on: possessing without possession, still possessed by the land left behind, solutioned by the gift outright of ourselves, and being possessed by the new land at last truly possessed.

She was amazed. No one had ever taught her to look at the language of a text. And when she showed me the dictated commentary, it was a two-page potted history of British colonialism in America. Whether my interpretation was "right" or "wrong," it was more alive to her than the one she had been taught. Clearly the teacher was terrified by a literary text and preferred to inculcate the notion that potted history is the meaning of the poem—which raises the question: so why bother to read or write a poem?

It was too late to undo the damage, so I rewrote six-line commentaries for each text for her to learn by heart. After the exam she called me excitedly to say, "I got the Frost!" As a Moroccan immigrant born in France she had really liked the poem. She also passed.

Now of course this is an outrageous example, from a local school, of the worst type of teaching that has always gone on everywhere. Also the

---

* "The Gift Outright" from *The Poetry of Robert Frost,* edited by Edward Connery Latham, the Estate of Robert Frost and (in the United Kingdom) Jonathan Cape as publisher. Copyright 1942 by Robert Frost, © 1970 by Lesley Frost Ballantine, © 1969 (in North America) by Henry Holt and Co. Reprinted by permission of The Random House Group Limited and by Henry Holt and Company, LLC.

subject was a foreign language, the equivalent of French in England or America, and the type of baccalaureate was not literary but commercial (so she should not even have had to comment on such texts in an oral, but rather commercial ones). Nevertheless, I was always astonished, during my twenty years of university teaching in France, at the way so many students would arrive hating literature, having learned simply to extract a content (love, death, colonialism) and to expand on that. I have learned since that some schools now teach literary texts through multiple-choice questionnaires (as in *le Code* for driving). In this case a question might be: What is Massachusetts? A) A mass selection process; B) an African tribe; C) a town in Bengal; D) a state in the U.S. An earlier generation in France had been put through the mechanical grammatical method called *explication de texte,* which could also kill a poem, being at its worst a dry picking out of parts of speech without relating them to how the poem functions. But at least it did look at the language.

This experience is all the odder because children and adolescents in France *all* respond enthusiastically to the more poetic texts of their favorite popular singers and know them by heart. It's true that there is today (and permanently) a catastrophic education crisis in France, and that this example may not (I hope) be universal. But it may serve as a warning, for the problems of illiteracy, fragmentation, lack of attention span, cultural heterogeneity (in itself good), exclusive focus on the contemporary, and swift teacher surrender to the lures of facility are by now quasi-universal.

‿

In the thirties when I was at school in England, extracting the content was the way literature was taught chiefly through Bradleyan descriptions of Shakespeare characters. So I have been appalled, in recent years, to see that content extraction, though more like ideological rewrites, should still go on. For of course, after the war, like everyone else of my generation, I went through (on my own, not with my Oxford medieval tutors) the New Criticism (from Cambridge and the U.S.), which taught close reading, and even reached schools in the forties and fifties, especially in the United States. This close reading addressed only poetry, not narrative, but I'll come to narrative in a moment. In fact, as a method it could not deal with anything as large as narration. The New Criticism showed how words and metaphors functioned in interaction, but according to the ideology of the time, it sought paradoxes and contradictions in order to resolve them into an underlying unity, often called organic, when indeed it wasn't transcendental. It sought, in other words, an absent totality.

So much for poetry. The method could not address narrative, and when one of its best practitioners, Cleanth Brooks, wrote *Understanding Fiction* with Robert Penn Warren (1959), it consisted of long extracts followed by general commentary, full of insights but hardly the close reading that had at the time so revolutionized the understanding of poetry. Serious criticism of novels was merely a more scholarly version of contemporary reviewing: sum up the plot approvingly or ironically, in more or less detail according to the space allotted and add a short sentence on style. This is, incidentally, what we still get in France, both in the press and in the few still surviving TV book programs, which have vanished elsewhere.

At about the same time as *Understanding Fiction,* Frye in *An Anatomy of Criticism* (1957) produced four increasingly complex theories of narrative based on anthropological and broadly Frazerian and Jungian interpretatons of myths and archetypes, another form of content extraction. These were fascinating and enriching, and had the advantage, for once, of treating epics, romances, plays, and novels on the same level, as narratives. This revealed very clearly why each was favored in this or that category but showed nothing about their respective structures. And, from the contemporary and subsequent Structuralist viewpoint, these categories were so confused in terms of theoretical levels, so empirical and disorderly, as to be scarcely usable except in a very subjective and empirical way (see Todorov 1973, for this criticism). Since Frye, this kind of analysis has become more rigorous and can deepen our understanding of the ritual forces behind narrative, on condition of remaining close to the text. But it is wholly an analysis of content. A few years later Booth published *The Rhetoric of Fiction,* which for the first time analyzed problems of narrator knowledge and narrator position. At last narrative structure was being seriously tackled.

Meanwhile, other phenomena had occurred: first, in the United States, came the rise of creative writing courses at the university level, much scorned in Britain at the time and still nonexistent in France today, but producing at least an awareness of language and structure. Second, in France, two phenomena arose in the fifties: the appearance of novels that were narratologically unfamiliar, from Beckett to Sarraute and Robbe-Grillet and Pinget and others—each author very different but all lumped together as *le nouveau roman,* which caused at least some critics, notably

Roland Barthes, to think about the nature of narrative; and the rise of La Nouvelle Critique, soon to merge with Structuralism, rising out of Russian and Czech Formalism and Structuralist (pre-Generative) linguistics, in many applications, anthropological, narratological, poetical.

Some aspects of Structuralism, when noticed at all, seemed oddly familiar to the English-speaking world, due to what I used to call the university gap. Barthes, for example, proclaimed the death of the author in 1968—long implicit in the Jamesian "showing" versus "telling" at the turn of the last century and again in the New Criticism, which was dogmatically interested only in the text. Barthes also proclaimed *polysémie* as a new discovery, although it had already been analyzed thirty years earlier by William Empsom in *Seven Types of Ambiguity* (1930) and again in *The Structure of Complex Words* (1951), both books, like Frye's, chaotic from a logical Structuralist viewpoint but nevertheless early and exciting attempts to analyze plurality of meaning. This *polysémie* also had its extreme practice, such as Joyce's in 1939. Inversely the Anglo-American scene (especially the Anglo-) rejected Structuralism as an aberrant mania for system. Or, when a few critics turned to it, it was ill-assimilated and naively used. Since those far-off days there has been much more fruitful exchange and interaction.

The great innovation of Structuralism, however, was a new attention to narrative structure—new, I mean, in the West—but it was much more abstract than Booth's very humanistic and humane attention. It came out of Russian Formalism, notably Vladimir Propp's work on the folktale (1929) but rapidly developed into many models, from A. J. Greimas and his semiotic rectangle or (1970) Claude Brémond and his bettering/worsening model (1966, 60–76), or Barthes and his pyramids (1966) or Tzvetan Todorov (1969) with his peculiarly naive "grammar" of the *Decameron* (the last two both tacitly dropped by their creators as each became more sophisticated and even personal), to more and more complex models (in Russia, Germany, France, the United States, etc.). Inevitably, at first the narratives were very simple ones (James Bond, for instance). Grammars of narrative were proclaimed as "universal," but few were used even at the time and fewer have survived, for once again the temptation, even the policy, was to extract not a content but a structure, often without reference to any text or, when applied to a text, killing it exactly as a potted history of colonialism kills the Frost poem.

One great exception even then was Genette's *Discours du récit* (translated as *Narrative Discourse,* 1980; note that in the French title *form* comes first). Genette, unlike Barthes, knew English and had read Booth. Nor did he ever lose sight of his exemplar text, Proust's *A la recherche du temps perdu* no less. He also revealed for the first time the muddled thinking that had been developing everywhere over the years since Percy Lubbock's *The Craft of Fiction* (originally published in 1921), the confusion of narrative instance and point of view, of narrative instance and moment of writing, narrator and author, distance, addressee and individual reader, indeed all the categories in the handling of time, mode, and voice. And although Genette has long since moved to other kinds of analysis, *Narrative Discourse* remains the best example of Structuralism at its (rare) humanistic best, even if, badly used, it could lead to students mechanically picking out analepses, prolepses, metalepses, free indirect discourse, and all the rest without any attempt to relate these to the whole, let alone to suggest the purpose and effect of such techniques in any one instance. But Structuralism did at least clear the ground for a renewed rhetoric, for a while anyway. The job of rhetoric is to name and describe all the logical possibilities. The job of criticism is to go beyond naming and to ask why and how, and to analyze the specific effect, which pure or purist Structuralism refused to do. That, they said (or Todorov said [1967]), was the job of criticism.

So pure Structuralism died, and Poststructuralism, almost contemporaneously, was born and survives, more or less. I say contemporaneously because Jacques Derrida's first three books all appeared in 1967, counterinfluencing Barthes out of his pure Structuralism, and the two isms ran parallel throughout the seventies; indeed I taught both, Structuralist models to first years, as all literature teachers in the American department had to, and, by choice, Poststructuralism to graduates, almost as if I knew that structural analysis was just an exercise to unteach the school killing of literature, but which they'd also have to outgrow later. Poststructuralism of the Derridean kind was soon called Deconstruction, and was of course much contested everywhere before becoming a banalized and misused term, a sort of blind substitute for demolition, or even (as once met in a novel) for thinking hard about an emotional situation. It can also be lazily dismissed, like feminism, with the fashionable prefix "post," which implies, as it did in Poststructuralism, that we need no longer bother about what preceded. Indeed, the terms *Structuralism* and *Deconstruction* are probably the last names of movements to contain some notion of their aim or method, as opposed to the merely temporal names that came into fashion around then, as if

Modern couldn't change its meaning to "old hat," as if the suffix *ist* in Modernist resolved this, and so on. The very vagueness of the present return to content analysis (or mere summary) seems to echo this vagueness of nomenclature (see chapter 1).

With Deconstruction came at last a brief return to close reading. I once heard an English lecturer in Bern say that Deconstruction was just another version of the New Criticism. I think he meant that both liked to discover paradox, ambiguity, and contradiction, but whereas the New Criticism sought to resolve them into an underlying or transcendent unity, Deconstruction laid them bare as aporia and multiple meanings. Even thus expanded it seemed an outrageous reduction, based on a strong element of truth. I am not qualified to deal critically with Derrida's complex "antilogocentric" philosophical edifice, not even enough to be wholly convinced by it, though I enjoy it. Here I am only concerned with it as a type of textual analysis. Deconstruction not only deals with far more varied texts than the usually short poems chosen by the New Criticism. It also brought in the notion that Deconstruction cannot be a totalizing or a colonizing method mechanically applying its key concepts to every text. On the contrary, it learned and taught how to think otherness, to recreate it: even the otherness of the deconstruction. It also brought in another new notion: that meaning depends, not on subjective identity but "on a conflict of forces, which produce interpretations" (Derrida 1971), so that any text, including the deconstructing text, can be shown to deconstruct itself: hence Derrida on Jacques Lacan on Poe's "The Purloined Letter" and Barbara Johnson on Derrida on Lacan on Poe, delightful as a one-off but fortunately not repeated for every text in existence.

This self-deconstructibility was also revealed from a very different quarter by Mikhail Bakhtin through his theory of dialogism and hidden polemic, and seems to me the most exciting aspect of literary language, perhaps of all human language, but from lack of time or insight we continually fall back on easier descriptive ways.

Moreover, apart from Bakhtin's splendid work on Rabelais (1970) and on Dostoyevsky (1973), the French and American version of Deconstruction at the time seldom dealt with narrative as such, let alone modern narrative. Derrida's early readings of Plato's attitude to "writing" in the *Phaedrus* (1972) and of Lacan's insufficient reading of Poe (1966) were rare exceptions and dealt with reversals of ideas rather than with narrativity. Similarly the Yale school of Deconstruction worked chiefly on Romantic poets, or Nietzsche or Rousseau, later tackling Hardy or Proust, while all around them truly Deconstructive novels were sprouting under the inherently meaningless name of Postmodern fiction. Here it was academic criticism that was irrelevant to contemporary fiction. Unlike the New Criticism, Deconstruction did not reach the schools but remained and perhaps continues under various guises in the higher spheres of academe—but only in the higher spheres. I remember doing a fairly simple deconstruction of Stephen Crane's *The Red Badge of Courage* for a collection of essays, which I was told only much later was meant for schools, and having a great deal of trouble with the editor, who kept correcting my sentences to say the opposite—a Deconstructive experience in itself. Nevertheless, Deconstruction deeply influenced and enriched many of our best critics.

But I am still discussing the seventies and early eighties at the latest. And the most surprising development for me has been the more recent, or maybe parallel, return, not only to the author—and I'll deal with that in a moment—but to pure content criticism, at its best of the type that structures the content, at its worst as reportage of the pre-thirties kind, updated: plot summaries or ideological rewrites, loose thematics, and cultural essentialism. One of the few advantages of growing old is recognizing the apparently new as old hat: one has seen or been through all the isms. I intend to name nobody, but I think such critics reduce and impoverish the writers they defend. All my life I have taught that if you deal with literature, of whatever origin, through content only, you miss a great deal (see chapter 1). I may, however, be too biased to plead this, for I also used to teach that poetry is about grammar, shocking my students to attention, showing for instance how Shakespeare's sonnet "When to the sessions of sweet silent thought" or, for that matter, Ronsard's "Quand vous serez bien vieille, au coin du feu," are also, or even primarily, about how far you can transgress the when-then structure (which transgression, incidentally, Yeats wholly missed in his version of the Ronsard poem, thoroughly weakening it). However, when I taught that poetry is about grammar, I did not neglect what was happening to the sessions of sweet silent thought or to the intimations of old age and regret; I merely refused to reduce the poems to that.

Now I'm well aware that all criticism feeds on extraction and reduction. If this were not so, criticism would mean copying out the whole text plus commentary, and some New Criticism almost amounted to this, since it dealt chiefly with short poems. Clearly this would be nonsensical with long poems and novels. This may well be the basic reason why narrative criticism is so difficult, so split up, so subjectively messy. There had arisen a situation in which, at one extreme, bare structures were extracted in a purposely reductive way, in the name of authorial death, of the irrelevance of evaluation and of subject matter—in the name, in fact, of an abstract grammar of narrative claimed to be so universal that it often revealed little more than bathetic platitude hardly more useful than Aristotle's beginning, middle, and end. At the other extreme was a return to the paraphrasing of plots and themes with an occasional justifying quote (in brackets and wrenched out of context), or even unsubstantiated claims of formal experiment in attempts to have it both ways and make an admittedly conventional writer seem innovative merely because feminine or ethnic or both, a "new" or unfamiliar content standing for formal experiment, the whole sometimes accompanied by dissertations on the critic's theoretical position or the state of the world or the discussed author's life, with little reference to the work in question—at worst no better than a potted history of colonialism with regard to Frost's poem. I exaggerate on purpose to signal the danger. Clearly both extremes are only extremes, and one of them, pure Structuralism, is long past. But the other extreme is still very much with us, as if narrative criticism had gone round and round Jakobson's old (pre-Deconstruction) diagram of communication (1960), according to the six functions emphasized. Sometimes an "outdated" diagram can still be useful to emphasize a point. For recall (meanings for a literary text in parentheses):

CONTEXT (world represented)
Referential Function
!

SENDER (author) —— MESSAGE (text) —————— RECEIVER (reader)

Emotive Function   *Poetic Function*   *Conative Function*
!

CONTACT (paper, waves, stone)
Phatic Function
!

CODE (language, literary conventions)
Metalinguistic Function

These functions are all necessary to any communication, but can (and, alas, are) analyzed separately according to need, the bottom two generally forgotten.

Back in the nineteenth century and at the beginning of the twentieth, the attention was all on the Sender, that is, on the author's intention, and even in Oxford in the late forties, when I was there, the teaching was still "first establish the author's intention, then judge whether this has been achieved"; or else, in Cambridge, on the Receiver—at the time, on the reader's pleasure—and whether that had been achieved. Both these were dismissed somewhat summarily by the New Criticism as, respectively, the intentional fallacy and the affective fallacy (Wimsatt 1946, repr. in *The Verbal Icon,* 1954), just as it implicitly dismissed all discussion of the world represented or referential function. All was in the text (poetic function), though in communication the text or message need not be a poem but could be prose, or a slogan (Jakobson's example at the time was "I like Ike").

Nobody has ever disputed that the author's intention, even when declared in the text, can be "wrong" or at least irrelevant, or not attained, in the sense that a writer may intend his poem to be a work of genius when it isn't; more explicitly, Milton wanted to "justify the ways of God to Man" and ended up, in some views, portraying a splendid Satan, a touching Man, and a rather boring God. Certainly the author doesn't begin to exist without the reader. But then, so can the reader's reading be "wrong" in that subjective sense, "plural" at least, or else interpretation wouldn't exist either.

Yet after the long wallow on the text, whether through the New Criticism or through Jakobson-type Structural analysis of poetry, the reader came back full strength and less subjectively than earlier. I remember a set of seminars we organized at Paris VIII in 1970 with as our guest Stanley Fish, then little known, who was one of the first to bring back the reader in an early essay allusively entitled "Affective Stylistics" (1970). Fish's work was being paralleled by the then-new Reader-Response criticism out of Roman Ingarden's phenomenological study *The Literary Work of Art* (1973) and its theory of gaps filled in by the reader. There arose many theoretical constructs, called the ideal reader (already in Booth 1961), the implied reader (Iser 1974), super reader (Riffaterre 1971), and others, with which I had much affectionate fun in my novel *Textermination,* on characters praying to the Implied Reader for existence.

But since the best of this reader-oriented criticism concentrated on the many ways in which the reader was encoded in the text, given, as it were, hidden instructions, the emphasis was still on the text rather than on real readers, though these also came in through the new history of reception (*Rezeptionsgeschichte*) and a sociopolitical type of criticism through Marxist, neo-Marxist, Freudian, neo-Freudian, and feminist criticism, which in fact expressed a return to the referential function of the world represented. It is as if criticism had moved from an implicit "the author intends," via "the text/the structure says," to "the reader infers," these attitudes, however, being only too often a lip service to current fashions and merely masking "the critic asserts." Indeed, the new emphasis on the reader, together with Deconstruction, produced the intense discussions in the New Hermeneutics of the seventies and eighties, and its problems, including the reactions against it, well described by Booth in *Critical Understanding* (1979). I summarize: if the reader's reading is supreme, anything goes, from pluralistic chaos—in the hope that the more voices there are the more truth will emerge, or maybe some view (the critic's own) will prove right and the others wrong—through five different possible reactions all the way to complete skepticism: There is no truth, all is relative, individual.

In that same interview quoted above, Derrida had already given a sort of answer to Booth's doubts: "I would never say that every interpretation is equal but I do not select. The interpretations select themselves. I am a Nietzschean in that sense. . . . So I would not say that some interpretations are truer than others. I would say that some are more powerful than others" (1971, 21). I have experienced many instances of this "anything goes" in the reader's interpretation as supreme, but one amusing trivial example will point it up. The protagonist of *Amalgamemnon* is a teacher of classics made redundant, often plunged nostalgically into Herodotus, and whenever Herodotus mentions unknown Europe, a modern query echoes: "But then, Europe, shall we ever make it?"—wrenching us to the present situation. One excellent critic and expert in Modern and Postmodern novels, Richard Martin, interpreted this as meaning "shall we (the British) ever make it into Europe?" I protested privately, gently (we're still very good friends, despite this tiny disagreement), but I'm not sure I convinced him. In a later reprint (Friedmann and Martin 1995, 149), in a generous attempt to meet my objection, he complicated his comment to read "expressive of British non-relations with the European Common Market and containing at the same time the colloquial punning use of the verb *make,* thereby relating the phrase back to the original myth," which still twists the simple verb *make* (as in "make an apple pie," which can never mean "get into an apple pie") and still prefers Britain as subject of "we," rather than (author's intention): "Shall we (Europeans) ever make (create) Europe?" The result is a having-it-both-ways blur, without much gain from any ambiguity. Seen in the simplistic Jakobsonian terms used above, this is what has happened:

1) The conative function (reader's interpretation), quite rightly in reader-oriented criticism, has taken over the first and leading role; the emotive function (author's intention, which may be "wrong") has for similar reasons been annulled.
2) The poetic function, here grammar, is ignored: the verb *make,* despite the phrase "colloquial punning," is in fact read in an idiomatic sense peculiar to English (which foreigners have to learn) instead of in its basic sense (first in any dictionary). This idiomatic sense entails altering the subject "we."
3) The referential function (world referred to) is ignored, and with it the historical aspect: Britain decided to enter Europe in 1972; I started the novel in 1978,[1] rewrote it over several summers (first abandoning it for a first version of *Xorandor*), and published it in 1984. The consequences are also ignored: the limited, parochial meaning Martin reads is now forgotten, insignificant (even the political name of Europe he gives has changed), while the wider meaning of *make* as "create" is still valid to this day, well over two decades later, and we (the Europeans) still haven't succeeded in making Europe.[2]

   This last point could give a general rule: "between two interpretations, always choose the wider one" (as I believe I once said to a student working on me), but on reflection this may well not be true. In a different case the narrower meaning might be more just, the wider one more banal (there's a good example in chapter 5). Or both may be valid (but then both must be given), or (as in Derrida, above), the "more powerful one" may be best. I am occasionally delighted by interpretations that enrich my original intention, and this might well have been the case here. But it seems not to be.
4) Back to the poetic function: the juxtaposition with Herodotus is more comical, more desperate in my "intended" reading: if Herodotus (from Asia Minor) has never visited Europe, can't imagine it, and says barmy things about it, the situation hasn't changed much.

This is perhaps a heavy-handed analysis for such a small item, but that is the author's situation today: even with devoted friends and fans (but for whose appreciation and loyalty I wouldn't exist at all), the author is more and more invisible, even when not using invisible constraints or visible complexities. All power to the reader, yes, if he's prepared to read—as indeed Martin was, in the rest of his article. This was (in my reading) just an unexpected and perhaps mutual misunderstanding.

⁶⁹

So much for the reader. Few schools of criticism, except critics of Postmodernism such as Brian McHale (1987), paid even implicit attention to either the phatic function (Jakobson's minimal example was "hello" on the telephone) or the metalinguistic function (the code used, which here would include playing with narrative conventions). But now the wheel has come full circle, and we are back to the referential function (world represented), with content summary, and to the emotive function (author).

Now it is perfectly legitimate to argue that in some cases mere content summary is precisely what is needed in reediting or writing about forgotten or neglected writers, in order to open up a field for later close reading. Perhaps. Or again, many writers, of any sex, race, or period, are more interesting for what they are saying than for how they are saying it, so that neutral content summary gives a fair and clear impression of them. However, the what without the how can easily date, being, like ideology, prisoner of its time. So, of course, can the how without the what, for nothing is more unreadable than a highly mannered narrative to the manner born dead. These are truisms, but often forgotten. Nevertheless, content summary, ideological rewrites, and loose thematics do not work with, and can be very unfair to, the many writers who are trying both to say important things and to alter the familiar forms of narrative.

The return to the author's intention (emotive function for Jakobson) is perhaps understandable in reaction to the long period when the author was, as person, ignored (New Criticism) or declared dead, admittedly a long time ago (Barthes 1968). I opened the first chapter by saying that the current paradox is what urged me to risk this book. Never have authors been so much in demand to explain themselves, at least orally. More curious still is the reliance on biographical criticism and the preference for autobiography; or, even more deeply contradictory, as I mentioned in chapter 1, on asking the author, at a time when the convention against an author reviewing himself or even writing critical essays on herself still holds. Asking the author, chiefly prevalent in the mania for interviews, from those of research students to those of empty chat shows (a plug in fact) that barely mention the book, is clearly a superficial side effect of author intention, except that, in the days of author's intention no student was allowed to work on a living author. What was taught was how to discover the author's intention *from the text*. The interview may be considered a widening of tools, but as a method it is A) restricted to living authors, B) greatly abused, and C) often degrading to the author, who is not necessarily good at the plug, or even at evading imprisonment in the interviewer's trivial ideas.

As to biographical criticism, I shall end with an interesting example of a critic not knowing a piece of biographical information and being the better critic for it. Susan Rubin Suleiman wrote a short essay on *Between*, using content summary, alas, but intelligently (1994). The novel is "about" a simultaneous interpreter. Now this is not in any sense an autobiographical novel. I have never been a simultaneous interpreter. But I invented the protagonist in an attempt to explore the state of bilingualism, which *is* autobiographical. To get away from my own state (French/English), I made her half-German, half-French, which produced quite a different background. Nevertheless, an author uses general experience, and I used my experience of international travel and hotels, far less familiar in those days than it is now. I'm inside her head the whole time (see chapter 3 for method), and I was interested in juxtaposing different types of discourses, notably those heard at all the international conferences, but also more personal ones from people of different origins. And one of those dotty discourses was that of the Vatican in proceedings for annulment. Now this *was* autobiographical. I had been trying for years to get an annulment of a brief and early wartime marriage so that my postwar Polish husband could practice his religion. This of course is not in the novel. My unnamed protagonist is married to an Englishman and merely wants to annul, as Suleiman puts it: "Because she wants to remarry? No. Because she is a practising Catholic? No. Because. . . ." Suleiman has been quoting the following passage from the proceedings:

— Un cottage? Que voulez-vous dire, un cottage?
— Hé bien mon père, une toute petite maison, à la campagne.

> A box a refuge a still small centre within the village within the wooded countryside within the alien land, where Mr Jones the builder who converts the bathroom says bee-day? Oh you mean a biddy. Yes I can get a biddy for you but you 'aven't got much room 'ave you? Ah si! Un cottage. The pale fat priest-interpreter looks over his half-spectacles made for reading the sheafs of notes before him. Un piccolo chalet. Va bene cosí? Un piccolo chalet?
> — Va bene. (Suleiman 1994, 172; Brooke-Rose 1984, 418)

She then goes on to quote a further passage "which occurs a few lines after the first, part of what Martin has called Brooke-Rose's "interest in verbal collage"—the priests have been replaced by TV newscasters, "archpriests of attualita," celebrants of instant news in an instant world. Their words are in turn interrupted by the explosive celebration of OMO—not a new brand of humanity but an improved (or so we are told) brand of detergent that "washes even whiter": "Da oggi con Perboral! Lava ancora piú bianco! Gut-gut. Piú bianco than what? We live in an age of transition, perpetually between white and whiter than white. Very tiring" (Suleiman 1994, 171–72, Brooke-Rose 1984, 418–19).

After further analysis Suleiman concludes:

> Why does the woman seek an annulment, even though she wants neither to remarry nor to reenter the Church? I would hazard a speculation related to history: to annul a marriage is to decree, with all the authority invested in the Church, that a certain event never happened. In other words, it is to do away with history—or rather, not to do away with it but return it to an earlier time, a time of wholeness, prior to the breaking (of the hymen). When she was a young girl, before the war, the woman visited, with her German boyfriend, the Church in Munich that holds the remains of "the frail skeletal nun in a glass case, Heilige Munditia. Patronin der alleinstehenden Frauen." During the war, she visited it again, with a different boyfriend but the church was damaged and the nun gone. Much later, now, she visits the church again, this time unaccompanied: the church has been "totally rebuilt" and the frail skeletal nun once more lies in her glass case. (Suleiman 174–75)

Now this is a much richer and truer (i.e., fictional, truer to the fiction) interpretation than any based on the fact that I used a bit of personal experience of a hilarious discourse, adapting it to very different and invented circumstances, for of course I was not in Germany during the war, nor do I have a half-German background, nor would I have wanted or not wanted to "re-enter" the Church, since I was never in it. Suleiman arrived at this fictional interpretation without knowledge (which might well have misled her) of that bit of personal history, simply through close reading and imaginative criticism.

Between was considered difficult at the time, partly because of its many languages (ten altogether, miming conferences and travel bewilderment). But as another of my insightful critics, Sarah Birch (1994), has said, the world of international travel and people knowing more than one language has caught up with it, and it seems almost straightforward today.

So here I am, having protested against the kind of criticism that summarizes content and turns to the author for explanation, deconstructing my protest by summarizing and explaining myself, if, at least twice, via (good) summarizing critics. I can only say, defensively, re-enter author but reluctantly, with a plea for an attempt to reunify all the many and now scattered ways of enthusing about a necessarily chameleon text and transmitting that enthusiasm without killing the chameleon through summary, ideology, a rigidly held theory, or imposition of abstract structures that have only a limited relevance to any text, using a sort of chameleon or even magpie criticism, that uses the best of past isms without fear of unfashion, and this or that theory if it can enhance understanding, but above all, genuine enjoyment, insight, imagination, a "gift outright" of ourselves, and the compliment of careful reading; a plea for the unsplitting of what I have called Splitlitcrit.

3

A Writer's CONSTRAINTS*

IN THE DAYS WHEN I was introducing first-year students to literary theory, I used to start with practice. I would ask the students to invent a short opening sentence for a story.

One such sentence was the following:

He sat on the chair, kicking the bed.

This isn't the most brilliant opening sentence imaginable, but it served, as almost any sentence would serve, to reveal two main features:

1) Any narrative sentence, even by unpracticed writers and without their conscious knowledge, assumes certain conventions. This one, for instance, starts *in medias res,* a technique going back to early epic, which produces a constraint: it arouses an expectation of explanation some time (who the man is, why he is kicking, and so on) in some form or another, either in flashback, called analepsis—usually marked by the pluperfect but also in the past—or else through dialogue, which can include thoughts in free indirect discourse (f.i.d.). I shall return to f.i.d. in a moment.

The sentence is also in the past tense (he sat), and uses one continuous tense (kicking), which arouses expectation of some punctual or singulative action sooner or later. These are grammatical con-

---

* Given as the James Bryce Memorial Lecture, Somerville College, Oxford, 2 March 1993, printed by Oxuniprint, Oxford University Press.

straints, but they are inevitably linked to the questions of content posed by the second feature that the sentence reveals, namely,

2) Any narrative sentence at once imposes certain "content" choices, which then become constraints. The writer must decide which part of the sentence to develop first: the *he*, who can be further described, given a name, or words to speak or thoughts to think; or the writer can hold back on that and develop the action of kicking—is it brutal, noisy, gentle, regular, intermittent, damaging, will it go on or stop, and if it stops, will it be because of a completely new action? Or the writer can develop the surroundings—the chair, the bed (is it empty?), the room. You'll notice that *the* chair, rather than *a* chair, already implies familiarity (hence the expectation of being let in on it), and this leads to the main decision, for above all the writer must decide pretty soon who is speaking: is it a dramatized narrator, and if so, is it someone inside the room and part of the action, or someone watching in the next room, or spying at the window (in which case he may not hear whether the kicking is noisy). Or is it our old friend the omniscient author, and if so will the author switch focalizations—for instance on someone else in the room—or will the author confine focus to that of the man kicking, and if so, will that view be purely external, as in film, or will the author go inside the man's mind, perhaps in f.i.d.?

These are familiar constraints, second nature to any writer, though inexperienced readers are usually astonished by the sheer number of decisions to be taken before the next sentence or the next. Indeed, these decisions may be invisible constraints to both naive readers and readers so experienced they no longer notice them. Every writer absorbs them by instinct, even sometimes as a child, and the early Structuralists often seemed ridiculous with their earnest codification of what we all know. The point was not, of course, to teach creative writing but to lay bare the structures for further analysis.

All writing, even nonfictional, produces such constraints, but fiction, being in principle not argumentative, or only indirectly so, and more free-ranging than, say, scholarly writing, is beset with constraints at every sentence. In addition, the writer is freer to break them. It is quite a shock, for example, when roughly in the middle of *Moby-Dick,* a huge novel, after we have been seeing every detail of the whaling ship from the viewpoint of the narrator-character Ishmael, a lowly deckhand, our identification with his viewpoint is suddenly switched to Captain Ahab's thoughts, by realistic definition unknown to the narrator, who then more or less vanishes from the story until he reappears as sole survivor at the end, to tell the tale. It is as if Ishmael had made a huge imaginative leap and himself become Captain Ahab, taking the reader—who follows him willingly—along with him.

It is the constant defamiliarizing of familiar constraints that I want to discuss now, in order to bring out the fact that, if conventions produce constraints, constraints can also rapidly become conventions and, through overuse or misuse, slowly die.

༄

Let us take one of them, f.i.d.[1]

I said earlier that one of the options for the author of our kicking man is to go inside his mind, and that one of the ways of doing this is through free indirect discourse. F.i.d. has had a long life and yet it is a relatively recent invention of the modern novel, first found, sparsely, in the seventeenth century, then rapidly developed. Before that, in classical and medieval epic or romance, a character's thoughts were given either in straight narrative sentences, that is, in indirect discourse, called *oratio obliqua* ("he said that," "he thought that"), or in direct discourse, *oratio recta*, that is, in dialogue, from "he spake," plus the words of the speech, to the modern "he said, she said," and so on, even if these insertions, called parentheticals, are mostly discarded today.

Indirect discourse reproduces thought or speech but as summarized by the author, so that we don't necessarily get the character's actual words. It shifts both tense and person: for example, in the future: "he thought that he would tell her" reports an implicit "I shall tell her" of direct discourse (spoken or thought). Plato dealt with the difference long ago in *The Republic* (3:392–93), distinguishing Chryses's prayer at the opening of the *Iliad* as first summarized by the poet, then given in the priest's words. Plato preferred the former, that is, Narrative Sentences, or "telling," as opposed to dialogue, so that "telling" became the dominant mode (I simplify) all the way to Henry James's famous inversion, "showing" versus "telling."

Free indirect discourse seems to stand between narration and dialogue. It keeps the past tense form of a Narrative Sentence and adopts the same tense-and-person shifts as indirect discourse but is apparently at the other extreme from narration, since it purports to give, through the vocabulary and syntax and exclamations, the actual speech or thoughts of the character, including remembered or intended speech, rather than the author's version of them, but with nevertheless the author's "apparent" control through the change of tense and the shift to the third person.[2]

Here is an amusing example from Jane Austen, in the scene where Mrs. Bennett bids farewell to Mr. Bingley in *Pride and Prejudice* [d.d. = direct discourse, f.i.d. = free indirect discourse, n.d. = narrativized discourse):

> "Next time you call," said she, "I hope we shall be more lucky." [d.d.]
> He should be particularly happy at any time, &c &c, and if she would give him leave, would take an early opportunity of waiting on them. [f.i.d.]
> "Can you come tomorrow?" [d.d.]
> Yes, he had no engagement at all for tomorrow [f.i.d.]; and her [f.i.d.] invitation was accepted with alacrity. [n.d.]

Who says or thinks "&c &c"? The character? The author? Or a narrator? I'll take up that problem, with this example and others, in chapter 7.

This extraordinary invention (f.i.d.), is here still fresh and startling. My point, which in my last critical book (1991) I added to the whole dispute, is that during its long development since the eighteenth century, f.i.d. has become a dead convention. With the author eclipse called for at the turn of the last century, writers began to use f.i.d. to filter complicated narrative information through the character's mind, including explanatory flashbacks. This is particularly salient in early science fiction, where scientists, for instance, are made either to exchange elementary facts in dialogue (d.d.) with each other or to think them on their own in f.i.d., elementary facts they must take for granted and that are really intended by the author for the reader. But f.i.d. is also misused in the realistic novel, thus killing both the convention and the realism for which it was invented. We do not offer information to ourselves in pluperfect explanatory flashbacks or conditional futures when we think. In other words, f.i.d. is a convention. And every convention has its constraints, which may be broken to enrich it (as we can see in Jane Austen) but not to weaken it or merely to give narrative information to the reader that the characters wouldn't speak or think. I shall be taking up this whole question of narrative instance in chapter 7, where we shall also see that such sentences, when not given as intentions and suppositions but as past actions or thoughts, can be syntactically identical to Narrative Sentences, and hence are ambiguous.

Long before I had become aware of any of this, I had stopped using f.i.d., for the simple reason that when, in the early sixties, dissatisfied with my early novels, I started experimenting with narrative instance, I switched to the present tense, in which f.i.d. is not possible, at least not as we know it, and certainly not in that particular use I made of the present tense, which I owe to Robbe-Grillet.

Despite many attacks on and dismissals of the *nouveau roman*, the present tense is now in frequent use, but without Robbe-Grillet's sublety or accompanying constraints. It is found in many novels, especially in feminist and Postcolonial novels, which are otherwise dealing with the kind of social and psychological problems Robbe-Grillet totally rejected. A constraint developed for a particular, limited purpose, for an externalization that merely suggests inner intensity—in other words, to get away from psychology and what Robbe-Grillet (1963) called *les mythes de la profondeur*—is being extended back into its traditional opposite. Naturally there are brilliant exceptions: for example, Muriel Spark's use of the present tense in her minute-by-minute theological thriller *The Driver's Seat* (1970), broken into as it is with omniscient prolepses in the future tense telling us that the protagonist will be found stabbed to death. Possibly Robbe-Grillet also would have kept the present tense for those moments, destabilizing the narrative. (See also chapter 7 for Spark's *The Abbess of Crewe*).

If I'm right about these two relatively new narrative conventions (f.i.d. and, more recently, the present tense, which bans it) and their later misuse, they each perfectly illustrate Sarraute's reversal of the old dichotomy between Realism and Formalism. Formalism, probably since Hegel (1807), was then regarded as superficial and decorative. Later, with the Russian Formalists and all that followed, it came to be re-emphasized as the basis of creativity. Sarraute in a way goes back to Hegel, though without the decorative implication, by brilliantly reversing his opposition, insisting that the true realists are those who look so hard at a changing reality that they have to invent new forms (f.i.d. earlier, the present tense now) to capture it, whereas the formalists are the epigones who come afterwards, taking over these once unfamiliar but now ready-made forms and pouring into them a perfectly familiar reality anyone can see (as in the twentieth-century misuse of f.i.d., and, now, already, the misuse of the present; see chapter 7 for more detailed discussion). When Sarraute said this (Sarraute 1956), she was in a sense still part of an old dispensation that regarded reality as pre-existent and merely to be "captured" by art rather than as a new reality created by the artist (or anyone) through language.

This brings me to the vexed question of "experimental" writing, or the "experimental" novel. What does it mean? Is it a genre? Just as "women's novels" seem often to be treated as a separate genre (out of fear? timidity? scorn? ignorance?), one often gets a similar impression with the word *experimental*: there is the Realistic novel, the Gothic novel, the detective novel, the thriller, the historical novel, the romance novel, the science-fiction novel, the autobiographical novel . . . , and, it seems, an unidentifiable category called the experimental novel, a ragbag of anything so far uncategorized or unfamiliar, undefinable because its constraints are either unperceived or different in each case. If one happens to be both a woman and an experimenter, one's work tends to be regarded suspiciously as doubly a different genre, not quite relevant.

Added to that, the phrase I've just used, "different in each case," increases the alienation, although it does perhaps best define *experiment* in the wide sense: *experiment* not in its scientific sense of reproducibility as basic requirement but "experimental" writer as someone who tries something different each time, which may indeed make things difficult for the labelers. But in a still wider sense every writer except the most formulaic tries something different each time, or goes further than he or she did before. It's a matter of degree, not of kind. One can experiment with all types of novels, from realistic ones to pure fantasies. To my mind, "experiment" (like "woman's" or "black," etc.) cuts across all genres, and, needless to say, experiments can fail; they can be imitative or pointless, like other writing, nor of course is technical experiment alone sufficient. Nor is it necessarily antirealist to experiment, though the experiment may put in question certain conventions of realism.[3]

Because I experiment with narrative conventions and language, and a bit differently each time, I have been called antirealist—among other things. I am not antirealist, if by realism one means representation, and I do not think that a writer can be antirepresentation: language is representational, and even a fantasy has to be rooted in realistic representation or cease to be narrative. The supernatural or even the most outrageous narrative infractions we see in cartoons and films with morphing special effects are ultimately only pleasurable in contrast to familiar expectations, and what matters is whether the conventions used are tired, and therefore unconvincing.

∞

I shall now try to be a little more specific about what I've been doing.

I first wrote four conventional, satirical novels, from 1957 to 1961 (i.e., too fast). And although I had no trouble publishing them and got immediate status as a writer and considerable attention (far more than after I started experimenting), I was dissatisfied, rightly or wrongly. Muriel Spark, a very old friend, told me in the eighties not to dismiss this early work as it's part of my "oeuvre." That's as may be, and very kind of her, but I cannot judge. I am only talking biographically, of a very real dissatisfaction.

In the third of my novels, *The Dear Deceit* (1960), I already threw my narrative machinery into reverse: the hero gets younger in each chapter—an antinarrative device, for readers are frustrated in their expectations of continuation at each episode. This device has been used since, by C. H. Sisson in *Christopher Homm* (1984) and more recently by Martin Amis in his remarkable *Time's Arrow* (1991). This could be called a constraint in the use of sequence. In my case, I think it also represented a way of distancing myself, for the novel was directly based on research I had done on my almost unknown father's life, who was much older than my mother and who died when I was eleven, in London when we lived in Brussels. Discovering by chance strange things about him (he was a thief and mythomaniac, as well as an Anglican Benedictine monk in the late eighteen-nineties, and was sent to Parkhurst prison), I later decided to find out more, contacting anyone still alive who knew him, reading up the case in the church newspapers and so on. The novel was a straightforward biographical task, but I changed myself into a young man, who appears first as a small boy learning of his father's death then disappears from the picture as we move from the father's deathbed to earlier and earlier episodes, ending with another small boy in Warwickshire and the young man (me) at the end, talking to his mother (mine), by then a Benedictine nun. I think it was the true fact of the two Benedictines, one at each end, with children in the middle (during the early twenties), that most fascinated me.

But the backwards narration only gives extra irony, with promises of love or ambitious projects already known by the reader to have gone wrong, and despite the experiment, each chapter is told in traditional narrative, as indeed are Sisson's and Amis's experiments, though Amis goes much further and moves back with each sentence, writing dialogue backwards. I may be wrong, but I feel that this is perhaps pushing the constraint further than it will go, constantly pointing up the trick, for we soon learn to read dialogue upwards. Clearly the end of that logic would be to write every sentence and even every word backwards. There are, in other words, constraints within a chosen constraint. At any rate, my own less ambitious attempt didn't satisfy me except as a one-off that was fun, and I never did that again.

Clearly composing backwards, in whatever way, is a structural rather than a grammatical constraint. There are many constraints other than grammatical ones. In *Such,* apart from my main narrative constraint (pronounless present tense; see chapter 7), it was a metaphoric constraint; in *Thru* it was part typographic but mostly theoretical, the sought-for impossibility of deciding who the narrator is (see chapter 5); in *Textermination,* metalepsis and the sought-for impossibility of recognizing all the fictional characters; in the two SF novels *Xorandor* and *Verbivore* it was the narration wholly in dialogue.[4]

෴

I have selected two novels on which to end this chapter's discussion of constraints: *Between* and *Amalgamemnon.* In each I use specific, grammatical constraints rather than the more general ones I have just mentioned (structural, metaphoric, metaleptic, typographic, or those playing with limitations of knowledge), let alone the ordinary narrative constraints known to all with which I began.

The protagonist of *Between* is a simultaneous interpreter in French and German, but she has an English husband. She lives between languages, between conferences, between places, in airplanes and hotel rooms, which look more and more alike. She has no name, and uses no "I" except in dialogue; in other words, I am inside her, stating in the present tense what she sees, says, thinks, hears—snippets of travel talk, slogans, conference jargon, reception talk, airport announcements, and so on, often in different languages. But the new constraint I have added is not to use the verb *to be.* That's very difficult, incidentally, it's so easy to slip in an apostrophe-s, and when I told my Italian translator about the constraint he actually found an apostrophe-s which I had to correct for the *Omnibus* edition. Nevertheless, after finishing the novel, I had so got into the habit that I went on avoiding the verb *to be* for months in my reviews, even for the *Times Literary Supplement,* which was anonymous then, so that one couldn't say "I"—an involuntarily double constraint that may have produced some syntactic contortions at the time.

So what were the reasons? There were two, the first of which was, I insist, realistic, or at least mimetic, in two ways:

1) My protagonist is constantly on the move, and indeed I also use, more occasionally, another technique, that of starting a sentence which continues in a grammatically correct way, but by the end of the sentence we are elsewhere in space and time.

   That is one sense of the verb *to be:* the plate is on the table; the tree is tall; I am, statically, here. Its omission should create, invisibly, the sense that I am not here, "I" (the protagonist) am constantly elsewhere or on the move, especially since "I" doesn't use "I," exept in dialogue.

2) The other sense is *to exist,* and its omission should create the impression, without a banal verbalized search for identity, that my protagonist has none, not in the sense that she is seeking one but in the sense, already explored in *Out,* that neither she nor others have one: we none of us have. Each of us is many; identity is wholly constructed and deconstructed by our world, in her case, permanently translating ideas not her own, permanently waking up in different hotel rooms, which are all the same but in different countries, as are, implicitly, all the conferences.

All this may not, of course, be directly expressed by the lack of the verb *to be* any more than it could suggest that I as author am not there behind the text, only that the relatively recent concept of identity has caused so much harm that I, for one, was deconstructing it as theme even then—I mean before "Deconstruction" occurred as a technique, although to this day many novels are still discussed in terms of a search for identity. But such deconstruction was not my conscious purpose, even if it occurred. The lack of the verb *to be* is meant merely to suggest all this subliminally, as do other techniques throughout the novel.

The second reason I chose to work with this constraint was stylistic, or more precisely, practical, work-centered: the imposition of a constraint as such. Avoiding the verb *to be* forced me each time to find another verb, usually more dynamic, active, even metaphoric, and this rejoins the mimetic reason of constant movement. But it does also prevent sliding into facility and cliché. This second reason applies to all the constraints I have used; they force me to evade the obvious, expected next word—invisibly so.

To give an idea of the resulting flavor (since all lectures by authors end in a reading), here is an extract from the second chapter, representing a still moment of meditation on the techniques of simultaneous translation. Yet the passage is full of movement, I hope, because of all those other verbs and the juxtaposition technique:

> Steadily, in well formed phrases hitting the German nail on the French pinpoint. Unless alternatively concision shrinks the abstractions like angels to a pinhead and the pinhead pricks the Gallic nuance which escapes like gas depending on the speaker's nationality in French, Hungarian for instance or Chinese or mediocre, depending on the theme the time the place the climate, whether canyons or mountains create different pressures and great holes of air into which the plane sinks suddenly with a lilt of the stomach as in the Výtah—Ascenseur. Privolavač it says, Appel.
>
> In der Luft gibt's keine Grenzen. The dark handsome Viennese leans right across from the left to photograph the Danube which from der Luft looks actually quite blue to prevent any true exchange of thoughts above the close breath and perhaps intentional nearness unless he genuinely wants to photograph die Donau für die Kinder with a tip of nose in the foreground and maybe a dark green shoulder or curve of bosom even and the enormous wing spreading back moving at speed over the Danube quite blue from der Luft and gone.
>
> Ah but airports have frontiers. And travel-talk ensues with Herr Helmut von Irgendetwas who travels in textiles as others travel in simultaneous interpretation. To inflate pull red toggle (1). To top up, blow into mouthpiece (2) in order to prevent any true exchange between the close breath and the leaning forward beyond keine Grenzen, obeying the innumerable instructions

that translate time speed height desire into locality and channel and the slow descent into matter. You will find your life-jacket under your seat. This life-jacket can serve on an unconscious person. Uw zwemvest bevindt zich onder uw stoel. Dit zwemvest kan dienen voor een bewusteloos persoon. Questo salvagente one day will have no frontiers and no passports per assistere anche una persona priva de conoscenza. Aber natürlich, selbstverständlich, hoffentlich und so weiter.

As I said, nobody, of course, noticed the absence of the verb *to be* until I mentioned it in an interview much later, whereupon it got (very) occasionally repeated without further discussion or exploration, and the one person I told sooner attributed it to the wrong novels. You might feel that therefore the supposed loss of identity in the popular sense would also go unnoticed, but then, that's rather the point, isn't it, and a mimetic point: you feel the loss of that kind of identity when nobody notices you. So the constraint at least satisfied me, if no one else. At least I had the above reasons. Perec's much more difficult lipogram seems to have had no such "motivation" (to use Brian McHale's distinction between Modern or epistemological instability, which still tries to motivate, and Postmodern or ontological instability, which does not). Perec simply chose *e* as lipogram because it's the most frequent letter in French. In other words, he chose it for the tour de force, which would then completely absorb him. He later wrote a novel with only *e* called *Les Revenentes* [sic] (1972) and for his much more readable *La Vie, mode d'emploi* (1978) he followed a rare chess grid for the knight's move on a ten-by-ten-square chessboard to decide the order in which to present the various tenants of the fictional building.⁵ As with Amis's *Time's Arrow,* which I deeply admired, I felt rightly or wrongly that this was not my way, that there are constraints within constraints.

In *Amalgamemnon* I experimented with a different constraint, which at first seemed more like an exclusive selection than an omission. Unlike the four previous novels, where the central consciousness of any one moment never says "I," this is a first-person narrative. But I decided to write it entirely in the future tense: a selection then, but an omission of other tenses. I later discovered, through one of my best critics, that it was a real lipogram, but semiconscious.

My original reason was technical, or rather, it arose out of literary theory. In *Discours du récit,* Genette had examined all the different narrative modalities that deal with time, viewpoint, distance, narrator position, and so on. Under narrator position he pointed out that although the narrator (I use his term) is free with regard to space, he must position himself with regard to time, since he must use tenses. The three possibilities are past, present, future. The vast majority of narratives tell of past events, some tell of simultaneous events, and some of future events. But the reader needs to know that the event has happened or is happening, and Genette insists that the future is only used in mini-narratives within narratives, such as prophecies, orders, threats, or proleptic information from the author, as in Proust, or in Spark's *The Driver's Seat*, cited earlier. Even the Apocalypse and science fiction are postdated from an imagined future and use the conventional narrative past tense.

And indeed, it is very difficult to use the future throughout, since it is antinarrative by definition. Maurice Roche, who used it in his first novel *Compact* (1966), in fact has different short sections in different tenses, each in a different typography (and, originally, different color, unreproduced, but now, after his death, about to be or perhaps already reprinted in color). In other words, he rings the changes. And Michael Frayn, whose novel *A Very Private Life* (1968) starts "Once upon a time there will be . . . " doesn't keep it up more than a page or two. So I took it as a challenge.

The second reason was, once again, mimetic. I insist on this word because I am so often called antirealist, when I am, on the contrary, a sort of naive mimetist, going back to essentials as if to strengthen them or to honor them. My protagonist is a teacher of classics who has been made redundant. She spends her time, when not with a macho lover, listening to the radio while reading Herodotus, which leads her into daydreams and invented stories. But this was just a setting, a mimetic pretext, in fact added on later to "motivate" this bizarre discourse in a specific character, rather than just a voice, but more especially to avoid the portentous tone the perpetual future seemed to bring. So I created this character. I tagged on a completely new first chapter installing her. When I say "tagged on," I mean I rewrote the whole novel in the light of this new first chapter, so that the bizarre discourse then falls into place, a sort of narrative with all the mini-narratives that go on in her head.

Nevertheless, despite the usual "about a redundant teacher" descriptions, she isn't the main point. For I was also, and again mimetically, trying to explore the pseudofuture we all now live in, the future of speculation about political events, violence, how people will vote, the risk of this or that action, what this or that leader will say, and so on. I don't know if you've noticed, but a large chunk of the news we hear every day is in the future tense or the conditional.

But I ran into tremendous difficulties. For one thing, as I've said, it's very hard to use the future for any length of time without sounding intolerably oracular (hence the mimetic and motivating framing). It took me four or five rewritten versions to get the tone right. For another thing, I had to make adjustments to my own constraint, especially in dialogue. People do not talk wholly in the future tense. So I widened the constraint to all nonrealized tenses (in fact, I used that phrase in the blurb, for this time I did tell, and as usual it aroused no interest): the conditional of course, and what's left of the subjunctive in English, the imperative, and, when forced to use the present, only questions and, possibly, negations. Strictly, I was wrong to include negations, but I'll come back to that in a moment. I also use the present in the modals *must, cannot,* and so on, and in the peculiar English future after *when,* in "when I go," and also in apparent exceptions such as "I promise," "I suppose," "I wish."

And what are those apparent exceptions? They're called, since J. L. Austin, performatives. I had stumbled on a completely different constraint. I say "stumbled" because, contrary to the image I sometimes get of being a very cerebral writer, who maybe kills her narratives with overconscious theory, I wasn't fully aware of what I was doing. That's usually how experiment works. One little idea leads to something quite other. And it wasn't until I went to a seminar on *Amalgamemnon* at Nanterre (Université de Paris X), given by a French philosophical critic, Jean-Jacques Lecercle, who then published his reading in 1991, that I realized what I had done. For he showed me that what I had in fact excluded were all constative sentences, called also assertive or declarative sentences by linguists.

But it was only a semiconscious decision. Lecercle didn't pick on those present tense negatives I had allowed myself in dialogue, then corrected without quite knowing why, and a few may have been left. I see now that clearly the negative transformation does not turn a constative sentence into a nonconstative sentence (the pot is on the table/is not on the table). My conscious aim had been merely to destabilize the narrative so that nothing could be said to be actually happening. But Lecercle's notion of what I had done is so beautiful, and so close, that I am adopting it, and discounting, as he may have done, those possibly uneffaced present tenses in the negative. And since I stumbled, and since the critic is so rare and enchanting who can see beyond the author's conscious "intention" to something greater, I had better end by leaning on him to summarize what I did.

Constative sentences are sentences of which it can be said that they are either true or false, and to evade them is to evade this obligation. Yet all constative sentences in a fiction, he says, following Austin, have an ambiguous status, since they are true within the fiction yet false as fiction. What I did was therefore to push this truism to its limit.

Philosophers, notably those who deal with the logic of propositions, have always had trouble with nonconstative sentences. You may remember that Austin excluded all fiction from his study, though in a way the sentences he gives as examples are themselves small fictions, for example, "he said, 'Shoot her,'" or his story about black swans in Australia. Various logics have been invented to deal with this problem, notably modal logic, which has been the most fruitful for the study of fiction, with its concept of possible worlds (the world of 1832, Balzac's world, and so on). But, says Lecercle, modal logic does not apply to *Amalgamemnon*. We're wandering, not in the fictional, but in language. Why?

A lipogram is usually discreet—as I said, nobody noticed the absence of *to be* in *Between*. But in English the auxiliaries *shall* and *will,* even abbreviated, even much varied with *might* and *must* and *may,* are very visible and audible, and in fact mask the real lipogram. They exclude the possible world solution because they are not logical modalities but modal auxiliaries (*modalités/modaux*), that is, elements of grammar, of the natural language. A modal is always virtually ambiguous: is it an innocent future? a question of will? a wish? a probability?

Lercercle insists that the future in *Amalgamemnon* is not teleological (otherwise it *would* be, and, but for my rewrites, very nearly was, unbearably portentous, and the teleological future is just what I forbade myself). It's closer, he says, to the Heideggerian *Zukunft* or going towards death, outside the present, ek-stasis. And he goes into four *Dasein*-ish consequences of my grammatical choice. But I have had to abjure the philosophical aspects of my choice (see chapter 1).

The ineluctable future is what my protagonist fights; she lets multiple possibilities come to her and play together. So once again, identity is blurred, and this also affects the ontological status of the characters she creates, out of mythical genealogical trees or, for some, constellations. One of her ex-students is called Anne de Romède, which gives her the name Andromeda. She herself, of Greek origin, is called Mira Enketei, *en ketai* meaning "inside the whale," Mira being a not very bright star in the constellation of the Whale, the whale recalling, of course, the prophet Jonah (and, more incidentally, the plane in *Between*, where the same metaphor occurs). Others call her Cassandra, or Cass, or Sandra. Far from having no name, she has too many, and this too has confused some critics.

This wordplay is carried over into the text, for further destabilization, with sometimes outrageous puns, and occasionally invisible ones, as well as the addition of the syllable *mim*, as in "mimecstasy," "mimagree," "mimage." For the novel concerns the mimetic fiction she is living, based on the play between the effect of the real and the effect of recognition. Recognition is what her selfish and useless mentor Willy expects, and what the reader desires, for it is the function of characters to constitute themselves clearly. But Willy is himself unstable, and his role is taken over at the end of the text by another boyfriend, even more useless, called Wally—a faint echo of "will" and "shall."

But the reader should get a clearer idea of the result if I end with the opening page. The first paragraph is fairly dense with wordplay I should perhaps comment on beforehand: the first line is calqued on Beckett's "I shall soon be quite dead at last despite of all," from *Malone Dies* (1958), the word *redundant* merely replacing the word *dead,* creating an equivalence, but only if one has the original first line in mind. The word *redundant* is used in its two senses, the social sense and that of information theory, as in *u* after *q,* which carries no information since *u* always comes after *q.* But I spell it *you* and *queue* which emphasizes the social sense. My as yet unnamed protagonist Mira can't sleep after sex and has withdrawn to the next room, where she is both listening to the radio and reading Herodotus, so that his various tales of kidnapped women starting wars weave in and out, the word *plagiarize* having originally meant "kidnap." That's the invisible pun, just as *Apollo apocalyptic* translates a similarly sound-echoing epithet (*apollonai,* you undo me), which is a pun in Aeschylus. Clytemnestra is called "the glory-gobbler," literally, because that's what her name means in Greek. These invisible puns do not block: they enrich, for some, but those bits of knowledge are not necessary to understanding:

> I shall soon be quite redundant at last despite of all, as redundant as you after queue and as totally predictable, information-content zero.

The programme-cuts will one by one proceed apace, which will entail laying off paying off with luck all the teachers of dead languages like literature philosophy history, for who will want to know about ancient passions divine royal middle class or working in words and phrases and structures that will continue to spark out inside the techne that will soon be silenced by the high technology? Who will still want to read at night some utterly other discourse that will shimmer out of a minicircus of light upon a page of say Agamemnon returning to his murderous wife the glory-gobbler with his new slave Cassandra princess of fallen Troy who will exclaim alas, o earth, Apollo apocalyptic and so forth, or else Herodotus, the Phoenicians kidnapping Io and the Greeks plagiarizing the king of Tyre's daughter Europe, but then, shall we ever make Europe? Sport. Rugger. The Cardiff team will leave this afternoon for Montpellier where they will play Béziers in the first round of the European championship, listen to their captain, Jo Tenterten, we're gonna win.

I could anticipate and queue before the National Education Computer for a different teaching job, reprogramming myself like a floppy disk, or at the Labour Exchange for a different job altogether, recycling myself like a plastic bottle, and either way I'd be a worker in a queue of millions with skills too obsolete for the lean fitness of the enterprise. Or I could hope for the best, which for me would normally arise out of dead men and women on a printed page, meanwhile anticipate on my severance pay if any and with my small savings make a humble down payment on a tumbledown small farm to go back to the soil as we all must, no sooner dead than briefly sung, to rear something or other, recycling weeds and words no sooner said than dung.

That would mean seeing the elegant portly man at the National Education Computer again who would during the burocrastination try insistently to exchange a word in someone's ear for a brief place in my life which he will imply will fall into disuse without his aid. The new generation will supertouchtype programmes and games to be superdevised by an elite of supertechnicians of communication I'll show you after hours he'll say.

Probably that would make the new generation the new high priests and oracles of pythian mysteries none will control himself or understand further, increasing gale eight, perhaps gale nine later, then becoming cyclonic in Fortes, occasional snow, good, becoming poor.

As you see, I have led you rather a long way from "he sat on the chair, kicking the bed."

4

ReMAKING*

I AM NOW GOING TO deal briefly with my autobiography, called *Remake*, which came out in 1996. It was presented by my publisher as an autobiographical novel, and one reviewer at least was puzzled. What is the difference? This is what I want to discuss.

I have always felt a deep prejudice against both autobiography and biographical criticism, at least with reference to writers. This is perhaps due to my early and long medieval training on poets called Anon., or poets of whom little is known but their names.

The previous novel, my twelfth, published in 1991, was ominously called *Textermination*. This had nothing to do with my extermination as a producer of texts, but rather with the slow (or rapid?) dying out of reading capacity. In that novel, hundreds of fictional characters from all regions and all periods gather at the Hilton Hotel in San Francisco, at a Convention of Prayer for Being: they all attend prayer sessions (pray-ins), separated into various religions, and pray in their various rituals to the Implied Reader for existence. I worked very hard so that no single reader should recognize every single character, for none of us has read everything, and most of us have experienced the anguish of arriving at a huge conference and knowing no one. The people running the conference are, of course, fictional, but they are *my* fictions, even if they seem nonfictional or "real" to the visitors from other fictions.

---

* Lecture given at a British Council Symposium in Solothurn, Switzerland, September 1996; published in *The European English Messenger* 5, no. 2 (autumn 1996): 12–17, and in *PN Review* 23, no. 3 (January–February 1997).

I play a great deal with these different levels of fiction. For instance, the opening (Christian) pray-in is interrupted by Muslim fundamentalist gunmen who want to kill Gibreel Farishta, one of the two main characters in Salman Rushdie's *The Satanic Verses* (1988); in other words, the *fatwah* is transferred from author to character, who, being a star Indian actor, appears in various disguises and always escapes. This the reader has to recognize, for no authors are mentioned. In other words, the allusive system assumes both that readers will have read the books out of which the characters present are taken (pleasure greater) *and* that they won't have read all the books or even have heard of them (pleasure less), and that this will differ from reader to reader.

In another type of play with fictional levels, one of my own fictional characters hosting the conference is a graduate student called Kelly, who represents the reader's own confusion. She finds herself on a vast list of forgotten characters nobody reads or invites, and therefore disappears. This is repeated, even more ironically, with Mira Enketei, the protagonist of my own earlier novel *Amalgamemnon* (which no reader will have read), who is briefly seen as one of the guests and at one point is supposed to be the author of *Textermination*.

I said the title *Textermination* was ominous. I don't know whether that was the reason, but after that novel, in which I had such fun, I was totally blocked, for several years. There's usually a longish space between my novels, but this is because I rewrite and couldn't do so in the academic year. In this case, I was already retired, so that did not apply. Even so, after I've finished and have sent off one book, I'm normally already toying with or working on another idea, however long it takes. This time there wasn't even an idea. I felt bereft. I now realize that I must have fallen, unwittingly, into a numerological superstition. I had written four fairly conventional novels, very fast, at the turn of the fifties and sixties. Then I started experimenting and wrote four novels with short prepositional or adjectival titles, *Out, Such* (that's the adjectival one), *Between,* and *Thru.* Then four novels with one-word—but longer and punning—titles, *Amalgamemnon, Xorandor, Verbivore,* and *Textermination,* making twelve. But I had also written four serious critical books over the years.[1] I'm not normally superstitious, and I think the numerological blockage was more an aesthetic than a doomful one: to write another novel would break that beautiful four-times-four sequence, making the list of novels thirteen and the list of books seventeen.

So when my publisher suggested I write an autobiography, my first reaction was naturally no, never. Then, tied up in my blockage, I thought, well, as an exercise, it might unblock me. And, after all, an autobiography is neither a novel nor a critical book.

Isn't it, though? Where are the frontiers? Critical writing is yet another interpretation, in other words another fiction grafted on the original. And as for fiction, what is the difference in epistemological status between, say, Defoe's *Robinson Crusoe* and his *Journal of the Plague Year*, which is neither a journal nor even a reliable documentary? I start, you see, with the beginning of the modern novel, to show the ambiguity at the source. As Oscar Wilde quipped, the nineteenth century as we know it is entirely an invention of Balzac. Or, later, as Barthes said on Balzac: "the realistic author spends his time referring back to books: reality is what has been written" (1974, 38). And today, of course, we are, through the media, faced with the problem of "faction," or the indistinguishability of fact and fiction, since even the most "truthful" documentary or reportage dresses the topic, using the techniques of fiction.

Or, to change the register, what is the epistemological status of, say, a Structuralist diagram such as the rectangle of contraries and contradictions from elementary logic (applying to any semantic opposition, e.g., masculine/feminine; nonmasculine/nonfeminine), used by Greimas more than thirty years ago in his narrative grammar to show the movement of an object O (the princess) from her palace to the villain's lair and back via the rescuing hero? As a representation of a narrative structure, it is a fiction, a theory about narrative movement, to be verified and proved, at least for simple tales. As a rectangle on a page it is an object, a visual fact. And this is the kind of ambiguity I was already playing with, partly by means of typographic display, in *Thru* (see chapter 5 for a close reading), when I was plunged into and teaching both Structuralism and Poststructuralism.

Clearly *Remake* had to be more narratively straightforward than some of my more experimental novels, although the difficulties were quite other. At any rate, I went all the way back to my beginnings, not so much as a writer but as a person (who is not normally represented as such in my novels). So I wrote down my life as I remembered it, in a conventional order, and the result was dreadful. The general formula, to exaggerate a little, was "And then . . . I—this, and then . . . I—that." It was my own life, my own experience, but even I couldn't reread it. So I put it aside.

An experience is not in itself of the slightest interest merely because it happened to oneself. We all know the bores who recount themselves but artlessly, or the semiarticulate who are interviewed on television after an event merely because they were there, or public figures asked for their reaction to some outrage and producing banalities. All I had done, in fact, was an exercise in (as Plato calls it) rememoration. The facts were "real" to me, but that was all that could be said about them.

Let me show you the difference with a brief example. In *Remake*, as I finally rewrote it, I describe a bare memory, more or less in the same form as in that first version, except that I say "the little girl" at this stage, instead of "I," and I'll explain that in a moment. After various primary schools in Brussels and London, my sister and I are suddenly given an English governess, in London:

> And mysteriously, to cover the transition back to Brussels, a brief governess called Miss Enoch, with an atlas. Joanne remarks triumphantly, France is bigger than England. The little girl looks and sees a sort of solid square for France and, for England, a crochety old lady backside to the continent with stretched out legs driving a motorcar into the Atlantic, Ireland as the wheel. But Miss Enoch turns to the world page and says Look, everything pink on the map belongs to England. The little girl looks at the dot of England and the huge expanses of pink and asks, Why?(11)

This is from the first chapter, and if you read it you will see that I do other things to the passage immediately afterwards. But the memory is true, including my childish impression of England. The bit about the pink areas of the map, however, I had already used in my earlier novel *Between*, about the simultaneous interpreter who travels from conference to conference and hears and sees many languages. But the novel is also about the state of bilingualism, and to get away from my own (French and English), I made her French and German, and invented a whole German background for her. Among her occasional prewar memories, we get this:

> — Und alles ROTE auf der Karte, das gehört ENGland.
>
> The schoolmaster glares around the class, looking for a scapegoat perhaps.—Und alles GRÜNE auf der Karte, das gehört FRANKREICH.
>
> The gangling girl in pigtails grows cold and pale even as a girl she always did look pale, uninteresting, then suddenly hot and flushed as the whole class follows the stony glare at the französiches Mädchen responsible for the green on the map slightly deeper than the yellowish green vastness of the Soviet

republics right up to Siberia or for that matter Brazil and then again not quite so bright as the green United States of America together with Alaska beyond the crimson Canada the pale pink of Greenland (pink?) and responsible also no doubt for the dark and pale ROT on account of the Entente Cordiale. (Brooke-Rose 1984, 520)

The complete change of circumstances (that is, from an innocent questioning of empire by a little girl of six in 1929 to an imagined envy of empire by an invented German schoolteacher in the thirties) transmutes the "real" memory into something else, which is fiction.

This brings me to my second difficulty: when I write a novel, I like to invent as I go, not to know where I'm going, what will happen, what a character will grow into, each sentence leading to another and gradually creating a scene, a person, which gives rise to another scene and so on. But here I had all my material ready-made, not just in my head, but in the two hundred pages or so of rememoration I had done, and there was nothing for me to do but to rearrange it. I had done this very flatly in that first version, and I wasn't in the least tempted merely to improve it, or, as Hegel would say (for whom "form" is mere ornament), to adorn it. If I altered it at all, I had to rewrite completely.

The obvious and first solution was to scrap the pronoun "I," and get some distance. But this would merely lead me into another trap: most autobiographical novels are written in the third person with a fictional name, or even with "I" and a fictional name. Indeed, most novels use autobiographical material, far more so than I have ever done.

And then I had a brainwave. I decided to scrap all personal pronouns and all possessive adjectives: no *I, you, he, she, it, we, they,* no *my/mine, your/yours, her/hers, his, our/ours, their/theirs.* Now this was a real challenge: an autobiography without personal pronouns. Suddenly, I got interested again. I had the constraint I needed.

For I had already, in two novels, adopted such punctual constraints (see chapter 3). I have described my conscious motivations, but also, and only half-consciously at the time, as I now remember *Between* especially, I must have been feeling for both contemporary and later deconstructions of the notion of identity as a male humanist concept, a deconstruction already (perhaps incoherently) incipient in Virginia Woolf. A book often does more than it knows. On authorial identity, I remember writing an article on the *nouveau roman* for the *Observer* in

1961, entitled "The Vanishing Author" (speaking descriptively, regarding the *nouveau roman,* not defending it or making claims) some seven years before Barthes's more famous essay "The Death of the Author" in 1968—though of course mine was more naively, if less finalizingly, dogmatic—and eight years before Foucault's demonstration that the concept "author" is a construct out of specific operations (1969), all of which had been said by Booth in 1961. In 1968, just after the publication of *Between* in November, I went to teach in Paris and plunged into Lacan's *Ecrits* (1966) and his displacement of the subject, and more enthusiastically into Derrida (1973, 1976, 1978) and his deconstructions of fixed notions of essential truth. In 1974 came the deconstruction even of sexual identity by Julia Kristeva, for whom the dichotomy between masculine and feminine is metaphysical. Woman, as such, does not exist, except as a construct of the patriarchal symbolic order, negatively and marginally constructed through her refusal of it. Woman is "that which cannot be represented, that which is not spoken, that which remains outside naming and ideologies" (1974 a, b). All this would presumably apply also to the appalling tragedies caused by the notion of ethnic or national identity.

It was extraordinarily comforting in the early seventies to read as theory all that I already had been groping for in *Out,* where I reverse the color bar, as it was then called, and imagine the whites, called the Colourless, discriminated against as feckless, through the mind of an old white man, and in *Such,* where I imagine a man who has died briefly and sees distances between people as a radio telescope sees the stars, and in *Between,* where my simultaneous interpreter only emerges through the travel sights and the conference discourses she translates—in other words, as in *Out* and *Such,* through what hits that consciousness. This objectified narratorless mode, which is the only feature in my novels directly developed from Robbe-Grillet (see chapter 7, where this is analyzed in detail), not only privileges the time of story over the time of discourse but, more concretely, never lets this central consciousness say "I" except in dialogue, or even have a name. In *Between,* the central consciousness has a job that is pivotal in the sense of indispensable, but it is nevertheless marginal, intermediary. Above all, because of a new constraint, she cannot really *be;* she is a construct, as identity is a construct, or, in Derridean terms, she is "always already" there, and always deferred, if only until the next conference. Or so I saw it then, though others may see it otherwise.

By the next novel, *Thru* (written in 1970–72), I was much more conscious of all these things. For instance, I make it particularly difficult for the reader to identify with any narrator or to know who she or he is; is it Armel Santores or Larissa Toren? Or is it the students in a creative writing class? Or, at another point, the Master of Diderot's *Jacques le Fataliste*? (See chapter 5 for a close reading.) Then in the following novel, *Amalgamemnon*, I imposed the future tense only—or rather, nonrealized tenses—to find that, in fact, I had excluded all constative sentences (see chapter 3).

Now the constative tenses, the verb *to be*, and pronouns are the most stable elements of language. They didn't, for instance, get replaced by foreign loanwords, even after the thorough invasion of English by French from the eleventh to the fourteenth century. To omit any of them, such as pronouns, creates a certain floating instability of the narrative. In the case of *Remake*, doing without pronouns and possessive adjectives naturally abolishes the gender problems of he/she, the power problems of I/we, we/they, and the possession problems of my/your/his/her/our/their. It also abolishes the deictics (situational words and I/you), so that we are partly in a historic mode (which can't say "I" or "you," as discussed in chapter 7), but only partly, since I use the present throughout. And although I can't use certain time and place deictics such as *yesterday, tomorrow,* and so on, I do use others, such as *here, there, ago,* or pointers such as demonstrative pronouns. So, as with my other novels, I privilege the time of story.

Secondly, doing without personal pronouns meant using names a great deal, since a pronoun stands for a noun. And this led me, oddly enough, back to Chomsky. You may remember that many of Chomsky's example sentences are about John, for instance in the difference of deep structure between "John is easy to please" and "John is eager to please" (the subjects of *to please* are different), of semantic constraints in "John builds a house" but not the passive transformation * "John is built by the house," or "John continues" but not * "John elapses." Other examples are in the reflexivity rule, "$John_1$ killed $John_1$": if both Johns are the same (coreferential, same subscript) the second must be replaced by a reflexive pronoun: "John killed himself." My problem of self-confrontation was resolved: John confronts himself. Except that I mustn't use the reflexive pronoun "himself."

This John, who starts as an example in linguistics, soon becomes split up into many Johns, $John_{13, 51, 73}$ and other subscripts, who acquire personalities, as in a novel, according to what they say: John the nasty piece of perk, John the "lit-critter," John the pedant, John the psycho, and so on, who keep interfering with the narrative, especially at the beginning when I can't quite get going.

And this led me, quite naturally, since I must overuse proper names, to the decision that all my main characters, that is, all the people who most influenced me from childhood on, who "made" me, those I call the mentors, must be called John, or a variation: so I call my mother Jeanne, my sister Joanne, my favorite aunt Vanna (Giovanna), a cousin Jean-Luc, my first husband Ian, my second Janek, with friends and lovers called Joan, Jean, Jane, Janet, Jon, Jock, Sean, Hans, and so on. Anyone not so called is not a mentor. And, of course, I couldn't be called so, yet have to have a name, which isn't introduced until chapter 4 of *Remake*, when "the little girl," remembered by "the old lady," is named Tess, not because of Hardy but as a play on *text* (which gave *textile* and *tisser* in French, and *tessitura* in Italian, the quality of a voice) and a further play on *tesselate,* to build up with small tiles: "The little girl's name is Tess. Only a name and memory can tesselate and texture all those different beings, the baby in Geneva, the little girl in Brussels, Chiswick, Brussels, Folkestone London and all the others to the old lady in Provence" (41).

Once I had found these constraints, I forgot all about my prejudice against autobiography. Why? Because I could now have fun with it—though whether the reader can share the fun is clearly a very different problem, since the constraints are once again invisible. I don't mean that I could turn it into fiction and invent, but that my ready-made material could be transmuted into an autobiographical novel rather than an autobiography. My exercise in rememoration, in other words, had produced no being I could recognize, although all the memories were "real," whereas *Remake* produced someone or other I felt happy with. Identity, in other words, is a fiction, made of language, and, like all good fictions, is open-ended and slightly unreal. So my publisher was right. I could even leave out items of "reality," if the chosen constraint made one impossible. For instance, when I mention the trilingual jokes of my family in Brussels: "And the family deranges the range with trilingual jokes, quelle est la matière, raped carrots, what is loose, have a good Fahrt, there is no what, taking something mit, grandpère a été délayé, like a sauce" (10). But I had to leave out others, such as "do not derange yourself" or "ça turnupera" for "it'll turn up," a phrase I use to this day (to myself), since I always mislay things.

And quite often I had to leave out an anecdote because the punch line needed a pronoun, a possessive, or the real name. One example with all three: the original of "Janek" is Jerzy, Polish for George, pronounced Yégé and often mispronounced "Jersey" by the English. Rayner Heppenstall, an earlier experimental writer friend of ours in the fifties and sixties, apparently said to Muriel Spark, who told me of it many years later: "Wouldn't it be nice to see Christine without her jersey?" But perhaps it was just as well the constraints made me leave it out.

Alternately, I may have later invented some of these, the only real memory being the fact of the bilingual jokes. This is made explicit in a later episode about my brief wartime husband, whom I call Ian, a musician who, to my disappointment, decides to study law, and who is fond of facile, foreseeable jokes:

> Ian sends for big books on Roman Law and the Law of Tort, and a nutshell series including *Carriage of Goods by Sea in a Nutshell,* chortle. The jokes become legal jokes, playing on set phrases, breaking and entry and aggravated buggery, conduct calculated to cause a breach of promise (Tess smiles), loitering with intent to feel. But perhaps the old lady invented these, the real jokes forgotten. (121)

The whole of chapter 3, which, before I have even appeared as a child, tells of my mother's death in 1984, at the age of 92, is based on a diary I kept at the time, and diaries, as I clearly observe in the text, overuse pronouns. So I implicitly (or almost explicitly) break my own rule, partly because I'm using a real document, partly to point up the contrast, when strong personal emotion is at stake. All this is explained in the last chapter, in a conversation between Tess and the old lady (one and the same person), and more allusively earlier, in the first chapter, which is really about the resistance to autobiography that I've been talking about.

And I mean "talking," although I have retyped this lecture, for it points up my initial paradox about talking versus writing about oneself. This is my weakest chapter, said my friend Richard Martin of the "make Europe" controversy (who kindly let me keep it), and I agree. Yet as a lecture it went down like a bomb, raising laughs in all the right places. Was that because I've learned to "act" what I read or because that's what people want, autobiographical material and anecdotes? And is it, as a written chapter, weak merely because of my deep reticence about autobiography? I can't answer those questions, except to add yet another personal item: as a writer, and like all writers, I need criticism, but unlike many I'm good at taking it, desirous of it, and obedient to counsel unless it goes absolutely against my conscious intention. Nevertheless, not a single one of my publishers has ever given me such advice: my first, second, and third loved all I wrote and would even ring me two weeks later to say so. My fourth has been the opposite, taking so long to react that any advice he gives is difficult to apply. This happened with *Remake* (which is the only book of mine he "loved"); indeed, it's the only criticism any publisher has ever given me, and it turned out to be regrettable: the final chapter, which dealt with my then last twenty years in France, didn't interest him. Moreover, a late but finally refused remarriage with a long-lost playmate cousin ("Jean-Luc") from the beginning of the book "shocked" him, though the *retrouvailles* after forty-five years, created, both in life and in the book, an almost magical rounding off—but "almost" indeed: like other remarriage requests, my hard-won independence was once again at stake. But by the time my publisher read the book, I was so out of it that I scrapped the chapter rather than rewrite it, ending the book of my life in 1968, twenty-three years too early, that is, never really catching up with the "old lady of 72" of the beginning. Like falling off a cliff, one friend said. *Mea maxima culpa,* but not only mine. As for my last novel, *Subscript,* my publisher took a year to react, then pretended to have read it but showed he hadn't by making huge howlers in the blurb, which I had to correct quietly. It is sometimes hard for a writer, whether experimental or not, to get so little good advice.

However, I have decided to keep this chapter, for those interested in biographical criticism, and merely say, well, the book enabled me to break the four-by-four spell. Which I never really believed in anyway. By now, however, if this book is published, I shall have reached fifteen novels and five critical books, hardly an improvement, anti-numerologically speaking.

5

Is Self-Reflexivity MERE?*

MY NOVEL *THRU* HAS been classified among Postmodern self-reflexive novels, occasionally with an implied "merely." Since I play a great deal with narrative conventions, I fully accept the self-reflexivity. However, I would like to try to show, with a close reading of the first twenty pages, that this self-reflexivity, far from being "mere," or an end in itself, is a means to another end, this end being the exact opposite of self-reflexivity as normally understood.

First a few general comments. *Thru* is indeed a novel about my involvement with and parallel alienation from literary theory, involvement as craftsman, critic, and teacher, alienation as writer, so that it was written to resolve the conflict, as long ago as 1971, finished in 1972.[1]

I expected to be rapped on the knuckles for *Thru*, and was; even the *Times Literary Supplement* reviewer was content to mention the Saint-Laurent scarf I happened to be wearing in the photograph (code: Paris = pretentiousness), but I'm glad I wrote it, even if, once I had done it, I was not interested in attempting the same experiment again.

In McHale's definition of Postmodernism (1987) as ontologically unstable (versus Modernism, which he calls epistemologically unstable), it remains my most daringly ontologically unstable text and so my most wholly Postmodern—and he treats it as such. It is among the three most attractive to my fans (with *Between* and *Amalgamemnon*), and the one I'm most proud of, even if its difficulty has caused problems.

---

* Lecture given at a Conference on "Fiction/Faction" at the University of Warwick in 1995, and, on my way back to France, in the University of East Anglia. Published in *Quarterly West, Twentieth Anniversary Issue* (autumn–winter 1996–97): 230–65.

Yet the basic situation is ultrasimple, and I will use content summary here *before* plunging into the opening (whereas most content summary would end and never plunge): Armel Santores teaches creative writing in a radical university, unsituated but probably America and not Paris as some have biographically supposed (let alone, again as some have supposed, the Sorbonne where I did not teach), since no European universities except East Anglia taught creative writing at the time, nor would French students be capable of producing this text in English as they sometimes seem to be doing. Armel Santores was once married or living with Larissa Toren, a teacher but of much more esoteric theory and in another university (not in the same one, as usually read), since, among other reasons, they write letters to each other. Armel Santores is an anagram of Larissa Toren, except that she doesn't find her "I" in his name and he doesn't find his "me" in hers. They may be inventing each other. All this is clearly said, though not in these opening pages. In fact, there is no clear narrator: at first we have an anonymous text describing facts, but later this or that bit of text turns out to have been written by this or that student in the creative writing class, with comments from the teacher; at another time by the Master in Diderot's *Jacques le fataliste;* or by Larissa. At one point, Jacques's Master, commenting on a scene with Larissa in it, quotes an obscure paragraph by Kristeva (1970, 83) on the author having to pass through zero, and Jacques falls asleep.

At the beginning, however, we know none of this, and (as in the Realist novel but more so) we slowly have to constitute an imagined situation out of stray elements: a car, with glaring lights forming magic circles in the driving mirror, observations apparently by a man and later by "the mistress of the moment," a nice but ignorant girl, going back with him to her place. The car has one of those driving mirrors that, when one leans slightly to use it as mirror, splits two eyes into four, the upper two in the hairline. Later, one of the students, Myra Kaplan, writes out a fully realistic scene between Armel and (presumably) the girl in the car, who is then given a name, Ruth, anagram of *Thru* and *hurt*.

This simple situation could, of course, have been narrated as a classical campus novel, with the thoughts and the teaching discipline of each character given in the usual modern misuse of free indirect discourse, author comment, flashbacks, or unnecessarily explanatory dialogue. But I wasn't in the least interested in doing that, or indeed in any "real" situation, which in my novels is only the basic material with which to do something quite other. I chose to fragment it from the start, using a typography that mimes either what is being said, or an object such as the rectangle of the driving mirror, which then becomes the rectangles of a timetable, into which one enters as into a rectangular class, or (much later) the broken tablet of the Moses Commandments, or, in this extract, the Greimas rectangle of contraries and contradictories as narrative model, or the Lacanian rectangle of desire.

Here I want to make the point that when I say "mimes" the driving mirror, I mean just that. I'm often called antirealist, and since I use realist situations to play with them and produce other discourse, in that sense it's true. But language is referential, and every sentence we utter is intended to be realistic in this more absolute sense. If I'm antirealist it's only in the sense that I have been trying, along with others, to alter or refresh the more fatigued conventions of a specific genre called the Realist novel. So I'm more of an anti-Realist, with a capital *R*. Thus every sentence in *Thru* represents a reality, however imagined, however destabilized, as we all are.[2]

All the themes of the novel are announced in these opening pages: textuality, sexuality, memory, Derrida's architrace and trace, story and history, the partiality of theoretical discourse, teaching problems, and others.

The page numbers I shall refer to are from the first edition, but as this was simply photographed for the *Omnibus* edition (the only one now available), pages 1–21 correspond to pages 579–99 in the *Omnibus*. As far as possible my comments will face the page of *Thru* they refer to, or, when brief, be on the same page, so that my comments may precede or follow. This is difficult for printers (not quite achieved in *Quarterly West*, where, also, the last two pages of *Thru* I was commenting on were missing). Because of these reproductions from *Thru*, this chapter will be twice as long as the others.

༺༻

The faulty driving mirror is typographed as an incomplete rectangle—the word *place* displaced to leave a gap. The eyes, which are in their proper place, are now right on cue, printed as the letter O, then another long gap to "ask us," as if the correctly reflected eyes posed a problem, not the other eyes further up.

This is a wider and taller rectangle, still about the four eyes, two of them "correct" on either side of the nose, this nose mimed as an upside-down triangle, echoed at once as a traffic signal for danger, together forming an X, this X then capitalized in the word "eXact," and recurring in the words *text, sex, exit,* and others, or as the design of the Greimas rectangle of narrative movement.[3]

The next two rectangles are both still about the eyes and the hairline. This is interrupted by the Barthesian question about certain holes in a narrative. The specific reference is to S/Z (original 1970 edition, 48), after Balzac's phrase "C'était un homme," about the old man who will later turn out to have been a castrato. "Qui parle?" asks Barthes, is it a scientific voice, transitory, later to be corrected, or a phenomenal voice, a constatation? It is impossible, says Barthes, to attribute an origin, a viewpoint. The English translation (1974, 41) more correctly says, "Who is speaking?" but I have preferred "Who speaks?" (later echoed on an Italian phone as "Chi parla?"). And here, of course, as yet we do not know who is in the car. A first answer is the French word for rear mirror (*rétroviseur*), which emphasizes the element of looking forwards to see backwards while driving forwards, explaining this but isolating the phrase "some others" in brackets.

IS SELF-REFLEXIVITY MERE • 67

First published in Great Britain 1975 by Hamish Hamilton Ltd. *Thru* copyright © 1975 by Christine Brooke-Rose. Reprinted by permission of Carcanet Press, Limited.

    Through the driving-mirror four eyes stare back
    two of them in their proper   place
    Now right on
    Q   ask us

to de   V   elop   foot on gas
how m(any   how)   eyes?

    four   two
    of them   correct

      on either side   ▽   of the
      nose   the other

two   ⚠   O danger
   slow   down

                  eXact   replicas

nearer the hairline further up the brow but dimmed as in a glass tarnished by the close-cropped mat of hair they peer through

The mat of hair is khaki, growing a bit too low on the brow the nose too big.

Who speaks?

le rétro   viseur   (some   languages
    more   visible than   others)

[Page 1]

The *viseur* (which also means one who aims) at once becomes "the vizir, grey eminence" behind the sultan, called "consultan" and later "insultan," listener, suggesting that the author's text is also a shadow murmur, a thought perhaps, listened to "how many times," as in confession. Then we are back in the car "to peer into how many / rectangles a thousand and one in which there is a flaw?"—the space suggesting a questioning of whether there is a flaw, a question within the question "how many times." The driver leans to the right to see his four eyes in the rectangular mirror, which reflects 1,001 other rectangles, other stories, the 1,001 Arabian Nights or Don Giovanni's *mil e tre* perhaps.

These eyes and their owner are then described from outside, either by the girl talking or thinking, though she hasn't been mentioned yet, or by the driver himself (the classic mirror scene in realistic first-person narratives as one way to describe the narrator); ending (in the third rectangle) with "the brow / which whoever speaks (Nourennin?) calls too low." Nourennin will later be met as one of the narrating students. So the "speaker" is no longer the *viseur* / vizir but, possibly, a new character of Arab origin.

An alternative answer to "who speaks?" is now "Some tale-bearer"—a punning mistranslation of Todorov's *homme récit* or *porte-récit* (1971), itself calqued on *porte-parole* or spokesman—heading a long rectangle in four columns that can also read downwards in bold capitals, linking the notion of Scheherezade having to tell a story or be executed, with other images I'll come to in a moment, while the capital punishment (first column) becomes capitals Baghdad, Rome, Athens, Istanbul, Neopolis, which downwards reads "BRAIN," the real writer, and the first fairly broad hint that some messages will, though less obviously, be acrostic.

or the vizir looming grey eminence behind the consultan listener how
many times leaning a little to the right to peer into how many
rectangles a thousand and one in which there is a   flaw?

   The second pair of eyes are less pale veiled by
   the reflected hair crinkly khaki flecked grey

   O but handsome all told whatever all is and who
   ever tells a young god yet the lower eyes lie
   blue to the tarnished replicas higher up the brow
   which whoever speaks (Nourennin?) calls too low.

```
                        Some tale-bearer
(O capital!                                         your
                        story or                    your
                        life
              wot no    story?
              no        life
punishment)   So that
Hang it all
                 no     life
                        story
              off with                              your
head          said the
chief         in-sultan to                          his
                        red red rose
              washed by
              once upon
              (some times)
              (other times)  purple passages
hanging                      suspen(I)s
              from the
capital       of
Baghdad
Rome
Athens
Istambul                busy anteroom
                              ⎧ st(anza)
                        con  ⎨
                              ⎩  (ante)
Neopolis
                        scarlet
```

The word WHICH is also an acrostic, the whole passage ending with the word *syntagmatics* split and spelled "SIN TAG MA TRICKS," leading to the "BRAIN WHICH SIN TAG MA TRICKS," or the brain tricked with shifty labels by some ancestral mother, memory perhaps or architrace. But "WHICH" also leads to the next rectangle.

We're back (or still) in the car, but the first letter of each line spells downwards, in acrostic, the word "creates," that is, "BRAIN WHICH creates." Creates what? The first letters of the next rectangle spell "death," and those of the following rectangles spell "she the truth."

Meanwhile the images on pages 2 and 3 have been suggesting the Queen of Hearts and "off with her head," Burns's love "like a red red rose," and later (on page 3) "like a white white rabbit / late / down the hatch / out of sight / dead (safe)" and a French nursery rhyme about a ferret, followed by the classic cinema's "Which way did he go? / Thatt-away," and the fisherman's "one that got away / that always gets away / safe / as a jack-in-the-box" (because it was a lie, of course, but will pop up again), "sitting beside / hiding behind / eyeing beneath / the grey eminence," and we're back with the *rétroviseur* and the in / consultan, who, however, now hears the deep structures below the performance (the surface structure). The gray eminence, the priest, the psychoanalyst, the transformational grammarian, knows you (the author or anyone) better than you know yourself.

IS SELF-REFLEXIVITY MERE • 71

```
                         WHORE of Babel        Whose?
                         HITE queen goddess      Who
                         Is always
                         Cramping
                         HIS styl                  us
                 under
                 perpetual   sentence
subject                      predicatimetable
                 just like   life
                             the scrapegloat of
SIN              TAG         MA                 TRICKS
```

    But when the muscular shoulders shift back to the correct position the cars that loom grey eminent into the retrovizor do not look double-faced or even quadruple-eyed top two through crinkly hair, for the hair has moved away out of focus together with the four eyes; the cars untarnished, with single metal grins between two pale gold eyes, one on either side, or else two smaller city slickers lower down but never both pairs together.

```
            My love is like a white white rabbit
                                                    late
down the hatch
                    out of sight
                    dead                          (safe)
earthhole though
          il court il court le furet
and which way did he go?
thattaway
hey follow that car
            you should have seen the one that got   away
                              that always gets      away
                                                    safe
            as a jack-in-the-box
sitting beside
hiding behind
eyeing beneath                             in  ⎫
the grey eminence the retro-vizir beyond the con ⎬ sultan
hearer of deep structures below the performance yes your
eminence I'm coming to that your reference moves up glaring
```

[Page 3]

Back to the driving mirror and a description of the glare of lights behind: A flick of a switch can darken the mirror, attenuating the glare but dangerously distancing the car lights, hence the phrase "but the glare is preferable / to the sudden isolation of almost not seeing behind / a head," which is then, apparently, signed, "Ali Nourennin," who, although we don't yet know who he is, may therefore have been writing these first three pages. This is followed by the teacher's comment: "To be discussed."

The sentences in the following rectangle read normally but are laid out as a timetable that we enter (so the sentences say), and we're in a class, with the uneasiness of the teacher and some teacher / student dialogue. The small rectangles of the timetable spell down on the left margin "ever escaping" (going on from "she the truth," which begins on page 3 and ends on page 4.

Below the timetable we're back with the dancing hoops of lights in the mirror, in straightforward description. The second rectangle at last introduces the girl: "She shifts the mirror to her rearward glance. It doesn't / work for her the mistress of the moment of sudden / isolation at not seeing back to the black magician who / fantastically juggles luminous hoops in the retro-rec- / tangular hey put my mirror back." The mirror illusion with the four eyes only works in one position, that of the driver, who now feels panic at not having the mirror to drive by, the word *moment* serving (as does the mirror) backwards and forwards: the mistress of the moment and the moment of sudden isolation. The black magician (who will later become a character in a dream told by the girl) here is the night juggling its shifting circles of light in the rear mirror.

The page ends with "So it needs adjusting. / Why at that precise point introduce this or that?" The question applies pragmatically to the adjusting of the displaced mirror but introduces a common narrative problem, posed long ago by Wayne C. Booth (1961): why shift the viewpoint (or the mirror) at this or that moment? Usually to conceal the first character's thoughts or acts.

BUT
the retrovizor has a bluish tinge. At a flick of a switch the
rectangle turns smoky grey to dim the dazzle of floodlights
undipped or even gently dipped but the glare is preferable
to the sudden isolation of almost not seeing behind   a
head

                                            Ali Nourennin
       To be discussed

entering a	roomful of	freshmanfaces	floating audio
visually over	rectangular	tables minds	into which you
enter unom	nisciently	for that time	table space
repeat per	form what	ever the deep	level comp
etence twelve	times a sem	ester nor is the	a(u)ctor re
stricted to	one technique	unless of course	he (who?) so
chooses he	can use sever	al in layers	through which
and out of	which he builds	up his effects	yes er
Paul? What	do you mean	builds up what	about the
intentional	fallacy yes	of course but	any message
narrative or	not has an e	mitter and a	recipient.
Garbage-can?	Receptor then	What does the o	mitter omit?

The dancing hoops. For the gold eyes when distant turn into
hoops (at night in the correct position) of luminous green
red amber white bouncing in out of through and through each
other narrowing to slim ovals vertical horizontal swaying
undoing swiftly changing shape as if juggled by a mad magician or by the black recumbent street beneath overhead bridges that make perhaps the optical illusion?

She shifts the mirror to her rearward glance. It doesn't
work for her the mistress of the moment of sudden
isolation at not seeing back to the black magician who
fantastically juggles luminous hoops in the retro-rec-
tangular hey put my mirror back.

So it needs adjusting.
Why at that precise point introduce this or that?

[Page 4]

Then the text moves back to the four eyes but with a further meditation on what they can reflect: only the "real" lower eyes see the "false" upper eyes in the mirror, which don't exist so can't reflect the gaze of the "real" eyes. The passage ends again with "the brow which / some teller or other thinks too low. Who? / Oh her."

The space indicates a pause before the question "who?" The answer is elided, and the answer to that ellision is "Oh her." And downwards only, center page, we read: "Who's she when she's at home?" a question that will be asked by Ruth about Larissa in the later realistic scene, which turns out to have been written by the student Myra Kaplan. I mean this happens later in the text, but it could have been written earlier and now be occurring in the man's mind. So, projecting backwards from that realistic scene we could imagine that here the man answered "Who?" with "Larissa," who is as yet unmentioned, or that he's merely thinking it.

Meanwhile these rectangles have been spelling down the left margin acrostically (since "ever escaping" on page 4) "Through swift" (and on page 5) "switch of signifiers."

The text is, in fact, attempting a simultaneity that we all experience but that sequential language can't achieve except with adverbs such as *meanwhile, later,* and so on. And we know since Einstein that there is no simultaneity without an observer who creates it.

IS SELF-REFLEXIVITY MERE • 75

Intensity of illusion is what matters to the narrator
through a flaw in the glass darkly perhaps making four
clear eyes stare back, two of them in their proper place at
height of bridge of nose and, further up the brow, the

other two, exact replicas but dimmed as in a tarnished reflection, tarnished by the hairline they peer through. A

second pair of eyes hidden higher up the brow would have
its uses despite psychic invisibility or because of.
Gazing they do not see themselves. They reflect
nothing, nor do they look at their bright replicas below
in their proper place on either side of the nose a
fraction too large according to whoever speaks in this
instance. Only these lower eyes, reflecting the
eyes of the real face as it leans for vanity to the
right, see the upper eyes, looking up at the brow which
some teller or other thinks too low.   Who?
                                                    Oh her.

                W
                h
                o
                '
                s

                s
                h
                e

                w
                h
                e
                n

                s
                h
                e
                '
                s

                a
                t

                h
                o
                m
                e
                ?

The new rectangle is fragmented into another decorative display of notions that could flash through the mind of either a teacher of literature or that of the author, who for the moment are fused, but not, of course, by means of commentary or free indirect discourse. The rectangle gets more and more stretched and distorted until it grows a long vertical tail. The quotations from *King Lear* (3.7) "Because I would not see thy cruel nails / pluck out his poor old eyes" and "Upon these eyes of thine I'll set my foot" are scattered through the text horizontally, and I leave the rest of the horizontal reading to the reader.

The word **STORY** in bold type spelled vertically at the top joins the horizontal "hYsTeRy of the Eye" (Bataille's novel *Histoire de l'oeil)*, "hystery" recalling both mystery and hysteria, then **MYSTERY** is spelled downwards, as are the Derridean words **TRACE** and **ARCHITRACE**, and the word **ENIGMA**, on either side. The two prefixes **PRO** and **EPI** open downwards into **GRAMMED** to read **PRO / EPIGRAMMED IN THE MEMORY'S,** which leads into the next rectangle's "blue lacuna of learning" (on page 7), this proepigramming first flanked on either side with the words **waX** and **TEXT, waX** recalling the wax tablets or early writing (stone and parchment written horizontally), as well as Freud's mystic writing pad as discussed by Derrida (1978).

```
                never              the      lesS
                this is                     noT
                                            nO
                           (My)
             the           h Y s T e R y    of The
                                                         Eye
becAuse I would noT         S e E thY       cRuel        Nails
boaRish                                     fAngs
                      pluck ouT                          hIs
             pooR old       (E    Xtract)   (Cruel
     Cruel   nAils)   uPon        These     eyEs of
     tHine
     I'll set    (C         R u El                    fanGs)
                 my         foOt  Poo R old eyes
     These      eyEs        hIs  eYes
pooR old eyes
beAm                                                         Mote
     Cruel                  fanGs
     Eyes                   cRuel                            fAngs
                            boArish
                            beaM
                              Moat
                              Etc
                            alreaDy    (all read eye)


                            naIls
                            Nails

                       upon These
                       eyes of tHine I'll
                            sEt

                       the  re Mote     sTone
                       Wide     Eyes    wEt?
                       pArch    Ment   waX
                       arXi    stOne      Trace
                              dRy
                            papYrus
                            eye'S
```

[Page 6]

With the next rectangle we are still in the man's mind (or the author's) but into pedagogic problems that speak for themselves ("a text within a text passed on from / generation to generation of an increasing vastness that / nevertheless dwindles to an elite," and so on).

After this, Thoth, the god of writing, is rewritten lispingly as a nursery rhyme—"How doth the bithy little Thoth / produthe an endleth piethe of cloth"—cloth being textile and text), which leads to another play on the linguistic deep and surface structures called competence and performance.

The next rectangle contains the Poundian "Hang it all, Robert Browning, [your] Sordello / and my Sordello?" of canto 2, but instead of Robert Browning and Sordello we have the story of "an eye" again, except that only the Bataille echo enables us to read "eye," for the word *eye* has been replaced by the earlier triangle for danger, here turned up again, like the nose of the beginning.

Then through the mock-jargon question "is not incompetent performance a non-disjunction at / level of deep structure," we are suddenly in the Greimas rectangle, with only the crossed arrows shown. This has been calqued on a somewhat personal version of the Lacanian zigzag rectangle of subject and object (hinted at by the phrase "to rewrite **I** as **O** and **O** as **I**," *O* also translating Lacan's *A* for Autre or Other), in fact here rewritten as **I** all round, leading to "should you start structuring your text [the **x** made of crossed arrows] thattaway / or the latterway?" The question is then put to the vote. All the names, including that of Ali Nourennin already mentioned (absentions overlap to page 8, see page 81), will become those of the students who are given marks some twenty-three pages later.

IS SELF-REFLEXIVITY MERE • 79

           blue lacuna of learning
and unlearning a text within a text passed on from
generation to generation of an increasing vastness that
nevertheless dwindles to an elite initiated to a text no-
one else will read by means maybe of the flick of a
switch for the overhead projector and diagrams drawn
into a boxed screen to the right of the desk with a
spirit-loaded pen thus not losing eye-contact.

           The quiver of the bhi on the beeswax

           How doth the bithy little Thoth
           produthe an endleth piethe of cloth
           when thought, that bithy little moth
           devourth it all like tho much froth
           leaving great holth, tho Thamuth quoth.

           a busy competent performance before busy bees
           who palp oscult measure time listen see
           smell taste imitate suck the performer dry.

Hang it all we have the story of an ⚠
O but is not incompetent performance a non-disjunction at
level of deep structure? I me if it be possible despite non-
equivalence to rewrite I as O and O as I

which has been suggested,
here,
you see,
                cosí   I

                I   I
     should you start structuring your te⋈thattaway
                                 or the   latterway?
Those for: Peter Brandt Barbara Darcy Francesca
Newman Robert Galliard Myra Kaplan Kathleen
O'Shaunessy Ali Nourennin Renata Polanska Lin Su Fu.
    Those against: Vittoria Charib Marie Faber Salvatore
Tancredi Michael Mandel Jean-Marie Fèvre Eliza Jones.

[Page 7]

These names produce five other names, so far unmentioned, in the permutations "unless Armel inventing Larissa" and so on, with a doubt about Marco ("or is it Oscar?"—a play on *marc* O and O *scar*), and other possible permutations, with a strange name "Tariel" (hero of a twelfth-century Georgian epic romance, presumably being taught in translation), and Marco again put in doubt ("or is it Stavro?").

This could suggest a woman's confusion about earlier lovers or the author's indecision as to how to name the characters.

Here, on the subject of confused identities, I want to skip momentarily forward to later passages when I shall be going much faster: in a subsequent conversation between the man and the girl (on page 11) she will call him Stavro once and Marco once, and the doubt will persist. And on page 13 the question is raised again: "Is it Marco or Stavro (or Armel)?" followed by the sentence "There has occurred however the foreshortening of / Armel into Marco / Laretino or is it Tarie / L ?"

A much later realistic scene with Larissa (well beyond these twenty-one first pages) will recall a "real" foreshortening as she looks through the judas eye of her door to see a black man foreshortened by the lens, who will turn out, coincidentally, also to be called Armel. But the confusion on page 13 is followed by two columned portraits of Armel, who is not at all like the low-browed man with khaki hair in the car at the beginning. These portraits are signed by Veronica (a new but minor character) and by his reflection, itself footnoted (inside the text) with a quotation on portraits by Jacques le Fataliste, and another on page 14 by Barthes (1974, 61–62). The confused implication of all this, at least on rereading, is that the man in the car is Armel, and later still Jacques's Master will refer to the confusion of brows, hair, and height at the beginning. But if the man in the car is Armel, thinking about his teaching problems, he is also a character in the realistic piece of fiction written by the student Myra Kaplan, in which the insults "nigger bastard" and "jewish slut" are used as erotic signals to action, without, of course, any indication as to whether they refer to fact; indeed, it will never be made clear whether Armel is black or white, nor does it matter to the narrative.

Meanwhile (again), from the end of page 7 onwards, from the rectangle beginning "blue lacuna of learning." The message down the left margin reads "agnosis," "Hole," "why," "NOT" (then on page 8 opposite) "Fictitious," "persons," which can be linked to Armel's or to the author's teaching / writing problems, meaning " I don't know, I have a hole in my knowledge" (the blue lacuna of learning).

Abstention: Paul Stradiver Julia Weintraub Neil Alder.
? Refusal of Vote: Saroja Chaitwantee.
a show of hands within a secret ballot
which is one way of introducing a cast-list.

   unless Armel inventing Larissa
     or Larissa   "   Armel
     " Armel   "   Veronica
     " Veronica "   Armel
     " Armel   "   Larissa
     " Larissa   "   Marco (or is it Oscar?)
     " Marco (?) "   Larissa
     " Larissa   "   Armel

The other possible permutations do not occur
for logical reasons: Larissa could invent Veronica but
in a limited subjective way in any case Veronica and she are
contradictories not contraries as Socrates explained
to Protagoras and Structural Semantics has just reinvented. While Armel could invent Marco or is it
Tariel and vice versa but due to the double standard
in practice would not stoop or merely would not have the curiosity. Clearly Marco does not invent Veronica nor she even
utter Marco (or is it Stavro?) they've never met besides
Stavro has no imagination.

On the other hand the hypotheses could have been
posed anticlockwise:

        Larissa   inventing   Oscar
        Oscar   "   Larissa
        Larissa   "   Armel
        Armel   "   Veronica
        Veronica   "   Armel
        Armel   "   Larissa
        Larissa   "   Armel
        Armel   "   ?

er something's gone wrong here there seems to be
room for some extra who why the mistress of the moment
since the man any man must be if not many at least
one up who will fairly soon be dropped for she does
not see by day the four lies in the retrovizor when
shifted to her forward gaze nor dancing hoops by night

CHAPTER 5

We are in the car with the mistress of the moment again and the flawed mirror. The phrase "er something's gone wrong here" on page 8 functions both backwards and forwards (like the mirror) to the list of names and to the mirror itself, and of course to the text, and this rectangle leads to a repeat of "But it needs adjusting" (on page 9 opposite) , and suddenly the girl is telling a dream about a fat black magician juggling circles of light, all the way down to "the show must go on can you interpret?"

The man answers, "the show within the show," but has been thinking (down the left margin: "What is Larissa doing now" or "Veronica."

But it needs adjusting.
Well then I found myself with a magician on a
helluva stage as his stooge you know in tights
and a sequin bodice and my bust like it was busting
tight out of it and I was handing him coloured scarves

i think and suddenly a prop was missing I forget his
stick I mean his wand anyway it was my fault he couldn't

Lift the white rabbit out of the hat and the crowd murmured
and even shouted as he signalled frantically like mad
right into the wings but they didn't get the message and
in the end he walked off leaving me alone on stage to cope
somehow in the glare of lights that hits the mirror and
swings left out of it beaming ahead rewritten now
as two small red eyes in a hunched black shape which is

delineated against forward floodlight the retrovizor re-
opening to the hoops dancing up and down and aside
in the rear distance luminous horizontal ovals oh
no, vertical ovals as if at quarter angle amber red
green white changing shape and juggled by the

night or by the tall dark house with blue eyes
or maybe by the black recumbent street who
was very short and fat for a magician more than

obese you've never seem anything so fat he tried to
reach the switches to calm the audience but he was so

Very fat and short so he lifted me in my tights and bodice
ever so firm under the breasts with them busting
right out of the sequins and I managed to switch them
off and as he brought me down we kissed half
naked ever so sexy and then we started wanting
it like crazy but I said no later we have to
calm the crowd so he got wild and dragged me
after him out of the theatre but I wrenched free
        saying the show must go on can you interpret
?
The show within the show
What?
of hands juggling

The girl, feeling his inattention, says "hell honey I guess I just fill the air for you," and a dialogue between them is created. Further down there is a second dream about a man jumping the plank and fighting an eagle in the water. This is typographically fragmented by the girl's interjections, obviously related to manual foreplay in the car during the slow drive, and capitalized downwards thoughts by the man: **"EXPECTED GES-TURES NO MYSTERY"** then, on page 11, **"WELL I WANT HER CUNT."**

within a secret ballet of the I
hell honey I guess I just fill the air for you sure that's what
i like about you oh I thought it was my big beautiful
true blue tits they're so fine too with a show of hands
entering under silk with a secret ballet of fingers on

tiptoe upon soft globed flesh the nipple now rising
hard between the lights the foot pressed gently purring
into a stop the is it sacred belly tensed to the show of
green fingers into the left thigh that jerks open to the
hot human humidity of a sexual humour secreted un-
secretly go on then

Doing what?
Oh filling the air. You do

it so much more convincingly
than the others (tit for

tat)
what others?
others who fill the air.   Oh

```
Well   you were giving      mmmmm         a class on British
history   for some        mystErious      reasoN
                                          Oh
                    yes eXite me          Mmm    how
in the royal                              naVy   they
                    Punished              Sailors
there               yEs                   There
                                          Er
            by making them Climb out and
er          walk the plank
            and all the planks sTuck out all    Round
like                  hEll honey                Yes     your
eminence              oh Don't                          like
guns I'm coming                 to that
                      Go on
so when they          droppEd                           into the
                      Sea
                      what The planks no the
```

[Page 10]

The dialogue itself is straightforward. At the end of the second dream comes the comment: "You're mythologising me. / Oh any time. And then you came with your car and said come / unto me I'll light the way and well / drove off"—the next phrase typographically mimes the bridge—followed by "Dopey relations you have with your magician men. / Yeah but he wasn't you Stavro that was the first dream / but he was short well you're short too but he was / immensely fat and couldn't have strangled an eagle / in the water for anything he'd have sunk you turn left at the corner / Hey I know / Yes you should by now but you always forget. / Okay can you see a spot?"

IS SELF-REFLEXIVITY MERE

```
                sailors silly a hUge eagle
                  boy   aRe you big
                    WEll he'd swoop
                down on thEm and they had to
                        eLiminate himmmmmmm
                    welL fight
                                It out
                              in the
                                  Water
            and if tHey
won                        they were hAuled out
            thEy               weNt free and you
         demonstRated            iT
            to the
                        Class you jumped the plank
                    and foUght it
out                              with the eagle and
        wrrrrrrrrrrrrrrrrruNg
                          iTs neck.
```

You're mythologising me.
Oh any time. And then you came with your car and said come
unto me I'll light the way and well

drove off

across the bridge in the scintillating foreign city

did you?   No I didn't
Dopey relations you have with your magician men.
Yeah but he wasn't you Stavro that was the first dream
but he was short well you're short too but he was
immensely fat and couldn't have strangled an eagle in
the water for anything he'd have sunk you turn left at the
corner
Hey I know.
Yes you should by now but you always forget.
Okay can you see a spot?
Usually there's one further up on the right. Here.

[Page 11]

CHAPTER 5

Page 12 begins with a sexually charged parking dialogue (spot . . . too small), typographed to mime the maneuvers, down to "You'll have to take her out and start again / Who sez? Some tale-bearer (off) or Other who has / got it all wrong / backing into too smalL a space / short / ening / the / man [those lines typographed as a backward maneuver] / who has no name till the mIstress / of the **Moment** / **Backing into a** / **fear** / o / **F U S I** [and, obliquely to the right] **ON,**" **Fusion**, the **F** doing double duty and the **O** landing in the middle of the word "explOdes" (the opposite of fusion) "into" (spelling down and across and down again) "reality," "some other textuality," "reality," "sex(t)uality." The crossed arrows of the Greimas / Lacan rectangles (now marked **U I I I** in the corners) form the main **x**, and the word **L I M B** spelled downwards in bold capitals, echoes the left marginal message that has gone on for the last four pages (from page 9 to the end of page 13): "two white thighs do it two white legs wo you daddybitch you titbitch you got it all wrong" (the *g* of vertical "got it" on page 12 also going off horizontally as "got it all wrong," referring to the car maneuver, but vertically to the girl, and more generally to the author composing the text). Then the Armel portrait by Veronica on page 13 spells downwards "wait was am seem icon image" (the name of Saint Veronica being an etymological formation meaning "true icon").

IS SELF-REFLEXIVITY MERE • 89

Too small.
It isn't. You'll have to back into it.
True. But it's still too small.
But Marco of course you can get in.
I'll say, if you light the way.
Tooshay! You kill me have you no male pride it's your car.
Come come honey it's your street.
hang on I'll lower the window. Turn full right
yes   now left   stop   straighten   oh lordy no you're
on the pavement   all crooked   forward a bit   straighten her
up   no   You'll have to take her out and start again.

    Who sez?   Some tale-bearer (off) or Other who has
got it all wrong

```
                  backing    into    too smalL    a space
                                short
                           ening
                        the
                     man
                  who has no name till the mIstress
                                 of the Moment
                                        Backing into a
          fear
                   o
                F  U  S  I
                      e
                      ╳         plOdes
                I  (t)  I       Nto
                               r
                               e
     some    other    text u   a l i t y
                      r e a
                          l
                          i               o
                       couldn't
                she be happy with y     o       u     in the
orbit of an eye and no referent without? Or with
the Other with he passed into hystery within?
```

[Page 12]

CHAPTER 5

So the scene is set: a university man acquiring, through dialogue, a name, Marco or Stavro or Armel, with a girl he only needs sexually as he thinks of other things, of Larissa, of Veronica, of teaching problems, of Derridean theory as later apparently expounded or taught by Larissa, while the girl tells her dreams.

Is it Marco or Stavro? (or Armel?)
There has occurred however the foreshortening of

Armel into Marco
Laretino or is it Tarie
L? of the accurate boymouth (removed?)

whose legs : his body : : his brow : his nose
relations in proportion quaternary conjunction
or disjunction with the possibility also of non-relations
non-conjunction   and even   non-disjunction a
game

Whereas well	Armel
Armel	however
is not like	equates
that at all but tall	rarity
with hair quite dark	of
and swept back grey over	mind with
splendid brow as stark	unusual
as Beethoven's	spirit and
making the nose (turned up)	the looks of a
seem small between the burned up	hero with a brow
eyes and blurred	as high as Beetho
evasive	ven's a small nose an
mouth	evasive mouth
it occurred in South	and hair swept back
Carolina	dark but silver
oh but	over temples
not muscular	retaliating eyes
indeed though	and the
masculine	troubled
and slim for	identity
grace and	of the
elegance	narrator.
(Portrait by Veronica)	(Portrait by his reflection)*

*Jacques, après avoir dit entre ses dents: "Tu me le paieras ce maudit portrait", ajouta. – Vous avez été fou de cette femme-là?
　　Le Maître-Et pourquoi haïssez-vous les portraits?
　　Jacques.-C'est qu'ils ressemblent si peu, que, si par hasard on vient à recontrer les originaux, on ne les reconnait pas. Racontez-moi les faits, rendez-moi fidèlement les propos, et je saurai à quel homme j'ai affaire. **
　　　　　　(Portrait of the portrait by Jaques le Fataliste)

[Page 13]

I shall now go much faster, merely quoting bits from page 14 on, without comment.

In the second rectangle on page 14 (after the portrait of the portrait by Barthes) someone is analyzing the art of digression, notably in faculty meetings.

IS SELF-REFLEXIVITY MERE • 93

> **Tous les signifiés du portrait sont "vrais"... tous ces sèmes désignent la vérité, mais même mis tous ensemble, ils ne suffisent pas à la faire nommer (et cet echec est heureux...) Dans le système herméneutique, le signifié de connotation occupe une place particulière: il pointe mais ne dit pas; ce qu'il pointe... c'est la vérité, comme nom; il est à la fois la tentation de nommer et l'impuissance de nommer... Ainsi un doigt, de son mouvement désignateur et muet, accompagne toujours le texte classique: la vérité est de la sorte longuement désirée et contournée, maintenue dans une sorte de plénitude enceinte, dont la percée, à la fois libératoire et catastrophique, accomplira la fin même du discours; et le personnage, espace même de ces signifiés, n'est jamais que le passage de l'énigme dont Oedipe (dans son débat avec le Sphynx) a empreint tout le discours occidental.
> (Portrait of the portrait by Roland Barthes)

Oh the moving finger points and having pointed itself out
moves on, will not stay for an answer, tetrapod
biped or tripod, two and a stick, a fang for an eye a foot
in it for an unintentional phallusy but an intentional
literality: gently dip but not too deep: you dip me
I dip you I I sir you dip us. So that today we shall make a
comparative analysis, taking these two famous classics, of the
art of digression. Those of you who attend (or even analyse) General Assemblies and Faculty Meetings may well have
concluded that it is not an art but a chaos. It is,
however, a very subtly planned chaos, it has the
odd, beautiful coherence of a neurosis. A pseudo-problem is
raised, to which a false solution is found, thus creating (by
design) another pseudo-problem. Neurosis has the cunning of
stupidity, and stupidity is a dimension anyone can fall into, however intelligent, indeed, part of the intellect can
rise suspended and watch, helpless in pain, the misuse of its own projected trajectory struggling alone, as if
cut off from itself, in a delirious discourse not its brother's
keeper.

These things do matter despite psychic invisibility
or because of in a text like the world or the human
body that merely
engenders

itself in
to

[Page 14]

CHAPTER 5

All of which leads, on page 15, to "the foot men [*les laquais de la bourgeoisie* was the phrase current in those days] who say / O in the mountains break fast tonguetables (thou shalt / eat thy prisoner) for a feted calf," which leads to an odd design of words representing bits of meat on a brochette, the horizontal line reading "a grid irony orguyastric," the *iron* in *irony* later becoming "eiron-monger" or (lower still) "It has all been dreamt up by the trait-or markster of the / comment [calqued on "mistress of the moment"], the tale-bearer as eiron-monger," all of which are allusions to the author, the word *iron* recurring in French in "a plot from fear of transfer ring a handful of / silver / displaced / condensed / metonymised." This is the backward pattern for the girl's phrase about the fat magician in her dream, which spills over onto page 16.

writing – for the foot men who say
O in the mountain break fast tonguetables (thou shalt

eat thy prisoner) for a feted calf

```
                        b
            t                       o
         a                  o
                                u       d
         f  n  h         a  d  t
←a  g  r  i  d  i  r  o  n  y  o  r  g  u  y  a  s  t  r  i  c→
         r     n  i         t     m        r
                                                e
         e     n     i         b     i
               d                     l
```

So poor Midas and other goldicondeologists prisoners of

well-planned desires for their own excrement obscurely
alimenting them while nevertheless consuming them up
regardless.

So more
or
less
literally

It has all been dreamt up by the trait-or markster of the
comment, the tale-bearer as eiron-monger hatching against
his homo-logos a plot from fear of trans fer ring a handful of
                             silver
    displaced
                 condensed
                                    metonymised
                                                  such a
                         man
                 would not
           fight
    the eagle in the

The passage continues in Armel's "retrospeculation" and "retrodiscourse" (recalling *rétroviseur*) and "Veronica [. . .]—true icon—/ who does not therefore exist / as Larissa does," an odd portrait of Larissa. Jacques interjects O and, later, on page 17, "ah" and "ee" and "eh?" with echoes of Wallace Stevens.

water for one thing nor wring its neck. Nor would he have four
eyes neither in retrospeculation nor even in any kind of
retrodiscourse as Armel might have and naturally
does the moment they are uttered as possibilities
epithets you mean
no: sapphires or crysoprases staring tetracyclops from bare brow.

         Clearly Veronica is in
         love – true icon –

who does not therefore exist
as Larissa does
(so?)
?

Who
has however an iconic nose
and eyes like Isis or even maybe Ra
    Jacques. – O
the day (or night)

is green
she plays upon a blue guitar

she does not play things as they are
hearing in the air messages un
emitted unadmitted mean

ingventing your desire with La belle si tu voulais (bis)
Nous dormirions ensemble o-la (bis)

and answering it unspoken with

No vale la pena el llanto or l'amor è un
altalena or love is just a four-letter word and
more: love is a bore, a soap op
era a telephone that doesn't ring

  in many languages from Lucan to Lacan
  she fills the air as well with
  syntagmatic silence – from Phaedrus to Freud
  Homer to Husserl and Locke to the Li Ki
  effortlessly displacing notions with a diachronic chord.

[Page 16]

CHAPTER 5

Then follow (prededing page) a French then a Spanish song, "in many languages from Lucan to Lacan" and other alliterative references, all crashing in a diachronic chord, followed by a conversation, on page 17, between Jacques le Fataliste and his Master.

IS SELF-REFLEXIVITY MERE • 99

        Jacques. – ee!
        Things as they are
    are changed upon the blue guitar
    namely
It is more difficult for a phallus-man to enter the I
of a woman than for the treasurer of signifiers
to enter the paradiso terrestre.
        Jacques. – ah.
Ah indeed. Larissa talks like that. The pathetic fallacy may
be used to fill the hermeneutic gap. Or in the dialectic
of desire, the subject is subverted and the object is from the start an
object of central loss.
        Jacques. –Eh bien! Monsieur, qu'avais-je besoin
        du portrait que vous m'avez fait de cetter femme?
        Ne saurais-je pas a present tout ce que vous en
        avez dit?
Ecco! In any case the mistress of the moment should be
changed, and no doubt will be in another moment though per
haps she could meanwhile be called, Ruth, for mixed reasons
of phonemic contiguity.
        Jacques. –eh?
        The Master. – work it our for yourself it's not very deep.
  So that now we have at last returned to the subject of
discourse, while still of the moment before being thru
and hurt (oo!) but who is we to dip royally
no collectively into an age-old narrative matrix before we
gouge out the I in order carefully to gauge its liquid
essence? the namers of things the silent obsessional
re-emitters of words who will therefore have their
mouths removed the spinners of texts that can
engender only text such as the cold street juggling
no hoops in no retrovizor and the sudden isolation of
almost not wanting anything now standing in
the wide street recumbent under great curved beams of
pale light equispaced but staggered each to the other
laterally, the quarter arches never meeting even on
an imagined curve except quite distantly along the can
yon of tall blocks all asleep all dreaming along the
boulevard as they diminish in size quite distantly
asleep whereas you standing out there in the

[Page 17]

100 • CHAPTER 5

On page 18 we're back in the car and there is a quarrel about listening, which leads to another decorative display on page 19 representing his inattention, with the words **CAN YON / LARISSA** (downwards).

    cold street come along, did you hear? I bet you don't know what I said I said you never tell me your dreams.
    I don't have any to tell.
    Of course you do they've proved it.
    Who have?
    Every ninety minutes of the night why didn't you know well fancy me teaching you something every one knows that, for a quarter of an hour you come up from deep level sleep and dream with electrodes no what are they called well yes electrodes I guess or something on the eyelids recording the movements up down and sideways called Rapid Eye Movements gee it's just like television you just don't remember honey and you need it like food and drink and sex too they're called R.E.M.'s.
    Not every ninety minutes then.
    Oh yes you do they tried depriving them of their dreams waking them up you see when those rapid eye movements begin so then they compensated and dreamt twice as much and if they deprived them like that for fifteen days they got to the borders of schizophrenia.
Were they allowed in?
Er well I guess I just fill the air for you oh I said that earlier.

IS SELF-REFLEXIVITY MERE

```
True,     that's what I like about You
Yeah                  I guess sO
       are You going to allow me iN?
                          Can         You
              beat that whY whAtve    You cOme for then
                          Now   cOme          along
           the                 C a N  YoN
           boulevard  Of       tAll  blOcks        all
           asleep    No        oNe         sleeper's
           dreams
   C Oincinding in exactlY    the same    quarter of
   A N                hOur                     everY
                          NinetY      miNutes      thOugh
              perhaps         Over(You)
         Lapping         weeN                      iNg
        eAch                  Other
         Ruth                 lesslY
         In                   eNdless
         Stati
         Sti       Cal            prObabilities
           According Achording to the    Number
              sleepiNg but
   Never         (You staying
                  Over
                  Night?) the same show

Cut
A diagram could
No doubt be drawn
You see
Oh
No.
```

[Page 19]

Finally on page 20, the Greimas narrative rectangle is drawn over a continuous text about teaching with an overhead projector and a spirit-loaded pen, or making love, then the "danger" triangle forms the Y of "Yet" for another meditation about the correct position for the four eyes and another about the teaching year.

IS SELF-REFLEXIVITY MERE • 103

In the box with a switch for the overhead projector tO
Note and a spirit-loaded pen, thus not loosing eye contacT
Or some still making love perhaps four eyes crossed foR
Riveting limbs, M or Y, opening crossing pentapod or ninE
Diagonals meeting In On which I enters O anD
Envelopes contraries contradictories subalterns as a staR
Rivets form substance floating up every 90 minutes or sO
To surface structure from deep level dreamlessness dowN
Over under electroded lids for a shared cigarette.

Yet when the shoulders return to their correct position, the eyes disappear all four (six? eight? or ten?) of them only the focus eyes remaining fixed on the road straight ahead but glancing up at the pale fish eyes one on either side (in the retrovisor the cars not double-faced at all) the silver grin here in this position cannot see if the brain too is equipped with another pair of eyes in the brow staring like jewels: lodged, perhaps, never to sally forth, in the mirror, condensed, a secret pair to reflect nothing except cars looming from behind over into the driving eyes that glance up at the blue perspective of fish eyes and down again retrowiser in daylight or in smoky grey

the year forms bluish slit-shaped holes of hours down days along implicit depths of weeks each one behind the other each slit a labelled letter-box translated into a rectangular room where the lesson of the day reproduces itself hour by hour in endless statistical probabilities which set end to end would no doubt extend and to a great extent exteriorise the text right off the page as far as

[Page 20]

This leads to an actual timetable with names of courses offered, one by Dr. Toren on "The Novel as Intentional Object" (not the intentional fallacy but a philosophical reference to Ingarden), Dr. Toren being, of course, Larissa Toren.

This timetable makes it reasonably clear that Larissa is elsewhere, since Armel does not appear in it and the courses are more fashionably complex than the creative writing course he will later be seen correcting.

In the wordplay design below, the last line is spelled backwards, then we read up column 2: "or else the show within the **SHOW WITHIN THE SHOW TILL COME THE REVOLUTION.**" The slogans of the early seventies thus pierce backwards through the context to express the feeling that all famous revolutionaries have been reactionary, racist, nationalist, tyrannical.

From page 14 on to this point the downwards messages have been reading, "ombilical chord struck to be if wo es war soll ich werden [*wo es war soll ich werden,* Freud's phrase on the id and the ego] was what is she in a name is she Iotaboo Echo danger men at playback."

I can't remember why I spelled *umbilical* with a French *o*—to suggest the **I** and **O** perhaps (though *I* and *You* would have done just as well).

On page 18 through 19 the downwards marginal words exceptionally include the inset rectangles, to read "I owe you nought no deal sweaty **CANYON.**"

On page 20 the Greimas rectangle reads on both sides (the right margin now justified), down and up, **IN ORDER TO,** and the next rectangle reads, on the left, "stop this stop," and on the right, downwards, "Order now order."

Here the downwards messages stop, and from now on we can read in a more straightforward way, or at least, there will be other typographies and even wilder ones, but they are less invisibly acrostic. The main themes have been stated, readers can continue on their own. The cessation of the acrostics is announced, ordered, even if nobody has noticed them in the first place, or noticed their cessation order. Indeed, one of the reasons for my offering this reading of an admittedly cryptic threshold or portal is that nobody has noticed. So now, at least the critic or reader can interpret what is there, criticizing or praising as they feel. They will find dialogues, letters being written during meetings, quarrels, and misunderstandings, students and others discussing the text, and so on.

IS SELF-REFLEXIVITY MERE • 105

Mars and Venus copulating under the net, the third day with the sixth day, though it could also be Wodinsday with Moonsday or or Thorsday with Freyasday but never on a Sunday or anyone of these juxtaposed with any non-contiguous other from the point of view of any one teacher or student for that matter with varying performance in each system country continent classroom of each institution of learning.

0900 1100	Discourse Analysis I: Initiation to Semiotics (Miss Chatman)	The Novel as Intentional Object (Dr Toren)
1100 1200	The Semiology of Cultural Images (Dr Medaware)	Initiation to Transformational Grammar (Miss Arbor)
1300 1500	Language as Subversion of Society (Dr Underwood)	The Inscription of Protest: Women's Lib. (Ms.Littlebrown-Fitzjohn)
1500 1700	Discourse Analysis II: The Semiology of Mass Media (Dr. Medaware)	Empiricism and Imperialism (Prof. Ngu-Rey)
1700 1900	The Inscription of Protest: Black Literature (Prof. Littlebrown)	Initiation to Dialectical materialism (Prof. Kreuzer)
1900 2100	Narrative as Object of Exchange (Prof. Kreuzer)	The Generation of Narrative Complexes (Miss Webb)

```
          within a text   passed on   from   generation   to
    g e n e r a t i o N    Of an Increasing vasTness fULl Of what neVER
                the mOre the less
                     dwIndles
                          To a
                     structUred
                          eLite      M   O      re or less
         texti    V     O    R    E
                  E     V    E    R
                  R     E    A    D
            to    O     R    D    E    R     else the show within the
                                 SHOW TILL COME THE
```

[Page 21]

CHAPTER 5

༄

The cryptic threshold is a kind of wake-up call or Dante-esque "beware all ye who enter," though, of course, it can have the opposite effect (go to sleep, don't enter at all). But having presented you with this threshold, I'd like to close with a much, much briefer glance at the end of the novel, which gives a strange example of misreading due to reading omission.

The novel (almost) ends with an alphabetical list of all names used or alluded to or quoted in the text, including the names of the fictional characters, each given an alpha, or beta plus, and so on. This has invariably been called an index, though I defy anyone to find a single page reference. In fact it is the result of a play on Genette's phrase "il y a des degrés de présence," quoted in English, "there are degrees of presence," just before the so-called index. Genette is referring to the presence or absence of an explicit narrator, itself an important element of play in *Thru*. Absence is absolute, he says, but there are degrees of presence; in other words, a narrator can be an occasional *I*, a dramatized but discreet observer, a participating character, or the main character. In English the word *degree* also means a diploma, hence the allocation of marks giving the degrees of presence for all those names or allusions throughout the novel. But these degrees are awarded by the students, at one point supposed to be the joint narrators in a creative writing class and not, as had appeared earlier, either Diderot's Master of *Jacques le Fataliste* or, even earlier, their teacher Armel Santores, let alone his ex-wife Larissa Toren. Moreover, if the marks are awarded by the students, who may or may not have been writing the narrative, it follows that the marks must be wholly arbitrary and therefore not a reliable guide to the degrees of presence of the characters, real or fictional, who make up the text. In fact alpha plus can be given to a name barely hinted at and delta minus to one of the chief presences.

༄

Now of course all this *is* self-reflexive. I have said several times since publication that this is a novel about the theory of the novel, a fiction about fictionality, a text about intertextuality, and maybe this misled people to suppose there was nothing else. But I hope I have shown here that there is more at stake than "mere" self-reflexivity, itself embedded and less showy than in some Postmodern novels.

And why is it so embedded? Because I am *also* doing the exact opposite of self-reflexivity, putting it, as it were, under erasure, by using language so mimetically that critics and readers who expect narrative conventions to indicate who's speaking, whether it's thought or speech, who the character is or why he's there, and typographic spaces or new chapters to change the viewpoint and so on, seem unable to grasp this direct, almost naive mimetism of how we act and speak and think at the same time, without telling ourselves who we are, even if it's also paralleled with direct mimetism of how a text starting thus *in medias res* needs to constitute itself slowly, in fragments, with trial repetitions and variations and doubts, but not through explanatory flashbacks and such. The old techniques, incidentally, could themselves be regarded as more self-reflexive, or at least more textually self-conscious, than their abolition, but we got so used to them we don't notice them as such.

Most fiction and all "serious discourse" would avoid such extremes as I have used here, but the basic procedures of both miming and representing thought are common to both fiction and serious discourse, and *Thru* is simply an exaggerated version of these procedures. It has been so consistently misunderstood and misquoted, even by enthusiasts, that I never attempted this kind of experiment again—indeed, I didn't need to, since writing it resolved my writer/critic conflict. But I'm deeply convinced that it's my most original text, whatever its faults, and that my later novels, whatever their qualities, made a few concessions.

An American critic, Robert Caserio (1990), writing in fact not about *Thru* but about J. G. Ballard, has written that some of the fears I expressed at the end of *A Rhetoric of the Unreal* (1981) had been "predicted in 1975 by a curious aspect of her novel *Thru,* where stylized and parodied discourses of disjunction, displacement, and indeterminacy, from linguistics to Lacan, are turned into a sublime poetry. The curious aspect of *Thru* is the way it makes one feel that the free-for-all thruway of the text can become a roadblock, and that what the road blocks is more important than the formulas and forms of mobility" (312).

Well, I hesitantly (if delightedly) accept both the sublime poetry and the roadblock, but would ask, tentatively, and truly quite modestly: If the poetry is sublime, what sublime poetry does not have roadblocks? We *learn* to read poetry.

But am I not hoist in my own petard? Are the roadblocks not equivalent to the blockings of fiction/faction we experience daily on the media?

Or are they groping attempts at a more technical understanding of those fluctuating "fic/fac" boundaries? It's not for me to say, but I hope I have shown that, except for jargon parodies, my sentences are correct and clear, my wordplay and syntax games are easy, and that the typographic roadblocks are there precisely to defamiliarize, to wake up the reader, to force him to read in unusual directions, to stop and think, to script the *texte scriptible* with me, to share and partake.

In all my novels, but more especially in this one, I am trying to make the novel once again do what only the novel can do, with words on a page, not film images or any methods the other arts do better than the novel can. And *tant pis* for readers who can't share in this scripting, this fiction was not written for them.

6

Interlude: EXSUL

AT THE BEGINNING OF chapter 1, I touched on one possible reason for my invisibility: my own hermit instincts and discomfort with PR and smart literary circles. During the nineties Susan Suleiman (she of the *Between* reading in chapter 2) asked me to contribute to a book about exile, and I did so.[1] The essay is impersonal and abstract, except towards the end (now expanded to include my own exile), and may not be an answer at all. Moreover it has nothing to do with narratology, and I include it here partly as a rest for the reader from the formal analysis that has gone before, which will return (rather more toughly) in chapter 7, with my lecture on my main lipogram (chronologically my last lecture), but also because *Thru*, just examined, was the first novel I wrote in exile, so that the reader may perhaps, after chapter 5, feel the various effects of exile discussed below, first somewhat generally, then a bit more personally.

༄

When I was a child in Brussels, brought up bilingually in a more or less exiled family (my maternal grandparents having left Geneva under a cloud, as told in *Remake,* my mother having left her English husband in London, where she should have stayed for contemporary *bienséance*), I used to think that the word *exile* meant "ex-*île*," out of the island, or, less etymologically, an island out of my world—not, I feel pretty certain, because of the British Isles, to and from which I was constantly trundled and to which I nominally and paternally belonged, but because islands are magical to a child, from *Treasure Island* via *Paul et Virginie* all the way to the island of solitudinous reading I loved to be in and hated to be wrenched out of. And are not many utopias and dystopias islands, such as More's, Swift's, and Golding's? Even science fiction's planets and galaxies and alternative worlds are felt as islands, *isolas* isolated from our round earth's imagined corners of reality.

But no: *exile* (Latin *exilium*, earlier *exsilium; exul*, earlier *exsul*, a banished man) was long thought to be linked to *solum*, soil, but is now (Andrews 1987) related to the root *sal*, Sanskrit *sar* ("to go"), Latin *salire/saltare*, and Latin *exsilio*, which meant "leap" or "spring forth." But then, later, in Old French, *exilier* or *essilier* meant "to ravage," "to devastate," a shift in meaning still traceable in *exterminate*, literally "to drive beyond boundaries."

Thus the clanging connotations are of suffering and even demolition in banishment, but also of leaping or springing forth into a new life, beyond the boundaries of the familiar (the island self, I obstinately add, since no man is an island, even in no-man's-land). "Thou paradise of exiles, Italy!" Shelley wrote in 1818 (*Julian and Maddalo*, 1.57). That's for the springing-forth connotation. But Pope Gregory VII's last words are said to have been: "I have loved righteousness and hated iniquity, wherefore I die in exile,"[2] a bitter adaptation of Psalm 42 ("Thou hast loved righteousness and hated iniquity, / wherefore God, even thy God, hath anointed thee / with the oil of gladness above thy fellows" [Revised Standard version]).

That's for the suffering connotation, a suffering felt as unjust, a punishment for righteousness instead of the promised reward. To be sure, Gregory VII (Hildebrand) was not a poet or other fiction writer, except perhaps in those last words, and in many ways deserved his fate in the deadly struggle for supremacy between the papacy and the Holy Roman Empire. The Emperor Henry VII had captured the Vatican in 1083, Rome itself surrendered in 1084, but Gregory held out in the Castle of Sant' Angelo. Then the pope's ally Robert Guiscard at last came to the "rescue," brutally sacking Rome and taking Gregory, almost as captive, to the safety of Salerno, where he died the following year.

It may seem absurd today that mere writers should ever have been considered powerful or influential enough to deserve exile, as opposed to political figures or, for that matter, to bakers and carpenters. But they have, and being writers, offer a good deal more variety than political figures do.

INTERLUDE: EXSUL · III

Literary exiles are very numerous. At random from memory, in roughly chronological, nonevaluative order, a sample would include Isaiah (and in a very wide sense, all Jewish writers of the Diaspora), Ovid, Cavalcanti, Dante (who departed from Florence under Charles de Valois), Petrarch (who went to Provence), Thibault de Champagne (who removed to his new kingdom of Navarre), Charles d'Orléans (imprisoned by the English), Voltaire, Mme. de Staël, Adam Mickiewicz, Shelley, Keats, Byron, Cyprian Norwid, Charles Baudelaire (who fled debts), Victor Hugo, Heinrich Heine, Oscar Wilde, Henry James, Joseph Conrad, Gabriele D'Annunzio (who also fled debts), W. B. Yeats, Edith Wharton, Tristan Tzara, Kurt Schwitters, T. S. Eliot, Ezra Pound, James Joyce, Gertrude Stein, Scott Fitzgerald, Ernest Hemingway, Djuna Barnes, Thomas Mann, Henry Miller, Radclyffe Hall, D. H. Lawrence, Max Beerbohm, Somerset Maugham, Stefan Zweig, Bertolt Brecht, André Breton, Christopher Isherwood, W. H. Auden, Malcolm Lowry, Witold Gombrowicz, Vladimir Nabokov, Paul Bowles, Jane Bowles, Lawrence Durrell, Samuel Beckett, Eugène Ionesco, Jorge Semprún, Luis Cernuda, Milan Kundera, Aleksandr Solzhenitsyn, Harry Matthews, Italo Calvino, Anthony Burgess, Muriel Spark, Ishmael Kadaré (one of whose novels contains an episode from which I quote, with his kind permission, in *Textermination*), and many others not in my head at the moment, all the way to the modern "foreigners" or Postcolonials who write in English or French today, from Kazuo Ishiguro to Salman Rushdie, an exile within an exile.

Clearly this list covers a great variety of exiles, from temporary to permanent (though the exile can't always know this); from early (such as Ishiguro, who came to England at six from Nagasaki) to late, *en fin de carrière* (such as Wilde). But the most obvious and commonly made distinction is between the following:

1. *Involuntary exile*, which is usually political or punitive (Isaiah, Ovid, Dante, Thibault, Charles d'Orléans, Byron, Mickiewicz, Solzhenitsyn, etc., alas). These can be further subdivided into those exiled for their books or their behavior (Ovid, Byron, Mme. de Staël, Wilde, Solzhenitsyn) and those who, as private persons, fled from political conditions or war (Gombrowicz, Kadaré, and others).
2. *Voluntary exile*, which is usually called expatriation and occurs for many more personal reasons: social, economic (including tax evasion), sexual (Radclyffe Hall and the lesbian group during the twen-

ties in Paris), or simple preference (Beerbohm retired to Rapallo, Ezra Pound chose Italy, Lawrence Durrell went to France, and so on).

Involuntary exiles may tend to be unhappy, poor, bitter (like Gregory VII), nostalgic about the society left behind, self-righteous; voluntary exiles may tend to be happy, comfortable, satiric about the society left behind, self-righteous. But that is clearly a useless generalization, with too many exceptions on any one feature, for instance Byron (who fled a sexual scandal but was rich, noble, and popular) or Wilde (who fled a sexual scandal but was broken by prison and poverty), while Cyprian Norwid, though a voluntary exile, lived and died in Paris in abject poverty and was buried in a pauper's grave.

It seems to me that there are more pertinent distinctions, which cut across the differences in causes and conditions. The first is formal and thematic (yes, the two *can* go together), the second linguistic.

༺༻

Formal/Thematic

In older times, well before the rise of the nation-state, when literary forms and themes were more restricted as well as more universal within a common temporal culture (classical, medieval, etc.), many writers in exile simply continued to write in the way they would have written at home. Among these are Ovid (who revised his *Fasti,* finished *Metamorphoses,* wrote *Tristia,* and made many attempts at recall, but died in exile), Petrarch, Charles d'Orléans, Thibault de Champagne (who wrote courtly lyrics), Shelley, Keats, Byron, Hugo (who wrote lyrics, romantic epics, elegies, etc), Voltaire (author of satires, tragedies, *romans philosophiques,* essays), and Mme. de Staël (writer of novels and essays). In other words, despite the language differences, if any, the formal and thematic idiom was close to the universal language of music (as for Handel, living in London, for instance). The analogy is inexact but broadly helpful.

With the development of Romantic realism in the nineteenth century, many exiled writers wrote about the society they had left behind. So a new distinction can be made between those whose themes look back, in either traditional or more experimental forms, and those whose themes, often with more formal experimentation, transcend the condition of exile. This distinction can be illustrated with, in the nineteenth century, Mickiewicz versus Norwid, or, in the twentieth, Joyce versus Beckett.

Mickiewicz, who left Wilno in Russian Poland after the 1830 insurrection, first for Russia, then Dresden, and finally Paris, was immensely prolific for five years. The whole of *Pan Tadeusz*, a Romantic patriotic epic with a Polish hero, full of passionate detail of landscape and customs, down to every different kind of mushroom, was written in Paris. Then, perhaps exhausted after that immense effort of total recall, he dried up, at least on poetry, although as national bard he became deeply involved with Polish messianism. A modern counterpart is Solzhenitsyn. Norwid's poetry on the other hand, though also in Polish, is not only more experimental but explores far less specifically Polish themes.

In a parallel if dissimilar way Joyce, though boldly experimental in form (if not in type of narrative authoritarianism; see chapter 7), continued to write about the Ireland of his youth, first realistically then mythologically in a wholly transformed, interlinguistic idiom that transcends not only his earlier realism but also, in that punning way at least, his Irishness. Beckett, on the other hand, also pushing the boundaries of novel or play beyond familiar form, writes much simpler English (and later French), yet leaves Ireland far behind, and his Postmodern successor Calvino also abandons regional or national locales and themes.

In a general sense this abandonment of the local is true of many modern writers. Thomas Mann's *The Magic Mountain* is not merely about a sanatorium; Djuna Barnes's characters are placeless; and so on. In *What Are Masterpieces?* Gertrude Stein said about herself: "I am American and I have lived half my life in Paris, not the half that made me but the half that made what I made" (1970, 62). Later she elaborates: "What is adventure and what romance. Adventure is making the distant approach nearer but romance is having what is where it is which is not where you are stay where it is" (62).

Those who make things "inside themselves," Stein goes on, do not need adventure but they do need romance:

> It has always been true of all who make what they make come out of what is in them and have nothing to do with what is necessarily existing outside of them it is inevitable that they have always wanted two civilizations. . . . There is no possibility of mixing up the other civilization with yourself you are you and if you are you in your own civilization you are apt to mix yourself

up too much with your civilization but when it is another civilization a complete other a romantic other another that stays there where it is you in it have freedom inside yourself which if you are to do what is inside yourself and nothing else is a very useful thing to have happen to you and so America is my country and Paris is my home town. (62–63)

Whether we agree or not with this elaboration (and I do), it is true that the American expatriates in Paris between the two wars were strangely immune to French influence, in much the same way that Joyce wrote about Dublin independently of Zurich, Paris, or Trieste. As Shari Benstock has said about the English or American women who settled in France during the twenties (and it applies to most of the men, including Scott Fitzgerald), they wrote about the English and the Americans, and "were not affected by French mores and customs," since it was "the need for separateness that brought them to Paris" (1986, 78), as well as, no doubt, economic and other advantages: the favorable rate of exchange, the sexual freedom, the liquor unavailable in Prohibition America, and "being geniuses together."[3]

Hemingway, with his Parisian, Italian, Spanish, and African locales, is a notable exception, but then he hardly remains in one spot and might be classed by Stein under "adventurer" (travel rather than exile). Perhaps the most exemplary exception, going back a generation or more, is Henry James, who shifted his subtle analyses from Boston to Europe, and more especially to the gulf between the two, skillfully inverting the cliché of Americans as vulgar and Europeans as civilized. His disciple Edith Wharton, on the other hand, though living in France, remained with New York drawing-room society.

The Jamesian shift is much more common today. Kundera is a good example, with *The Unbearable Lightness of Being* (1984) mixing Geneva into a basically Czech story. Salman Rushdie is another. *The Satanic Verses* (1988) is a real clash of Indian/London as well as Secular/Islamic cultures. Kazuo Ishiguro moved from Japanese locales and themes to a tour de force in *The Remains of the Day* (1989), in which the thoughts and emotions of a typically British butler pierce through his pompously distancing, alienatingly correct idiom.

Apart from the last two, all these exiles—whatever their home/abroad themes or their familiar/innovative forms, whatever lands they left or went to, in whatever condition, Babylonish exile or prison, poor or relatively moneyed—nevertheless wrote in their native tongues, or at any rate in tongues they learned as children.

Linguistic

The question of language is more complex, and examples of writers who adopt a language not their own are much rarer. Joseph Conrad is the modern archetype, writing all his work in his third language, English. Apart from two poignant short stories, Conrad never wrote of Poland, but wrote instead of the sea, of Southeast Asia, the Congo, South America, Marseille, London. The other apparent exception, *Under Western Eyes* (1911), with its eastern European revolutionary theme, has a Russian hero and a Moscow locale, and takes place partly in Geneva. As in all Conrad's novels, the essential solitude and despair of exile is transmuted away from Polish specificity.

Conrad was born in exile (near Berdyczow), in the sense that this once Polish part of the Ukraine had been incorporated into Russia with the Partitions, although the idea of Poland and the Polish language remained very strong there. But Apollo Korzeniowski, Conrad's father and a literary man, was politically active, and the family was further exiled when Conrad was seven, first to Vologda, north of Moscow, then back south to Chernikow, not far from Kiev. Eventually, after his mother's death, Conrad returned at least to Lwów (Lviv today, in Ukrainian), then part of Austria, and ended up as an orphan in Cracków (also part of Austria then) under the guardianship of his maternal uncle. Conrad's dream was to go to sea, and at seventeen he left for Marseille. In other words, he was born an involuntary exile in the east of Europe who became a voluntary exile in the west. But he was deeply read in Polish literature, a complex background.

Even today, Ionesco, Nabokov, and Beckett are rare examples of complete linguistic assimilation, which possibly gave them the distance needed to transcend regional/national themes and move into those of the human condition everywhere.

The phenomenon of language change, however, also cuts across postcolonial exile, since many writers from our ex-empires write in the ex-imperial languages, French and English. The Spanish/Portuguese situation is different, since those languages stamped out the native ones, at least in Latin America and for literary purposes, and became the first and native languages of anyone with any education at all, in much older ex-empires that achieved independence earlier. But the Nigerians Chinua

Achebe and Wole Soyinka, the Somali Nurruddin Farah, the Algerian Rachid Mimouni (and many other African writers), Rushdie (and now many other Indian writers), who learned English/French young (and perhaps did not even know the local language or did not live in exile) all chose the ex-imperial languages over the "native" (?) idiom.

This modern phenomenon, though still unusual, is less and less rare as frontiers become more porous, as was the case in the Middle Ages. But it is an exact inversion of the medieval situation, when the ex-imperial language, Latin, though much debased, was the only literary language but was eventually stamped out by the new vernaculars. The effort to create a new literary language (Provençal, Languedoc, French, Tuscan, Spanish, Middle English, Middle High German, etc.) or, earlier, simply to continue in the old vernacular (Gothic, Old Saxon, Old Icelandic, Old High German, Anglo-Saxon) must have been an equivalent challenge, with this political and social difference: the medieval effort, though in each case individual, was also a generalized (sometimes condemned) struggle in favor of native, popular language as against a dying official one, whereas the modern effort of writers who use a language other than their native one is a purely individual struggle to merge into and contribute to the (as yet) not quite dying official language in order to reach a wider public, rather than be restricted to a language this wider public can't be bothered to learn.

And yet, despite this inversion, the modern individual who decides to create in an idiom not his own, or only secondly his own, is surely making the same qualitative effort as that of Dante trying to create a new literary language out of his own spoken and popular idiom. That is, the effort is as great, the result at its best is as fresh, as cliché-escaping, as enriching, as that of Dante; unless the exile, or the postcolonial, on the contrary, tries to follow the clichés (in language and narrative structure) of the ex-imperial culture, as happens, in my humble opinion, with both Chinua Achebe (e.g., in *Things Fall Apart,* 1958) and Ben Okri (e.g., in *Dangerous Love,* 1996).

How then are these various clashing features of exile (involuntary/voluntary, home society/new society, own language/alien language) experienced today? Clearly with more education, exchanges, travel, tolerance (at least at educated levels), and political upheavals everywhere, exile is less unusual, almost banal. But such a vast subject would deserve a whole book, examining each writer and each society in detail. Perhaps it has received just such attention in the new postcolonial discipline, which I have not kept up with. But since, more modestly, I have experienced both aspects of all those distinctions, myself as expatriate English writer but also earlier by proxy as ex-wife of Jerzy Peterkiewicz, a Polish exile writing in English, I shall end with a brief but more personal treatment, first of him (in the original essay), then of myself (added now, replacing a section on George Gissing and "inner" exile).

༄

In 1958, the *Times Literary Supplement* (May 18, 1–2) published a long front-page article entitled "England Is Abroad," reviewing three English novels by foreigners: *An End to Dying*, by Sam Astrachan (Yiddish culture); *Black Midas*, by Jan Carew (Guiana); and *Future to Let*, by Jerzy Peterkiewicz. After more than forty years there is no point in summarizing the reviews or the books, but it was the first time, to my knowledge, that the question of foreigners writing in English was raised in the *Times Literary Supplement* (then still anonymous).[4] The article dealt first, and at length, with the situation of the English novel. It starts: "Provincialism, like rheumatism, is the name of a disease which has as many cures as it has causes. . . . Provincialism is a kind of cultural rheumatism, a stiffness in the joints, a pained paralysis of the executory organs, an insidious and obscure malady that will in time deform the very structure of a language, altering its every statement into the posture of parody" (1).

I would qualify the metaphor by adding that rheumatism is a conscious pain ("pained paralysis"), whereas provincialism is unconscious and self-satisfied. The author goes on to suggest that the English idiom

> was already in decay before the first World War. Already, by 1910, we find that many of the most accomplished writers in our language originate on the fringe of the English-speaking world and, more importantly, that they made no attempt to cover up their origins by conforming to the standards of the metropolis. On the contrary, they demand that London should accept them as they are and even suggest that it would benefit by following in their outlandish footsteps. What is more, London did. The centre of gravity of English literature shifted. (1)

To be sure, the author is here thinking chiefly of the "American influx," in terms of which, he complains, this remarkable revolution is too often considered; and, more particularly, of Yeats, rather than of writers from European or colonial cultures. On Yeats, he comments that

> had he been born a century earlier than he was . . . Yeats would either have written within the English conventions, or he would have been a much more modest poet than the one we know. He could not have been both an Irish poet and a great poet because there was no cultural context in which a great Irish poet could exist, unless perhaps, he wrote in Erse. The power of the English language was such that he would have been transformed by it into an English poet who happened to have been born in Ireland, just as Swift and Burke are English writers though they remain Irish men. (1)

Similarly there was no context (not even at the time of the article) for an African or Indian writer to become a great writer in French or English. In other words, Yeats would have been like Latin writers of the late empire or the Middle Ages (Macrobius, for instance), whose land of residence or origin is irrelevant even if known (as with Gregory of Tours, Matthew of Vendôme, or Geoffrey of Vinsauf).

Of the three writers considered by the article, Peterkiewicz was unique in having learned English late, in his twenties. Conrad was thus a frequent comparison in reviews of his English novels, and, like Conrad, he was attacked by his compatriots for "betrayal," as are, I believe, certain postcolonials today. But his situation, like his novels, was completely different from Conrad's. For one thing he had a Polish literary career behind him. In that sense at least, he is more like Nabokov or Beckett, changing language in midstream.

Born in 1916, Peterkiewicz (Pietrkiewicz) left his Polish village in Dobrzyn (northeast Poland) at fourteen, to study in Wrocław and to conquer Warsaw, where he was quickly recognized as a highly original poet and soon was editing a literary review. He was twenty-three when Hitler, then Stalin, invaded Poland in 1939. He escaped to Romania, where he fell very ill, eventually arriving in France, and escaping again in 1940 to England, still too ill to join up. The Polish government in exile helped him to attend the University of St. Andrews in Scotland, where he recovered, learned English, and obtained his first degree. In his autobiography (1993) he describes how he couldn't understand why a lecturer kept talking about Ovid, only to learn later that the lecturer merely pronounced "of it" in an emphatic way. That's how little English he knew at first.

I met him in the British Museum Library in 1946 when I was twenty-three and just demobbed, preparing for the Oxford ex-service entrance exam and later about to go there as an ex-service and grant-supported student. He was twenty-nine, finishing his Ph.D. thesis in London, and continuing to publish articles and poems in the exile Polish press to survive.

Then, slowly, came the mutation, over the next six or seven years: he not only stopped writing poetry and turned to novels, he also turned to writing novels in English—strange novels, both sad and funny, and deeply original. By then, of course, his English was fluent, and he was learning Spanish. And there occurred, equally slowly, a Jamesian shift in subject matter, from wholly Polish to partly Polish to totally free and experimental. Let me give slightly more detail (restricted here to content summary). His first novel, *The Knotted Cord* (1953), was partly autobiographical, about a boy in a Polish village, who, after an illness, is dedicated to St. Antony by his mother and dressed for three years in a Franciscan habit. In the second novel, *Loot and Loyalty* (1955), the scene shifts to Scottish mercenaries in seventeenth-century Poland (the exile situation reversed, with Poland then a powerful kingdom), including one Tobias Hume, a historical figure who composed songs and who, in the novel, gets involved with a newly imagined version of the False Dmitri. The scene shifts again in *Future to Let* to an Englishman caught up, via the exotic Celina, with Polish exiles in London.

After 1958, the Polish scene is over, if the essential solitude of exile is not, and the subsequent novels are among the most unusual of the time, or even, I would suggest, of the period since. *Isolation* (1959) also features an exotic foreign woman in London, but she is South American and a diplomat's wife, who meets her English lover in dramatically secretive ways and places, with a comic and melancholy eroticism that is part of the charm. *The Quick and the Dead* (1961) is literally about the dead and the dead living, in a weird, limbo locale (nominally the Canaries), not in the least like a ghost story but both violent and gently poetic. These works are completely out of the Polish/foreign versus London isolation.

That Angel Burning at My Left Side (1963) returns east to the borderland between Poland and ex–East Prussia (now Mazury), with a hero searching for an unknown father, but it soon shifts to other regions, in sections named "East," "West," "North," "South," in that order, ending in Italy. Then comes my favorite (with *Loot and Loyalty*), *Inner Circle*

(1966), written in a spiral structure of recurring layers called "Surface," "Underground," "Sky," that are apparently, but only apparently, unlinked. "Surface" describes a future people who emerge out of boxes to a much reduced living space on the surface, having barely a square meter each to stand on; "Underground" is the perpetual journey of a schizophrenic boy, Patrick, on the London tube (Inner Circle Line); and "Sky" is the story of Eve, already separated from Adam, living in a world of animals that is invaded by apes, with whom her daughter goes off to live. The link is in the title, the inner circle of solitude, of exile, echoed in the spiral structure. The treatment is like skating on thin ice, a light and graceful dance over cold, unseen depths.

The last novel, *Green Flows the Bile* (1969), about a dying British fellow traveler on a last visit to Eastern Europe, returns to a more realistic, satirical, even oddly prophetic vein, and was the first to be less well received. I myself like it less, but this may be subjective (and my liking it less didn't prevent me, despite early premonitions of a long marriage crisis, from persuading my then-publisher to take it).

Why then was this highly original writer forgotten? Partly, perhaps, because the British could welcome a foreigner as long as he remained exotic, much as men could welcome women writers as long as they remained domestic; partly because he came too soon to be truly comprehended; partly because England finally woke from its provincialism so that many other innovative novels, notably postcolonial and Postmodern, began to attract all the attention; but mostly, I would venture, because Peterkiewicz stopped writing novels, though he continued to write in English (including essays, radio plays, an autobiography, and translations of Karol Woytyła's poetry, commissioned by the pope he had become). Sheer persistency can also be part of survival. Conrad, after all, did not pierce through until his twelfth novel, *Chance* (1913), though his friends and admirers blamed him for yielding to sellerdom.

And why did Peterkiewicz stop? He stopped after I left in 1968, but I have to insist here that this is only an answer to "when?" and that there is no clear connection: literary gossip might say that he couldn't have written his novels without my support in English, or even, who knows, that I wrote them. But the second hypothesis is impossible (we're too different, as anyone would feel who knows his early poetry and plays in Polish, which show the real continuity), and the first is ridiculous. His English was perfect, nor did I ever correct more than actual and rare mistakes, as any editor might, and I took great care never to alter his *ostra-*

nenie, the defamiliarization, the poetic oddity of his style. I contributed only encouragement and enthusiasm, and I learned more then from him than he would have from me, even if I learned even more later, on my own. Indeed, I started four or five years after him, and we always wrote together, on holiday, reading chapters aloud and commenting. Perhaps he missed that magical partnership-in-variance, as I may have at first, the only difference being that I continued without it. Indeed, from *Out* to *Between* (when I left), he had less and less to say that was of any help to me and seemed either to disapprove or not to understand what I was up to—or else he was already emotionally elsewhere.

But the writer's block is always mysterious. Perhaps, unusually sensitive in mid-marriage crisis, he got discouraged by the bad reception of the last novel. Perhaps the sheer distance from his origins was too great, and though so well assimilated, he suddenly felt the gulf. Conrad, after all, could and did revisit Poland. Peterkiewicz was blacklisted by the Communist regime and did not return to Poland until 1963, for research, well after he had become a British subject and lecturer, then professor in Polish literature at London University, and so was "safe." And even then he was followed, as indeed even I was when left on my own during two later visits together. Now that Poland is free, he is welcome there again; his poetry is republished; his English works translated. Yet despite England's neglect, he prefers to remain there, but also to get away, to Spain, shuttling between the two.

༄

I also am astride two languages and cultures, though in very different ways. I left England for practical not political reasons. As a freelance, I couldn't survive on my own in a separate flat but needed a job. I was offered one in Paris in the middle of my marriage crisis, during which nobody I knew and worked for helped me in that respect, just as, after finishing my Ph.D. in 1954, it had been quasi-impossible for a young woman then to get a job in the university, so that I drifted into literary journalism and translations, as I tell in *Remake*.[5]

At any rate, I had to trust a purely verbal invitation as to the job, let alone the salary, and had to obtain two advances for unwritten books just to get away, or at least to buy a broken-down old car. The first book (on Pound) I wrote at once, the second (naively entitled *A Rhetoric for Reality*) I grew out of even envisaging after a year in France, but by then

I could repay the publishers, and it very eventually became *A Rhetoric of the Unreal* (1981).

As the new University of Vincennes, a sop to the 1968 students, wasn't ready to start until January 1969, I left, in early November 1968, for the "Pound castle" in the Italian Tyrol, during the appearance of *Between*, which I had finished there in 1967. Mary de Rachewiltz, Pound's daughter, welcomed me like a mother (though she was two years younger), and I wrote my Pound book in five weeks, surrounded by snow and Poundiana. I revised it in Paris, but that first draft, in its very swiftness of inspiration (I had been an anonymous Poundian for the *Times Literary Supplement* and for Faber and Faber for ten years), did much to restore my confidence.

Nevertheless, I arrived in Paris in a relatively demolished state. It would be tedious to recount here either the process of that demolition (after thirty years, we're now, more or less, "good friends" again) or the alienation of the reconstruction, bit by bit, as an immigrant in France before Britain at last and reluctantly decided to join Europe. I tried to do so twenty-five years later in the last chapter of *Remake* (1991), but, as recounted here at the end of chapter 4, this last chapter didn't interest my publisher and I scrapped it.

My difficulties weren't due only to post-'68 tumult but to the French system. It's true that alienation through administrative petty power is such a common experience that it took a Kafka or a Courteline to make literature out of it. By the nineties, I had long adapted to it (although the *bêtise administrative,* as the French themselves call it, continues [see Brunet 1998]). It is the dark side of the French *art de vivre,* and everyone seems to accept it as normal. If I mention it here it is only because it is relevant to exile: to start exile demolished, to have to reconstruct one's being, if not an identity, bit by bit in an unimagined atmosphere such as that of '68 (strikes, violence, aggressive students, and every topic, however pedagogic, politicized in endless haranguing at faculty meetings, as well as the incredible rudeness of officials), was probably as difficult for me as Peterkiewicz's early struggles in St. Andrews—more so, for he was young then, and now I was forty-five.

First, the '68 tumult, far easier to accept than the archaic French system, but a small shock at first : to be interrupted, for instance, in an English conversation class as I tried to launch a topic, a student saying: "C'est dégueulasse, c'que tu dis-là," was hardly part of my Oxford or London experience twenty years earlier. Amazingly, for I'm normally an after-thinker, I met it head on: "Say it in English," I said, which he couldn't, so I wrote all the rudest words I could think and won over the giggling students. I have to add that I thoroughly approved of the change in teacher-student relations brought about by 1968, and more so by this new University of Paris VIII, so I don't regret these initial little shocks. I probably learned as much, morally, from students during those twenty years as I imparted academically.

However, the French system teaches nothing but despair or resigned acceptance. To survive unpaid for six months, for a different example, living in a hovel and borrowing right and left, simply because it takes that long to get "inside the machine,"[6] was like being jerked back to the poverty of student days or even that of the first fifteen years of marriage, but worse, for none of my/our bedsits were hovels, and at least we were young and carefree and in love.

To be declared *inapte au travail* by a revengeful doctor, merely because I had burst out laughing and called the medical for immigrants *une comédie* (urine sample, weighing, measuring, and passing in front of him for a quick auscultation, "très bien, très bien—comment, une comédie?"), saying it could reveal nothing about tropical diseases or operations, and then being hauled in to reveal my operations (thus proving my point): this was my first lesson, underlined laughingly by the president of the university, who received the notice: "Ce travailleur ne remplit pas les conditions sanitaires pour travailler en France." I felt dirty. Meanwhile, of course, I was working. He told me how to appeal, but added, "never criticize the administration."

Oddly enough, I received the same advice recently, at this end of my French career. I was comically recounting my application for a handicap parking card to my physiotherapist. The administration thought I was asking for a national card (blue), linked to a pension, which I didn't need and couldn't have, whereas I was asking for an international one (orange), for parking only, possessed by Lorna Sage, confirmed as existing by the police and delivered by . . . the very section I was dealing with, which had never heard of it. It had gone on for months, each attempt at explanation treated as an appeal, since officials don't read either explanatory letters or the forms they send for filling. Indeed I have yet to receive a relevant reply from any administration, when there is a reply. My "kiné" said, "You must say *mon dieu*, do you understand the language of this document? Comme vous êtes intelligent!" I gave up, because I finally had to stop driving altogether, and so informed them. A year later (in December 2000) I received a letter from Amiens in the north (I living in the south, the French version of decentralization being merely to delocalize the central authority), asking me if I was maintaining my "appeal."

Still, even as deep irony, never criticize, and, thirty years later, flatter, such an attitude means that nothing can change. Nor does it, for the entire system is conceived always to put all effort on the public, not on the administration, so the public cheats too. It's the *maladie française*: every new law is immediately twisted, so that the lack of both civic sense and minimal efficiency runs through society from top to bottom, in every domain, both public and private, in favor of the *chacun pour soi*, which leads insidiously to a generalized *j' m' enfoutisme,* until any attempt to get anything done (four years for a telephone in 1972, before the technological leap, and in 2000, three months instead of five days for an e-mail address and compatible cable) gets not only clogged with inefficiency but also with total indifference, which creates frustration. Hence the French propensity for riots, revolutions, blockages. Hence also the severe braindrain of scientists who can't stand it any longer.

"Republican" rhetoric, though few are duped, also boasts daily about human rights while the officials are profoundly racist and xenophobic: "Alors, c'est comme ça qu'on fait en Angleterre," yelled a whistle-blowing policeman soon after I arrived, when I had slowed down the car, looking for a street. Or, when at the end of an unusually empty boulevard St Michel I stopped to ask the way to the Préfecture, the policeman told me roughly to go and park (impossible there) and to come back and ask him, so that by the time our altercation was over I really was blocking the traffic as he said, and he suddenly took two seconds to tell me: over the bridge and turn right. This was the attitude as long as I had a British number-plate and right-wheel drive—regularly, about anything. At the Préfecture, the policewoman at the entry desk, having told a Vietnamese girl where to go for naturalization, turned to me, next in line, unknown but white, and exclaimed furiously: "Ça, c'est une future française!" Perhaps this was only post-'68, which had destabilized the police? Yet by the time I had to renew my *carte de séjour* ten years later, the discourse at the end of the queue in the Commissariat had at best merely inverted to what I call *racisme à l'envers*: when I asked, just to fill the air, if it would take long to get an appointment at the Préfecture, the woman looked at my papers and said: "oh non, vous êtes quelqu'un de bien."

This certainly hadn't helped me at the beginning. The university had told me, racistically, "Oh, you don't want to be mixed up with all those

Portuguese and Spaniards [also not yet in the European Union] and Arabs, we'll do it for you," referring to getting the residential permit, and later the work permit, but they were wrong, fortunately for ideals. It wasn't being "mixed up" I minded, it was seeing how all these people were treated, including myself. Apart from the constant scorn and rudeness to people who mostly couldn't understand anyway but could hear the tone of voice, the story of my work permit alone was more than Kafkaesque. I was given an address, rue de Vaugirard, which (after long queueing in each case) sent me to the rue de la Folie [*sic*], which wouldn't accept my application in two handwritings (mine and the university's) and, the second time around, noticed my professorial salary on the front page and told me it wasn't here, it was at the Ministry of Labor, which sent me back to the rue de Vaugirard, which at last accepted my application, leading six months later to the medical and my "inaptitude." Was I glad when at last old GB decided in 1972 to enter Europe (done 1973) and I didn't need a work permit, only a *carte de séjour,* making one area, at least, where I could evade the administration. And indeed that is how one survives serenely in France: by having as little to do with its administration as possible.

Retrospectively, I came to understand the deep and permanent feeling of exclusion I had merely imagined in *Out:* not only what all immigrants and refugees must go through a million times more unpleasantly the world over, but also, more lightly, what my ex-husband must have gone through in the forties for two decades, even if the inefficiency and the xenophobia were (perhaps?) more superficially courteous than French officials could ever manage.

It's true I had no language problem, French being my native tongue, even if it had to be relearned as lunatic political and administrative jargons.[7] But I had been born in Geneva and brought up in Brussels, then England, and underwent a rude culture shock on discovering that my childhood language was also that of such a quarrelsome, self-centered, and self-righteous people.

Or maybe I was just learning the language of adults, the language of the world, rather late after many relatively protected years? Looking back, I saw that even the war years, though I spent them reading the entire war daily from the enemy point of view, had been in a hut in the decoding center at Bletchley Park, where I was collected by bus every day, surrounded by intellectuals, never having to face that enemy. Nor did I later ever have to face any kind of British administration (passport office excepted, and that was smooth as honey in comparison) merely to be allowed to exist. I had, I now saw, been very spoiled, allowed to take minimal politeness and efficiency for granted. Even in the nineties, returning from a lecture tour in the U.S. and landing at Orly for a connection, I knew from the rudeness within minutes and for two hours that I was back in France.

At any rate, I came to understand that even when one knows the language, exile can be an astonishingly destabilizing experience if one is not a rich American expatriate but tries to settle as part of the system, as Peterkiewicz and many others did. I also came to understand how, in 1961, he and I walked round and round Times Square after he received an invitation to Ann Arbor, to decide whether he should accept the chair in Polish studies there, which London had not been prepared to give him because of his Polish origins: now that so many foreign names appear everywhere, we forget how late these prejudices continued, like those against intellectual jobs for women. For in the end what decided him against it was the idea of yet another huge cultural adjustment, but at, precisely, age forty-five. Instead, he showed the letter to the School of Slavonic Studies in London, and the light blackmail worked. This is sad in a way, but it was the only way.

What it all amounted to then is that I was a semivoluntary exile but, unusually, going back to my first language, though shrinking from it , not writing in it (except for occasional academic articles), and never writing about the country I lived in. This is my only brief attempt to compensate, perhaps, for that scrapped chapter. Indeed, none of that immediate and daily experience of being an immigrant was ever worth fictionalizing, nor does any of it get into *Thru,* apart from a comically disintegrated academic context and the mocking use I make of Structuralism and literary theory generally, mingled with other elements that make the university in the book far more American than French. But it took me a long time to start writing again, after such a painful adjustment. The adjustment, moreover, prevented me from taking full advantage of my freedom, keeping up my Polish or my Spanish, for instance, at the university I taught in. I could have taken yet another degree. On the contrary, I plunged into Italian on holiday, and such seminars as I found time to attend were in linguistics or literary theory, part of the "new" personality I was forced to find.

Despite all this regrettable *haine* and pettiness, which does such harm to the intelligent, witty, cultured, and bon vivant side of the French character, and which most tourists don't see, exile is an immense force for liberation, for recovery, for extra distance. Everything is new. It is undoubtedly a leaping forth. I began, in fact, a second career, as teacher, scholar, and writer, teaching as short-term guest in the U.S., Montreal, Israel, Switzerland, publishing more and more, writing all my best books, driving all over Europe and America and Mexico. I met completely new people. I met Barthes, Kristeva, Todorov (but on thesis juries or conference panels, as colleagues rather than as myself a writer, of no interest to them), and many others. The very first writer I encountered, in 1969, was Maurice Roche and his delightful Brazilian wife Violante. Possibly Roche's exciting first book, *Compact* (1966), which he gave me, influenced me for *Thru*'s typography; I can't remember. Two years ago, when I could still drive, I went to his funeral, in a neighboring village; ours was a thirty-year friendship.

But there is a price to pay in exile. The distance can seem too great, the alienation as writer too burdensome—at least for one who shies from other expatriates or "being geniuses together" (if there are any). The language of writing can feel more and more remote, while the language of living, though close and quotidian, remains somehow alien because it is not one's creative language.

For instance, in 1969, Monique Nathan at Le Seuil wanted to bring out *Between,* provided I translated it myself and was presented as a French author. To her astonishment, since I spoke French like a native, I refused. I was not only far too busy learning the twisted ropes in a (both politically and administratively) highly jargonized university, but I also knew that French was not flexible enough to do all the wordplay and syntax play I had done in English—or, if it was, that I couldn't do it (Maurice Roche could, perhaps, who wanted to, but charmingly never got around to it). Besides, where is the fun in redoing what one has done? Well, Beckett did, and brilliantly, but I knew I couldn't. What little time I had I needed to write new novels, not the same one in French. Supposing I had accepted, and succeeded, would I now be a French writer? I doubt it. For I rapidly learned to steer clear of French literary circles and their cavalier manners, at least professionally.

So why did I stay, after retirement? It's a good question. Before and after retiring, I made several attempts to stay long enough in England to decide whether to return. I learned that London would be too tiring if ever I had a difficult old age (which has proved the case), but also, and more important, that changes in time are more off-putting than changes in space. At the beginning, I could make invidious comparisons: I remember telling a French colleague that in London I used to send a Christmas card to my tax inspector and would get one back (well, counterwishes on an acknowledgment card), or that in England, where of course there is red tape like everywhere else, the administration was still felt as a service, and every letter is signed "Your Obedient Servant"—a formula, yes, but unimaginable in France. He simply laughed: How naive. And no doubt that has changed in time. Or I'd think: a British bobby would never be as rude, as xenophobic, racist, or violent as a French policeman or a Préfecture official. True in the sixties, when I left. But when I saw TV reports on the British police during the miners' strikes in the eighties, or the discovered fabricated evidence in cases like the "Birmingham Six," I learned to stop comparing. After twenty years abroad—now more than thirty—I discovered to my astonishment that I feel far more alienated in England than in France. This is the process that, for a real immigrant, would be called assimilation. Although nothing would induce me to become French, with time I must have learned to accept and laugh with, and even cherish, French failings, while absence has made me not fonder but less tolerant of English ways of alienating, which are more devilishly subtle but just as unacceptable—for living among, I mean.

So is the real reason for exile social? My most loyal publisher and friend, Raleigh Trevelyan, who published me from *Out* to *Thru* (and, I believe, was fired with a golden handshake for accepting the latter), had said to me several times that I'd get on much better if I were "on the spot," meaning, I suppose, reviewing in the right papers and going to the right parties, which was what I was doing in the late fifties and sixties, and happily escaped from. For if such success as I had then was due to that, I didn't want it again. Besides, the literary world has also changed, and I have no illusions that an infirm old lady who can't go to parties or indeed be part of the reviewing world would suddenly "pierce through" merely from being "on the spot." As I said earlier, I'm proud never to have owed any such "piercing through" as I did get to legups from friends.

Unlike my one-time writing partner, who, once "the foreigner" to my Englishness, has "assimilated" and feels relatively at home in England, I am now the foreigner there, nor does my country greet me, as his does, with enthusiasm and republications of my work. It's almost as if he had unconsciously maneuvered me into changing places. So here I am, my work finished, like his, and happily waiting for the end, preferring to feel mildly alienated in a sunny part of France to feeling more than mildly alienated in my own country. I even enjoy it. Very possibly it echoes the perpetual nonbelonging of my childhood, experienced even then as a treasured status: Switzerland as ever neutral, Belgium as, on the contrary, always part of another country until 1830 and later the battleground of Europe. Alienation is also an inner exile. And exile is, more than living at home, a form of protected serenity and isolation. My "identity," if any, is "the lady who lives in that house."

Rooted in all types of exile are opposing desires: the desire to integrate/not to integrate; the desire to identify with the society left behind rather than with the society lived in (Mickiewicz, Joyce, the American expatriates, Solzhenitsyn); the desire not to belong to the society left behind but to the society lived in (James, Conrad); the desire not to integrate either with the society lived in or with the society left behind (Norwid); and many more ambiguous Postmodern variations (Kundera, Calvino, Beckett, Ionesco, Nabokov).

It seems, then, that despite an English tendency to neglect its writers who have chosen to live abroad, exile is not in itself a sufficient explanation for inattention to what I actually do. I could not, for instance, have thought spontaneously of so many names if all writers in exile had vanished from the record (as no doubt many others did). Most of them have or had other qualities that transcend exile, and maybe I have not.

It's true I do nothing or very little to help. I don't self-promote, nor does my publisher do it for me. I refused really to compromise and continued to do my thing, accepting failure. Failure happens to the vast majority, after all.

Ultimately, is not every poet or "poetic" (exploring, rigorous) novelist an exile of sorts, looking in from outside onto a bright, desirable image in the mind's eye, of the little world created, for the space of the writing effort and the shorter space of the reading? Mine has been a particularly active and interactive life. But this kind of writing, often at odds with publisher and public, is the last solitary, nonsocialized creative art, which is why it may well disappear. Even self-promoting websites are thoroughly socialized. Music needs performers, painting often needed teams in the past, as it now needs experts in modern inventions such as electronics or acrylics or plastics, as sculpture and architecture always did. The dramatist needs production and actors, the best-selling author needs media hype, the scriptwriter is the most minor in a vast list of contributors to a film. Reading is also becoming more and more difficult, fragmentized. It used also to be shared aloud, but is now the last solitary activity. The circle of light on the page, the escapes from it in stray thoughts and imaginative leaps: an inner circle within the island of exile, is that not also an island, the reader or writer in ex-*île,* exsul?

7

The Author Is Dead
LONG LIVE THE AUTHOR*

I HAVE KEPT MY MAIN constraint or lipogram (no past tense narrative mode) to the end because it is not a constraint affecting just one novel, like the *to be* lipogram or others discussed earlier, but a narrative technique that permeates nearly all my novels since I started experimenting (from *Out* onwards). It is a technique, moreover, that I perfected during all those years without, I now realize, always being as sure as I thought I was of its full implications, narratological, linguistic, and philosophical. I therefore decided to describe it fully in this lecture, together with those implications, hoping for an answer, if not from my own meditation, then perhaps from that of my few readers.

This century began with a growing resentment of the author's guiding presence in every sentence, the enveloping of every fact with comment. Authorial guidance was given in **Narrative Sentences (NS)**, as opposed to speech or thought by characters: **Narrative Mode** versus **Speech Mode**, each with a different grammar.

We tend to forget that epic and romance (both classical and medieval) and the early modern novel consisted overwhelmingly of NS and little

---

* Lecture given at the University of Helsinki, September 1999, published in shortened form as "Narrating without a Narrator" in the *Times Literary Supplement,* 31 December 1999, 12–13. To clarify difficult points, I have slightly expanded the original lecture here and there with more examples.

dialogue, for historical and stylistic reasons going back to Plato, who preferred indirect to direct reporting, telling to showing, as I mentioned in chapter 3. Open any book by Defoe or Swift, and you get pages of uninterrupted NS that would make a novel unreadable today. With Sterne and Fielding we get more speech forms, not only from characters but in playful author addresses to the reader; then with Jane Austen dialogue elegantly enters, but it develops slowly and not always so wittily; characters are fixed psychologically and socially through speech. With James comes the claimed preference for showing, but in fact the NS, more and more complex, still largely dominates.

This distinction, however, was rarely formulated, or formulated correctly. As late as 1966 well-known Structuralists such as Barthes and Todorov were still confusing narrative and speech, both stating that to narrate is to speak (see, e.g., Barthes 1966). It precisely is not.

The novel, in fact, has been making a huge effort, particularly in the twentieth century, to shake off the authoritarianism of the traditional narrative mode. At first, one solution was to take even the NS right inside the character as free indirect discourse (see below); another was to get away from that and allow far more direct speech mode, either inside the character (interior monologue, as in, say, Joyce) or as dialogue with outside viewpoint but no comment (as in the "anti-Modernists" Hemingway or Waugh, as opposed to James or Woolf). An extreme version of that was the novel wholly or almost wholly in dialogue (as in examples by Henry Green or Ivy Compton-Burnett), but this, as Sarraute later commented, was pushing the novel into the theater, where it is bound to be inferior (Sarraute 1956).

However, some indication of who was speaking—and how—was thought minimally necessary, and continued late, for example, Iris Murdoch: "she thought, her heart sinking a little" (*The Unicorn*). These parentheticals, as linguists call them, and their desperate variants, already parodied by Joyce in *Ulysses* (1922, in several sections but especially "Wandering Rocks"), were later attacked by Sarraute as "symbols of the old régime" (1956). In 1968 John Barth parodied the parenthetical by lengthily naming it instead of using it: "'Why do you suppose it is,' she asked, long participial phrase of the breathless variety characteristic of dialogue attribution in nineteenth-century fiction, 'that literature people such as we talk like characters in a story?'" (Barth 1968).

But parentheticals and narrative comment are only one type of author intrusion, and easily jettisoned. They had already vanished in *Tarr* by

Wyndham Lewis (1918), but kept recurring: Peter Ackroyd, for instance, whom I much admire, was still parodying them with italics in *Hawksmoor* (1985) but soon suppressed them. I stopped using them from *Out* on. Another easily jettisoned guidance is in chapter headings, fulsome in the nineteenth century, then dropped, now more discreetly reappearing.

A much more pervasive feature was the past tense, which has always been used as reassuring guarantor of real events. In 1953 Robbe-Grillet used the present tense throughout in *Les Gommes,* as did Beckett in *Molloy* (original French version, 1950), and Sarraute in *Le Planétarium* (1959). Their uses of the tense are, however, very different from each other, and had been partly foreshadowed by others, as will become clear below. By 1963, in *Pour un nouveau roman* (*Towards a New Novel,* 1965), Alain Robbe-Grillet was naming the use of the past tense as *the* distinguishing mark of the traditional novel. It's true that the French narrative tense, the aorist or *passé simple,* also called *passé défini,* started dying in the seventeenth century and is now fully dead (i.e., purely literary, never used in speech), unlike the past in English or other languages, where the gap between literary and spoken language is less dire, so that it's astonishing that the French revolt came so late.

There had been many attempts to get free of this past tense Narrative Sentence (NS): in nineteenth-century fiction, brief passages in the historic present are used for vivid descriptive (non-action) scenes before safe return to the past; and the present tense is favored for universalizing moral or social comments from the author. Or of course, much easier, the handing over of narrative to a character inside the story who, unlike Robinson Crusoe and other early I-narrators, are allowed to pass from the classic NS to the present and other tenses of Speech Mode. Already Dostoyevsky's *Notes from Underground* (1864) is a non-stop monologue by the hero. So are diary forms, and, earlier, epistolary forms (still predominantly in narrative mode, though). And of course the varyingly rhythmed (chopped, telegraphic, or unpunctuated) interior monologues of Stephen, Bloom, and Molly in Joyce's *Ulysses* (1922). As a narrative tense, however, the present was first experimented in 1874 by Flaubert in *La Tentation de Saint Antoine* (three earlier versions from 1839 to 1870), and in 1887 by Edouard Dujardin in *Les lauriers sont coupés,* then by Gertrude Stein; and by Joyce, first very occasionally as historic presents for sudden vigor in *Ulysses* (where the conventional distinction between past-tense NS for any activity and all-tense speech forms is still automatic); then coming into its own in *Finnegans Wake* (1939). But here Joyce purposely blurs the very distinction I am talking about, so I'll return to him below.

Tense didn't really become a narrative issue till the fifties. Beckett's earlier novels were in the past tense, as was Sarraute's earlier work. Camus's *L'Étranger*, written in the present perfect or *passé composé* of **Speech Mode** with its famous first sentence "Aujourd'hui, maman est morte," appeared in 1942. In fact, Louis Ferdinand Céline had forestalled him in *Voyage au bout de la nuit* (1932), written in an ultra-colloquial French, i.e., **Speech Mode,** a mixture of present perfect, present, imperfect, but also aorist still, perhaps unanalyzed then because the amount of dialogue masks the **Narrative Sentences,** all however pronounced in the first person of **Speech Mode.** The astonishment *L'Étranger* caused in France, however (e.g., in Sarraute 1947, discussed in chapter 1), was at an I-narrator so empty, so "absent from himself" (as recalled by Robbe-Grillet 1984, see 150, n.13). Tense was not properly discussed. Proust's frequent *présents d'écriture* ("j'entends la rumeur des distances traversées") were not dealt with until Genette on "Voice" and "Narrative Instance" (1972, 234–35), and strictly speaking are author interference in speech mode (see Benveniste below) rather than narrative. His famous first sentence in the present perfect, "Longtemps je me suis couché de bonne heure," had after all appeared in 1913, even if it wasn't really analyzed as tense until Serge Doubrovsky devoted a whole article to just that in 1971. But Proust at once continues his narrative, more traditionally, in the imperfect (continuous past, "mes yeux se fermaient" / were closing . . .), so well used by Flaubert as ideal solution to the dying aorist, whereas Camus's entire short narrative is in the present perfect. The narrator's "absence from himself" has in fact little to do with tense, it is achieved through the I-narrator necessary to speech mode describing only outside events, never himself or his reactions. In other words, content.

In 1966, a Structuralist linguist, Emile Benveniste, clarified the distinction between *histoire* and *discours* (history / speech). So as not to create confusion with Genette's later use of *discours* for "treatment" and *récit* for "story," from the Russian Formalist *sjužet/fabula* (the how and the what), I have here preferred Narrative versus Speech. Benveniste's distinction is entirely about the how, two types of telling, one for history, which uses a particular type of impersonal sentence to tell of events, and the other for the speech system (i.e., for addressing the reader or, in the novel as in life, for characters/people to address each other). Here is Benveniste on the NS used for history: "Nobody speaks here, events seem to narrate themselves. The fundamental tense is the aorist, which is the time of events outside the person of a narrator" (Benveniste 1966, 241).[1] If the aorist really expresses "the time of events outside the person of a narrator," this would explain the death of the once imposed *passé simple* in speech—and a possible difference of attitude in English and other languages, where the past tense can and does also belong to the speech system. There is no dead aorist.

The main point here, however, is that the "historical" past tense is speakerless, and—as Benveniste had previously demonstrated that historical narrative also ignores audience—it is not only speakerless but addressee-less. Moreover, it has its own grammar, and this is true of other western European languages: it has three tenses, the aorist, the imperfect (including the conditional depending upon it), and the pluperfect. The NS is also limited to the third person, which thereby has a different value (a nonperson) from its value in speech, where it is opposed to a *je/tu*. The NS cannot address an audience without saying "I" or "you" or using the present, the present perfect, or the future, that is, without passing into *discours,* or Speech Mode, thus ceasing to be NS.

In other words, the NS of historical narrative is outside the personal system of speech and cannot use its tenses. Nor can it use its deictics: it has to say "then" for "now," "there" for "here," "the next day" for "tomorrow," "the day before" for "yesterday," "the following year" for "next year," and so on (cf. Camus's first sentence, which is in speech mode); it should even avoid deictic verbs, which situate the speaker in space (e.g., "came" versus "went").

The tenses of **Speech Mode** are the present, the present perfect, and the future. The French imperfect or continuous past, which in English is the past progressive (was going) or iterative (would [often] go), seems to belong to both historical narrative and the personal speech system, *pace* Benveniste. Hence Proust could use the imperfect for the dead aorist throughout his long narrative without causing much shock or even notice. And, in English, the past tense is also part of the speech system. As I said above, there is no dead aorist.[2]

It may seem contradictory to talk of a revolt against author intrusions and at the same time to cite a Structuralist's dictum that in the NS "no one speaks." It isn't really. Benveniste is talking about the historian's sentence, and one of the sources of the modern novel is the chronicle. But the struggle to "speak" despite the speakerless sentence started early, with first-person narratives (as in Defoe and Swift) or author interference in the first person (Fielding, Sterne), or in varyingly fulsome chapter headings (Fielding, Dickens, Trollope, and epigraphs in Kipling); or by imposing a "personal" (e.g., more lyrical or opulent) style on the "impersonal" and distancing past NS (Thackeray, Meredith, sometimes hard to read for that reason), or a complex one (James).

By the thirties of the twentieth century the author's control was felt as omniscient and godlike. It was felt in the use of the distancing past tense and its distancing deictics, in the distancing third person even when plunged inside a consciousness (James or Woolf); it was felt even in the outside viewpoint with minimum comment and more dialogue, not only with the parentheticals that went with dialogue, but also in indirect discourse, which is a summary of what a character actually said, as well as in free indirect discourse, which I'll come to in a moment.[3] The last two devices (indirect and free indirect discourse) vanished, more or less, in the *nouveau roman*, with its brand-new, startling present tense and its equally startling variations.

It is not the use of the present tense as such that is original, as we have seen, but how it is used. Let us take four examples from the fifties, mentioned above, in order of "newness" rather than date:

1) Beckett, *Molloy*, 1950 (1955), opening:
   I am in my mother's room. It's I who live there now; don't know how I got there. . . .
2) Marguerite Duras, *Le Square*, 1955, opening:
   L'enfant arriva tranquillement du fond du square et se planta devant la jeune fille.
   "J'ai faim," déclara-t-il.
   Ce fut pour l'homme l'occasion d'engager la conversation.
   "C'est vrai que c'est l'heure de goûter," dit-il.
   La jeune fille ne se formalisa pas. Au contraire, elle lui adressa un sourire de sympathie.
   (The child came quietly from the end of the square and stopped in front of the young girl/ "I'm hungry," he declared. / This, for the man, was an opportunity to start a conversation. / "It's true it's tea-time," he said. / The girl made no objection. On the contrary, she smiled at him pleasantly. [My translation])

3) Nathalie Sarraute, *Le Planétarium*, 1959, opening:
Non vraiment, on aurait beau chercher, on ne pourrait rien trouver à redire, c'est parfait . . . une vraie surprise, une chance . . . [. . .] Une merveille contre ce mur beige aux reflets dorés. . . .
(No really, you'd have to look hard, you couldn't find a word against it, it's perfect . . . a real surprise, a piece of luck . . . [. . .] A sheer marvel against that beige wall with golden tints [my translation; unbracketed ellipses original])
4) Robbe-Grillet, *Les Gommes*, 1953, opening (my italics):
Dans la pénombre de la salle de café le patron dispose les tables et les chaises, les cendriers, les siphons d'eau gazeuse; il est six heures du matin. Il n'a pas besoin de voir clair, *il ne sait même pas ce qu'il fait.* [. . .] *Bientôt malheureusement le temps ne sera plus le maître.* . . . *Enveloppés de leur cerne d'erreur et de doute, les événements de cette journée, si minimes qu'ils puissent être, vont dans quelques instants commencer leur besogne.* [. . .]
Mais il est encore trop tôt. [. . .] *l'unique personnage présent en scène n'a pas encore recouvré son existence propre.* [. . .]
(In the shadowy depths of the café the owner is arranging the tables and chairs, the ashtrays, the soda-siphons; it is six o'clock in the morning. / He doesn't need to see clearly. *He doesn't even know what he's doing.* [. . .] / *Soon, alas, time will no longer be the master . . . Wrapped in their ring of error and doubt, the day's events, however minimal, will in a few moments begin their task* [. . .] / *But it's still too early.* [. . .] *The only character present on the scene has yet to recover his own existence* [. . .]. (My translation)

Beckett, in this particular matter of tense, has dropped the past NS for the conventional pronouned speech form, as in, say, Dostoyevsky's *Notes from the Underground* or Céline's *Voyage au bout de la nuit*. This is the only "legitimate" use of the term *narrator* (see Banfield, below). The opening line echoes that of Camus but "my mother" gives more distance than "Maman."

Duras is still using the traditional past tense NS to introduce the man and girl, but once the child is gone, taking with him the double quotes and the parentheticals, the whole of Part 1 is in dialogue (designated with mere dashes), therefore in conventional speech forms. Part 2 repeats the scene almost exactly (my italics indicate the slight changes): "L'enfant arriva tranquillement du fond du square et se planta *de nouveau* devant la jeune fille. / 'J'ai *soif*,' déclara-ti-il." Duras, in other words, still uses the convention of past tense for narrative. But she will soon adopt the present tense, if not always dropping the parentheticals but emphasizing them, for example, in *La Maladie de la mort* (1982, my italics): "*Et puis elle demande:* Vous voulez quoi? / *Vous dites que* vous voulez essayer [indirect speech for several lines]. *Elle demande:* Essayer quoi? / *Vous dites:* D'aimer." And in most of her later novels the present tense is used vividly, dramatically, to increase the emotion, and sometimes omnisciently.

With Sarraute, we are plunged into speech forms (various tenses), but inside the consciousness of someone, receiving a piece of furniture (a *bergère*). As in Robbe-Grillet we do not know whose mind we're in, there is no "je" (in the opening), but (as in James or Woolf) that mind is represented by the third person ("elle fait un grand effort, elle capte, elle tire," 19), getting more and more excited, gushing internally, but *not* narrating.

Robbe-Grillet, however, uses the present tense of speech form throughout the novel, paradoxically to replace its antagonist, the authoritative but speakerless omniscient past NS. In this he has been much imitated, but he will add two further paradoxes later, with *La Jalousie* (1959) and others. Here, however, he is giving the supposedly speakerless speaker the same omniscience as the traditional author, in both present and future.

In other words, these differences, in these early examples, may be gropings against the authorial authority, difficult to jettison, still there. But each will develop in various and specific ways. Here I am only concerned with Robbe-Grillet, who most influenced me with his paradoxical use of the present tense to replace the past tense NS. But here perhaps not quite "au point"? His second novel, *Le Voyeur* (1955), makes an interesting alternation of past tenses (*passé simple* and imperfect) for "real" variants, and the present tense for fantasies (as had Flaubert for St. Anthony's temptations).[4]

With *La Jalousie* he will go further than Camus or his own contemporaries in two respects: first, and paradoxically, by using the present tense of the speech system and its deictics, but with all the impersonal speakerless tone of the past-tense NS. That is, not just for momentary vividness as in the historic present; nor in direct address to the reader, like Sterne or Fielding; nor as a playful "look-at-me," like the Postmoderns; nor as inner speech or "sub-conversation," like Sarraute; nor even with occasional omniscience, as here. Rather, he uses the present tense as a "scientific" present tense (as in a scientific law, or indeed as in our own critical language). This is clearly derived from film, but only a certain type of film, with a quasi-neutral camera. Robbe-Grillet was originally an engineer and must have also felt the similarity between the speakerless past-tense NS and the scientific use of the present tense; since the traditional NS had become less and less impersonal and speakerless, he must have decided to replace it with a speakerless (scientific) present. He simply puts down objectively all that hits his central consciousness; in detail—too much detail, some said, which can create a rather obsessed observer.

In the second paradox, he limits this new present-tense NS to one conscience, unlike the traditional past-tense NS, which is far freer to go where it pleases, but like a scientific sentence limited to one experiment or result at the time of utterance, yet (and this is his great sublety), constantly varied with other possibilities, even at times, corrections. The "regard" evokes a detective rather than a scientist: "To the right, a simple shape, more blurred, already covered by several days' deposit, is nevertheless still discernible; at a certain angle it acquires sufficient clarity for its outline to be followed without too much difficulty. It is a kind of cross: an elongated main shape, like a table knife but wider" (Robbe-Grillet 1959, 10).[5]

The third paradox, and much more important to me, is that he never evokes an act of seeing or a consciousness, that is, there is no seer, only the seen, no *énonciation* ("I was convinced," "surely," "it seemed," etc.), only *énoncé*.[6] This is why I used the phrase "all that hits," above, rather than "all that his central consciousness observes." There is no act of observation. Moreover, he dispenses with the first or third or indeed any personal pronoun normally attached to the present tense, just as science can. For instance, in *La Jalousie*, we never know who the jealous person is whose objectivized registrations we follow: "She takes a few steps into the room, goes over to the heavy chest and opens its top drawer. She shifts the papers in the rear of the drawer better, pulls it a little farther out of the right-hand side of the drawer, leans over and, in order to see the rear of the drawer better, pulls it a little further out of the chest (11).[7]

Such a text can give two readings of him: as an observer of detached, scientific objectivity, or as an obsessed character, the latter chiefly because of the detail. Genette mentions this double reading, which he tells us derives from the emphasis laid either on the story or on the narrative discourse: if emphasis is on the discourse, as in the interior monologue (he gives as examples Dujardin, Beckett, Claude Simon, and Roger Laporte), the story seems just a pretext and can disappear; if it is on the story, it's the narrative instance that tends to disappear, as, almost, in the "behaviorist" Hemingway-type novel (though this is still in the past tense) and in early Robbe-Grillet and *l'école du regard*, the utmost in objectivity (1972, 231). Genette gives *La Jalousie* as an extreme example, but does not mention either the absence of the first person, which effaces the looker, or the paradoxical "scientific," non-speech mode use of the present tense for NS, which, as far as I know, I am formulating here for the first time.

Either way we are there, inside him, feeling both what is described and a nonevoked, nonrepresented reaction. This comes from the astonishing use of the NS, in which "no one speaks," but used in the present tense, in which someone necessarily speaks, yet we don't know who, since he never says "I", or anything about himself; he is the very "no one speaks" of the NS. We have to construct him, not even from what he says (as in most novels), but from what he sees. I have to add that Robbe-Grillet is wholly rigorous about this only in *La Jalousie,* and that alone is what truly influenced me. In *Dans le labyrinthe,* for example, there is an initial "I" in the first sentence: "I am alone here now, safe and sheltered" (my translation), who then vanishes and does not return until the end, after the soldier's death, when he comes back as (at least at that point) a doctor. In a traditional novel this brief initial and final presence would indicate that he has been telling the tale, like Conrad's Marlow, whom we wholly forget during the normally dramatized story. But here he vanishes after that first "I," quite "unrealized," to use reviewers' jargon, and his reappearance is equally indifferent to us. In between, however, the same "no one speaks" present tense I have been describing obtains throughout.

This startling change of narrative technique may well have been foreshadowed in French by Proust, Céline, Camus, and Beckett's *Molloy,* but not in that paradoxical mix (the present tense used in NS in which no one speaks). All four use the present tense with its conventional first-person pronoun, so that we're wholly in **Speech Mode.** Flaubert comes the closest to using the present tense as NS, yet he reserves it for hallucinations (another kind of paradox). Sarraute uses it as "silent" speech form rather than as NS, expanding what she calls her *sous-conversations* like "tropisms" (her critical comparison, from biology) through more and more emotion and ending up (as she had said of novels in dialogue) in the theater; whereas Duras, who also made films and wrote scenarios, uses it also as NS, as does Robbe-Grillet, but a NS emotively as highly charged as Sarraute's inner dialogue. Indeed, in Sarraute's later novels we hear our old friend the omniscient author telling us things the character can't know (such as "she can't hear"), but they are told in the present tense, which thus seems used for greater immediacy and emotivity, rather than for "scientific" objectivity. Only Robbe-Grillett, in *La Jalousie*, has fully achieved what so impressed me, a form that I used and played with and, I hope, developed, and which I shall call the scientific present tense.

Between the highly emotive and the scientific uses of the present tense outlined above lies an interesting experiment of 1974 by Muriel Spark, the delightful *The Abbess of Crewe*. Written in the present tense, it has neither the gush of Sarraute's subconversation nor the cold obsessive detail of Robbe-Grillet, precisely because the humor of author omniscience has returned from banishment at last (or, in the case of Spark, never let itself be banished). She ignores Sarraute's condemnation of parentheticals:

> "But we're something rather more than merely Benedictines, though, aren't we," says Sister Winifrede in dark naivety. "The Jesuits—"
> "Sister Winifrede," says the Abbess in her tone of lofty calm, "there's a scandal going on." (Panther 1984, 8)

Nor is Spark afraid of author explanation: after a comic description of the Abbess of Crewe's parlor and the two-foot statue of the infant of Prague "adorned with its traditional robes [. . . with] such large and so many rich and gleaming jewels it would seem they could not possibly be real," she adds: "However, they are real." Similarly she slides into the pluperfect (which conventionally goes with the past tense NS) for flashback information to the reader ("the Abbess had said to her closest nuns," "the Abbess had said to her two senior nuns when she began to reform the Abbey"). The book is thus near to the early Robbe-Grillet of *Les Gommes,* which, as we saw, has not quite jettisoned author guidance, but it is very distant from *La Jalousie* and *Dans le labyrinthe,* where, through neutral NS and minimum dialogue, we can only construct a speakerless experiencer from what is seen.

As for Joyce, the supposed father of it all, he is a special case of the diametrical opposite. In *Ulysses* Joyce still uses the past NS for all activity or event whenever he's not reproducing a character's thoughts, which are in **Speech Mode.** But he does seem very aware of the problems posed by both **Narrative** and **Speech Modes,** for he visibly avoids pronouns in the telegraphic speech mode of Stephen's and Bloom's interior monologues, so that a sudden "I" is all the more visible, and turns to other genres in order to use the present "allowably" as narrative; for example, the question-and-answer form of "Ithaca," which allows (inconsistently) pronounless answers, and the dramatic form of "Circe" with its long or short stage directions in italics, in (inconsistently) pronounless present tenses ("looks behind") or participles ("shuddering," "shrinking") or adverbials ("hurriedly," "in an oatmeal sporting suit," etc.), through which all the character mutations are achieved.

But already in "Sirens" the whole classic question of who speaks is being blurred, as if Joyce were already practicing for *Finnegans Wake,* as Jean-Michel Rabaté showed in his monumental thesis (1980, 52, and throughout). Here, Bloom's thought, for instance, includes a phrase of Stephen's from a scene Bloom did not attend). By *Finnegans Wake* Joyce is intent on creating an infinitely changing speaker to replace both the authoritative NS *and* the sociopsychologically differentiating speech forms of the classic novel. Thus endless speakers change into each other to tell of events, "tales within wheels," in both narrative forms (for events) and speech forms (for apostrophe, insult, etc.), both in a constantly reinvented idiolect, or private language, so that who speaks becomes intentionally blurred by that drowning stream of "punsciousness," which, however enchanting/repelling, ingenious/infantile, enriching/irritating (etc.), cannot avoid a "look-at-me" tone, an epic voice, perhaps, of Shem the Penman, though constantly escaping, the too idiosyncratic voice, in fact, of the author, very visibly "doing his stuff." The NS, in other words, is (like Meredith's but more "modern") too richly rhetorical to be in any way assimilated, either into the traditional speakerless past-tense NS it successfully destroys, or to the impersonal scientific present tense of Robbe-Grillet. Indeed, both Joyce's narrative sentence and speech forms together constitute its exact opposite. To Joyce, the author was still God, in a way, or at least self-fathering.[8] And it was, I believe, Robbe-Grillet's trebly paradoxical mix (an impersonal present tense, yet speakerless, yet single-visioned) in his use of the NS that led Barthes to announce the death of the author (Barthes 1994).[9]

Of course Barthes was referring not to the real author, who has toothache and marital troubles, but to a critical construct. Indeed, this real author had already been dispensed with less dramatically six years earlier by Booth in his pre-Structuralist but landmark book, *The Rhetoric of Fiction,* and had been replaced with the term *implied author,* meaning the image of himself the author gives. That term didn't really catch on as a construct for the organizer of the text, since it evokes the reader's image of the author, and did so well in advance of the reader-oriented criticism of the seventies. At any rate, the word *author,* even as critical construct, became taboo. So critics, surprisingly docile about dogmatic announcements (even suspected Structuralist ones), all started using the word *narrator* instead, and I hope I have clearly enough distinguished the author's NS from his speech forms to make the term *narrator* sound truly redundant, for it blurs important narrative instances: indeed, the word *narrator* now designates anything from a first-person hero to a fictional observer-character who can be very varyingly present and very varyingly reliable, to a mere substitute where traditional criticism had said "author," or used the author's name. Joyce's purposeful fusion, through idiolect, would never have sunk to that level of confusion; indeed, all his extratextual pronouncements show that he knew exactly what he was doing.[10]

The author also narrates, in case anyone had forgotten; she is the teller, that is, uses narrative sentences. He always has. But these were by definition impersonal. Yet even when remaining impersonal and unstylized, an occasional stray "I" in nineteenth-century omniscient author–type novels betrays the tension.

෧෮

This classic question of who speaks led to a strange dispute, during the seventies and eighties, between some linguists, notably Banfield, and a few literary critics who held on to the traditional view that there are two voices in free indirect discourse (f.i.d.) and who were unable quite to give up author intrusion, so merely changed the critical word *author* to *narrator.*

Just a brief reminder for those who might need it (and apologies to others): indirect discourse summarizes what a character says, with no guarantee of the actual words used: "I'll kill you" (direct discourse) becomes "He said he would kill me." The "I" becomes "he" and "shall / will" becomes "would." It can even be wholly narrativized as "he informed me of his decision to kill me." That's the most distant.

Free indirect discourse follows the same tense and deictic changes as indirect discourse: future becomes conditional (*would*), past becomes pluperfect (*had, done, said,* etc.); but it is "free," that is, it's not always attributed with a "he told me / thought that." And it can go on a long time when representing thought. Here is an invented cliché example:

> He walked down the street [NS]. Would he find the courage to tell his father? Yesterday, there'd been nothing but trust. But now, Oh God, yes, he was afraid.

In indirect discourse this would be "he wondered whether he would find the courage to tell his father." And in direct discourse, "shall I find the courage to tell Dad?" But you notice that *yesterday* and *now* and the exclamations "Oh God, yes," which belong to direct discourse, sound quite normal. This paradoxical intrusion of expressive elements from direct discourse (speech) into a past NS is unique to modern fiction, invented in the eighteenth century (with its first traces in the seventeenth), developed brilliantly by Jane Austen, and culminating in E. M. Forster, Flaubert, Woolf. It can even be part of a dialogue. Here are two typical examples from E. M. Forster's *A Room with a View*:

> A conversation then ensued, not on unfamiliar lines. Miss Bartlett was, after all, a wee bit tired, and thought they had better spend the morning settling in; unless Lucy would rather like to go out? Lucy would rather like to go out, as it was her first day in Florence, but, of course, she could go alone. Miss Bartlett would not allow this. Of course she would accompany Lucy everywhere. Oh, certainly not; Lucy would stop with her cousin. Oh no! that would never do! Oh yes! (1990, 36)

> Of course Miss Bartlett accepted. And equally of course, she felt sure that she would prove a nuisance, and begged to be given an inferior room—something with no view, anything. Her love to Lucy. (161)

In the first quotation, Miss Bartlett and Lucy are in Florence; the conversation is rehearsed, perhaps ironically, either during or after, in Lucy's mind (this would be Banfield's theory) or by a narrator (as in the two-voiced theory). The second quotation opens chapter 14, after another invitation to Miss Bartlett has been discussed at the Honeychurches (Lucy being against). It is not immediately obvious whose consciousness we're in, but when we read on we're more clearly in Lucy's mind, Lucy echoing Miss Bartlett's style in her head later, or while having the letter read to her by Mrs. Honeychurch. Both examples (given in Banfield, but not specifically commented on) are good cases for the two-voiced theory of "narrator" irony, and this is what Banfield's book argues strongly against. According to her theory we are always in a character's mind, either in reflective consciousness or in unreflective consciousness (see below; here, the stating of the names illustrates nonreflective consciousness). But rather than get her complex linguistic arguments wrong, I'll use my own favorite example from Jane Austen (already quoted in chapter 3, where I promised to return to it): Mrs. Bennett bidding farewell to Mr. Bingley in *Pride and Prejudice:*

> "Next time you call," said she, "I hope we shall be more lucky." [d.d.]
> He should be particularly happy at any time, &c &c, and if she would give him leave, would take an early opportunity of waiting on them. [f.i.d.]
> "Can you come tomorrow?" [d.d.]
> Yes, he had no engagement at all for tomorrow [f.i.d.]; and her invitation was accepted with alacrity. [narrativized d.]

Such swift changes of register are frequent in Austen. But who says "&c &c"? The two-voiced theory supporters would hear narrator irony about polite formulas, "but in Banfield's theory, though she would use linguistic argumentation, it would represent the character's own awareness, at a nonverbalized semiconscious level (formulas he could add but does not, or formulas he is adding and still uttering, while thinking '&c &c'), but which we are not given."[11]

Much more often, however, there are no such deictics, and the sentence is formally just like a straight NS. Here is a famously ambiguous example from Jane Austen's *Emma:* "He [Frank Churchill] stopped and rose again, and seemed quite embarrassed [NS]. He was more in love with her than Emma had supposed."

That last sentence reads as a NS like the first, coming from the author (or narrator in modern parlance) and therefore, by convention, is true within the fiction. But on second reading, when we know that Emma was gravely mistaken, we can only read it as Emma's thought, in free indirect discourse.

Banfield, from whom I have taken that last example, is an American literary critic and a linguist, which is rare. She has rigorously analyzed this kind of sentence of free indirect discourse, which she prefers to call Represented Speech and Thought, so, as it's more accurate, I'll do the same from now, abbreviating it to RST. It's more accurate, not only because it can represent both speech and thought, but because this type of sentence does not "imitate" speech or thought but "represents"—re-presents—it. This is an important distinction, to which I'll return.

Although Banfield starts from a slightly revised version of Benveniste's distinction *histoire/discours,* her analysis is not Structuralist. She uses the later and sounder argumentation of Generative Grammar. Her book is called *Unspeakable Sentences* (1982), because both narrative sentences (where no one speaks), and sentences of RST are specific to the Narrative Mode, whereas direct and indirect discourse can occur in the personal speech system. These two types of sentences, NS and the sentence of RST, are both speakerless, literally unspeakable in the Speech Mode of the personal system.

Banfield's book is a rigorous attempt to answer the traditional view of RST (f.i.d.) as representing two voices, that of the character and that of a so-called narrator. This view has to attribute different bits of the sentence to one or the other. She cites many literary examples given by holders of that traditional view, demolishing them one by one. For instance, we read, in Emma Bovary's consciousness, "She loved [imperfect, *elle aimait*] the sick lamb, the sacred heart pierced with sharp thorns, or poor Jesus falling as he carries the cross." The traditional view has always read this kind of sentence as author—or now narrator—irony about pious sentimentality. For Banfield we are inside Emma's mind, but she is not consciously "saying these words" to herself; they "re-present" her vague thoughts and feelings.

Banfield blames the modern silencing of the author for these various double-voiced formulations and for introducing "the notion of a narrator as a created *persona* distinct from the author alongside the notion of point of view," which includes evaluation (183). The author, she says, is "expunged" but "reintroduced as narrator who is responsible for all the sentences in the text, as the speaker is in discourse."[12] She defends another theory, which "sees author and narrator as distinct constructs of literary theory" where "'narrator' is restricted to cases when the author does create a narrator, namely the first person narrative" (185).

How does she prove this? She modifies the deep structure tree to account for such sentences, placing an E for Expression above the $\bar{S}$ and proposing two main rules, 1E/1SELF, and PAST + NOW (if a "now" can be inserted, it is RST). These, with a few other important points, enable her to show that there is no syntactic evidence for a second evaluating voice in RST. One of these important points is the distinction she makes between reflective and nonreflective consciousness, between the *cogito* and other states, a distinction philosophers have long groped for (she cites Russell's example of avoiding a puddle while talking, and another from Sartre) but which already existed in narrative technique. Sentences of nonreflective consciousness are often ambiguous. But there is no syntactic reason why "she loved the sick lamb" should be interpreted from a perspective outside the character's consciousness (Banfield 1982, 210). In Banfield's theory even the author's apparent evaluative interventions (in RST) represent the character's nonreflective consciousness. Nor can nonreflective consciousness ever be inner speech and remain nonreflective (211). In other words, it's not interior monologue. I shall return to this point.

Well, the author is back, responsible for every sentence in the text, even those said or thought by characters, and I was very glad of that, at least in my status as critical construct, particularly since most of my own narratives are narratorless, and I don't like to see constant references to my narrator (or to my view) when in my case only the character-experiencer (even if invented by me) can be meant. But, Banfield insists, even as construct, the author is not represented in the text; the author can only be inferred through interpretation.

Most of Banfield's book is devoted to syntax, but she also deals with her opponents' semantic arguments, which posit either an "empathy" of the narrator or an ironic commentary. On empathy, which is linked to the ambiguous RST sentences, she invokes a consistency criterion: the facts of the fiction must be consistent with one another. For example, the sentence about Frank Churchill being in love with Emma can't come from an undramatized narrator, nor can the character's value judgments. The following sentence would be "anomalous" (and so marked by ?): "?She loved sweet Jesus, the fanatical Nazarene" (Banfield 1982, 215).

As for irony, the classic case for the dual voice theory, she insists that "one can argue that RST is the main vehicle for irony [. . .] without thereby implying that this is an argument for the dual voice position. For the ironic reading of a sentence cannot be treated as part of its meaning, in any accepted sense of linguistic meaning" (Banfield 1982, 220). The two meanings of an ambiguous sentence have exactly the same syntactic and semantic structure. With irony we are beyond grammatical or even semantic rules. The irony is provided by the reader (which is why it can also be missed). Irony is a way of reading. "There is nothing to which the notion 'narrator's point of view' can be semantically attached that is not equivalent to the character's point of view" (Banfield 1982, 216).

When Banfield's book came out, I gave a paper on it in France and devoted a whole chapter to it (of which this is a much more careful reconsideration) in my *Stories, Theories and Things*, which, however, did not appear till 1991. I retired in 1988 and have not at all kept up with such disputes of literary theory (I have no idea who "won"), mainly because I wanted to write more novels. But such academic criticism as I do read continues blithely to use the term *narrator* for every sentence, so I assume nobody's taken the slightest notice.

୬୦

Curiously, however, Banfield makes no mention at all of Robbe-Grillet's paradoxical attempt to use the present tense for "unspeakable" Narrative Sentences, which are impossible in her system, nor indeed of anyone else's much more conventional use (i.e., with a pronoun) of present-tense narrative. Nor does she address Joyce's represented thought in the present tense, also impossible in her system—or rather, she would call it inner speech (see below). Her book concerns only the two traditional types of "unspeakable" sentences, the NS and the sentence of RST, both in the past tense. But she stops at Faulkner, Woolf, and Joyce. As we saw above, Forster's use, though as witty as Austen's, is already a little less clear as to whose mind we're in (hence the early-twentieth-century notion of a narrator voice). Indeed, this two-voice ambiguity is already felt in Flaubert, who was the first to develop the French imperfect to slide in and out of RST and NS, i.e., character reaction and author intrusion. By the time of Joyce this can be quite muddy. Why? This is my own opinion that I tack on to her thesis, but which an attentive reader will have guessed: because, just as he killed the (ultimately Aristotelian) notion of fixed sociopsychological discourse for characters, Joyce killed RST (f.i.d. to him). It only occurs (like parentheticals, but far less frequently) when he is parodying traditional styles, notably in "Wandering Rocks," "Scylla and Charybdis,"

"Cyclops," "Nausicaa"; Banfield's examples are few, but they are from these sections. Joyce killed RST (a version of author-controlled NS) by representing thought in Speech Mode. But not everyone read Joyce, and even the killing of RST took a long while to trickle through.

And during this long while, RST came to be very lazily used (and so died, more slowly) as a way for the author to pass narrative information to the reader—filtered through a character, since author intervention was by now unfashionable. It's a stock method in early or mid-century SF, for instance, where a scientist is made to think technical but elementary stuff (in fact, this is author intervention for the reader, whom the scientist in this genre should not be aware of). These thoughts are extensions of my invented but cliché model above ("would he have the courage to tell his father?"), which can go on for ages ("would he have the courage to press the button? He hadn't told Jim that his calculations," etc.), even with long flashbacks in the pluperfect. In Robbe-Grillet, of course, as in most *nouveaux romans,* f.i.d./RST vanished together with the past tense. In my view f.i.d./FST have now become, like the past tense, a mark of traditional narrative.

Theorists and critics are often slower to grasp what a few oddball writers may actually do, and even experimenters can't always formalize what they are doing. We grope. Ricoeur's three volumes on Time and Narrative, for instance (1983, 84, 85), no doubt interesting philosophically, are less so on the rare occasions when he analyzes time in three specific novels, Woolf's *Mrs. Dalloway,* Mann's *Zauberberg,* and Proust's *A la recherche,* where he concentrates wholly on organized content as part of his theory of triple Mimesis (Time in the World, Time figured by the Poet, Time refigured by the Reader). For example, although he mentions free indirect discourse once elsewhere, he never notices that all the time effects in *Mrs. Dalloway* are achieved, not only, as he says, through changing consciousnesses but, as he doesn't say, always in free indirect discourse, past tense, third person, which is not true of, say, Proust. And this makes a profound difference of effect on the reader, theoretically but not, in fact, taken into account. Similarly, Robbe-Grillet defended the present tense but said nothing about his paradoxical use of it, and I myself have been unable to formalize my own extension of it for interviewers or students working on me, until very recently, for this paper, using Banfield but finding she stops short of it.

Very possibly, however, Banfield would say that the present tense can only represent inner speech, that is, interior monologue (cf. above, "Nor can non-reflective consciousness ever be inner speech and remain non-reflective consciousness" [211]). I assume she would regard Sarraute's "subconversation" (her "tropisms") as inner speech. Clearly these are not dialogue, yet they are in speech form; as conversation, however "sub," they do seem to be "inner speech," and they did lead Sarraute to the theater, and not necessarily inferior theater.

Not being a professional linguist and speaking only as writer and critic, I feel that no two types of text seem further apart than any novel by Robbe-Grillet and (say) Molly Bloom's interior monologue in Joyce's *Ulysses* or Stephen's in "Proteus" (etc.). I happened to prefer Robbe-Grillet's solution, as less messy. As for my own efforts, a writer is notoriously not a good judge of her own work, so if I say that my fiction is in a speakerless (therefore narratorless, addressless and impersonal) NS in the present tense, yet from inside a character, *and* that it represents both reflective and nonreflective consciousness, in other words, a modern form (speech form) of RST, Banfield would call it inner speech and presumably dismiss my claim (my feeling) as grammatically impossible in her system.

However, in her refutation of the two-voiced theory, Banfield insists that "it is only a false impression that sentences of non-reflecting consciousness somehow show the author's ordering hand more than those of represented thought" (212), and she adds, "This is because reflection can have a linguistic realization, but, *since non-reflective states cannot*, their style must necessarily be other than what the character would have himself said" (212, my italics).

In other words, we do not reflect, or even "nonreflect," in RST. James's complex sentences do not "imitate" what Maisie thought but "represent what Maisie *knew*" (Banfield 1982, 212). Here the author is very much present and doing the representing. And after more argumentation and example Banfield concludes: "The artificial nature of represented consciousness which emerges in the analysis of sentences of non-reflective consciousness can thus easily extend to represented thought. It represents a reflection but not necessarily one cast in language the character might have used" (213).

If RST (whose rules are 1E/1SELF and PAST + NOW) is "artificial," a late but long-lasting literary convention, couldn't that convention have unwittingly been changed, by Robbe-Grillet and then myself, to an impersonal speakerless (narratorless) present, equally artificial (we do not reflect in an impersonal speakerless present either)? In principle, this new convention would *not* be imitating inner speech (because "scientifically" speakerless and impersonal), but in *practice* (here I speak only for myself) it would be miming it whenever the situation demands a direct, almost naive, mimesis of the moment, as an exact parallel to the expressive elements from direct speech forms that get inserted into the authorial NS in RST, rather than being a representation by a very stylized authorial voice. It is a sort of fusion of Narrative Mode and Speech Mode, or Speech Forms, taking over the speakerlessness of NS and RST. The enormous distance between this "new RST" and inner speech (*La Jalousie* versus Molly Bloom) would then be functionally if not stylistically reduced, as it does seem to be in fact. But I must leave this for others to judge.

༄

This brings me back to my own practice. I took over, and I hope extended, Robbe-Grillet's paradoxical use of a speakerless present tense for narrative. Robbe-Grillet himself gave up novels a decade ago, and his autobiography, though still in speech forms, uses the first person conventionally (Robbe-Grillet 1984), as does his last novel.[13] But innovation has a strange way of surviving. In those distant days (the late fifties), there was active prejudice in England, led by C. P. Snow, against that whole new fashion from France.[14] But who even mentions C. P. Snow now, or his followers? His type of prejudice against experiment persists, and has even grown, but the novel nevertheless has changed, not, of course, directly or only due to the *nouveau roman* but also due to Joyce—though indirectly, since what he did was the direct opposite—and probably due to Beckett and other explosions of the time, from the Beat Generation and the Postmoderns on. And if Robbe-Grillet himself is also perhaps no longer read, some of his technique has insidiously survived, in a way that Snow's has not. In any case, if any novel is truly dead, it's the classical novel written almost entirely in NS and RST (f.i.d.), with occasional dialogue (and its parentheticals) to perk things up.

Certainly speech forms have won, even in the past tense, which in European languages other than French belongs both to Narrative Mode and to Speech Mode, and even in French modern novels the dead *passé simple* is replaced by the imperfect or the more natural present perfect, not just in dialogue but in NS.

But the present tense is also extremely current now, though conventionally, in pronounced narrative instance. For instance, Peter Ackroyd plays sensitively with tenses and alternating he/I pronouns in the hallucinatory last few chapters of *Milton in America* (1996). In fact, it crept in more and more during the eighties (thirty years after the resistance discussed above). It is current simply as a tense, requiring and getting a first person. Indeed, we're flooded with first-person narratives at the moment, in both past and present. But the present has not been used, to my knowledge, as new NS in speakerless, narratorless narrative (a modern RST, if I'm right, see above), which paradoxical use is what gives Robbe-Grillet such a distinctive tone.

Even as tense, it's often misused. Indeed, it's difficult to use as narrative tense, for all the grammatical reasons I have touched upon, not to mention traditional philosophical paradoxes such as the nonexistence of the present or St. Augustine's triple present and its twists and turns up to Husserl and Heidegger. It's also difficult to use for stylistic reasons: at every sentence the constraint excludes easier slidings and forces one to find an alternative. But a constraint is also a limitation. Robbe-Grillet's shifts in time, for instance, are necessarily unmarked, since the present excludes other times, and the reader does have to work. Indeed, the author does allow himself occasional pasts (but present perfects, not the dead past definite), which are all the more startling because rare, when the present would be obscure, for instance, when contrast is needed: "Dehors il neige. Dehors il a neigé, il neigeait, dehors il neige" (Robbe-Grillet 1959; "Outside it is snowing. Outside it has snowed, it was snowing, outside it is snowing"). Like any constraint, the present tense is a limitation, but one that allows greater concentration on one aspect, simultaneity.

The present tense is also difficult to use for more generic reasons: the present is the predominant tense of lyric poetry, apt for lyrical description, less so for fictional action, which has for so long depended on the "guarantee" of the past NS, so that the use of the present for action recalls those brief historic presents for vivid (but nonaction) scenes in the classical novel. The present tense is also the tense of general statements and universal questions, the novelistic equivalent of "scientific statements," such as authors loved and still love to make in their intrusions, which can sound either dogmatic or banal. This is true at least in English, which, unlike French, also has the progressive present ("is snowing") for simultaneous action and so tends to reserve the normal present tense for generalization.

Consequently, young writers who think, a little behind the times, "ah, the present, that's the latest thing," and then merely replace the past in the traditional NS by the present, achieve, to my mind, little more than the critics who have merely replaced the word *author* by the word *narrator*. Here is a recent example, I won't say from whom, only that there *is* a first-person narrator (so it should pose no problems, yet does):

> She smiles, a little sadly. "Making music and making love—it's a bit too easy an equation."
> "Have you told him about me?" I ask.
> "No," she says. "I don't know what to do about this subterfuge."

No, it's not from a woman's magazine, though it well might be, and the present tense can't alter that. It contributes nothing, and what Sarraute called "the symbols of the old régime," the parentheticals, are still there (the only narrative bits in this quotation). But here I have to add the surprising detail that Banfield has a section on parentheticals as a type of speakerless sentence exactly like the NS, according to various criteria I can't go into here. The parentheticals, in other words, represent our unreflective consciousness of speaking, or of another speaking. So if Banfield is right, Sarraute and most of us who objected so long ago to parentheticals as author intrusions would be wrong technically, if right stylistically (those forms were exhausted and have almost vanished, except as ironic emphasis).

Nevertheless, the present tense nowadays often reads like a mechanical replacement of the past NS, regardless of true effect. The omniscient author is heard, indeed has made a triumphant return, and I hope will kill the merely substitute narrator, but the present tense in such cases seems reduced to mere vividness, like the historic present.

Much more important than the present tense as such, in my own technique, is the speakerless present from inside a consciousness, as impersonal, speakerless (narratorless) narrative. I have played with the first person, unnamed except by others (and differently, so thoroughly destabilized), but retaining the impersonal, speakerless observational NS, for example, in *Amalgamemnon*, where I also, however (and contrary to the "scientific" present described above) rule out not only the present tense but all constative sentences, which must be true or untrue, by using only the future and other nonrealized tenses for Narrative Sentences, which is also impossible in Banfield's grammar (see chapter 3). More conventionally, I've also used two first-person narrators in permanent dialogue, that is, permanent Speech Mode (two computer whiz kids trying to dictate their story into their pocket computer, the dictating altering the nature of the dialogue, as in *Xorandor*); and I also went back to a slightly more explanatory narrative, but in a mostly viewpointless present tense in *Textermination*, except when directly quoting the novel each character comes out of, as in the opening pages. In this novel, the topic itself made such demands on the reader's powers of recognition that I decided to make the narrative style a bit more familiar, though there is a metaleptic joke between two of the characters about the narrative they're in, even using free indirect discourse.

But mostly, since *Out,* I have explored a narratorless present tense in the same paradoxical way as Robbe-Grillet, as a neutral, detached narrative "representing" or miming a consciousness, both reflective and unreflective. In other words, I, the author (not a narrator), put myself inside a character to "represent" (not initially to mime) that character's observation abilities as well as unreflective awarenesses. I have, however, extended the method in using it for mimed moments as well, such as sudden change, or interjections, or brief dialogue.[15] I have extended it also in using it for fantasy and science fiction, in not limiting myself to one obsessive consciousness, in rejecting Robbe-Grillet's unconvincing rejection of metaphor, in adding other constraints of my own, and in using it for multiple viewpoints and changing them without warning (as in *Thru* and *Next*), which means that the reader has only the content to identify whose consciousness we're in. It's one of my many ways of slowing down the reader, forcing him, as Ezra Pound said of his ideograms, "to stop and think," that is, to read more attentively. Of course, it can also make him stop altogether. That's a risk I've always taken.

And I'm taking another here, of once again, as in those Snowish days, being labeled the *nouveau roman* in English—not that anyone could show why, as I have just done, by isolating Robbe-Grillet as an influence, purely on this one detail of narrative technique. For my influences are much more various, including Donne, Sterne, George Eliot, Hopkins, Mallarmé, Pound, Kafka, Beckett, Borges, Calvino, Derrida, Deleuze, Bakhtin, Maurice Roche, and many others, for this or that—even including the fourteenth-century Langland, though luckily nobody calls me sub-Langland or Langland in Modern English.

These aren't just tricks. I called my narrative technique a constraint, and, believe me, it's hard to use rigorously. It's a limitation which refuses some of the familiarities of language in order to focus with great intensity on one less familiar aspect, the constant impact of outside phenomena on an active but not always reflective consciousness.

My latest novel, *Subscript,* should give a very clear notion of what that means, as it is peculiarly suited to using language "artificially" (as Banfield would say) to "represent" even nonconscious beings. I have blended my speakerless narrative with a vast extension of an old convention that lends words and consciousness to creatures that have none or little. It starts inside a prebiotic chemical reaction at the beginning of life and continues on right through evolution to early humans four to three million years ago, stopping around 11,000 years ago. The only author intrusions are the chapter headings, but they are blatant, to mark the contrast: "x million years later." They are "intrusions" because the creatures I'm inside of can't know time or years or numbers. Even so, I also mime certain moments, such as the sudden formation of a eukaryote (nucleated) cell when the prokaryote cell I'm in is swallowed by another and becomes a nucleus ("Plonk!"), and is proud of being a center. There are several such foretokens of the human psyche through animals to humans, for instance, the vertical stance of the tiny picaia while feeding, or the slow acquisition of language as they chip stones this way or that and echo the noises to go with the movements.

I have said of my other, one-novel constraints that they force me to find another word. Certainly I've always tried to avoid the expected word. But here this effort became a different constraint: a delicate balance between the convention of language for no-language, a style for epochs stripped, not only of all mod cons but of all mod connotations, so that occasional phrases like "division of labor," even inside the cell (a tongue-in-cheek comment from the author) should both make local sense and jar. Apart from these tongue-in-cheek exceptions, I don't use any words denoting concepts the creatures couldn't have at the time I'm describing, such as *left* or *right* or the inside of the body or distances or even, earlier, *the sun, the moon, savanna,* nor of course names of periods or continents or places, and I use no metaphors such as, for example, "a *lancing* pain" millions of years before the lance was developed from the pike and the spear, or "a *needling* curiosity" before the bone needle was invented some thirty thousand years ago.

To mark the growing consciousness of my creatures, I add an extra constraint I've used before, but graduated: there are no pronouns at all at first, then, very slowly, *it* comes in, then *they, them,* and later *their.* There's a distinct shock at the first *we* opening chapter 8, when the creature

I'm in is still a small presimian mammal. Towards the end, when all the pronouns have appeared, the female creature I'm in still never uses *I*.

This time, because it's even more important than previous lipograms, I am telling. Not in the blurb, which merely gets mindlessly repeated, but in a privately prepared table of chapters with details of when and which pronouns come in. This I gave to both my publisher and my literary executor, to help possible translators, if any, who could otherwise, especially in Romance languages, bring in an unwanted reflexive (pronominalized) verb, often equivalent to an English intransitive; or fall into other traps in the Slavic languages, which can do without pronouns altogether except for emphasis.

It occurs to me now that, in the very lateness of man's appearance (halfway through the novel; language appears even later), I have once again unwittingly created a barrier for the reader, who is used to reading stories about human beings, not animals, except in fables, children's stories, and cartoons, wholly controlled by an outside designer. But I place myself inside their "consciousness"; for at least nine chapters, I grow from cell, to multicellular organism; to a finless, boneless fish called picaia (or maybe a lancelet, but anyway I can't say so); to a tetrapod lizard to a "synapsid," then "therapsid" or "mammal-like reptile"; to a small pre-simian mammal called a tarsier; to a chimpanzee (all unnamed). Once again, I have put my fun before the reader's easy access. And of course, I may have failed altogether in my "intentions," as described above, when I discuss "the delicate balance between the convention of language and no-language."

The paleontologist who kindly read it for me said he knew exactly where he was, but then that's his terrain. The less-specialized reader may feel lost, and I'll certainly be scolded for that. But the constraints forbade me to use zoological or geographical or other terms that were unknown to my protagonists. Even giving them wouldn't have helped the modern reader, since what my creatures see, in each chapter, is a climate and a vegetation very different from those of modern times.[16] However, as with *Textermination* and all those hundreds of characters, the reader can also let the anxiety of recognition wash over him and enjoy the story. It's the other extreme from having the author coddle the reader (trust me, it was so), wrapping every fact in the reassuring safety of the past NS.

8

Two
CODAS

THAT'S WHERE MY LECTURE ended, and that's what this book has been about: the profound difference between author authority (**Narrative Mode**) and character fallibility (**Speech Mode**). However, I opened it with the notion of something difficult. Not for the reader to read, but for the author to do. In chapter 7, I said that the present tense I had been discussing had "not been used, to my knowledge, as . . . speakerless, narratorless narrative . . . which paradoxical use is what gives Robbe-Grillet such a distinctive tone." I have just discovered such a use. This brief chapter will therefore consider, first, the question of difficulty, and second, this odd discovery.

༄

In practice I'm always told, to my surprise, that my books are difficult, but I am less surprised now since preparing that last lecture.

I'm convinced (but won't insist, in case I'm wrong) that the type of difficulty I am often taxed with forms part of both period and gender differences I have long accepted but which ought to have passed, that is, a notion of difficulty which among Modernist males excited dream teams of decipherers for decades (including myself for Pound at least), which I wouldn't have wanted, having hated the cult aspect of Pound studies; but, inversely, with the one token exception of Virginia Woolf, such difficulty has elicited only condemnation for women writers, even now, and this I don't want either, even if that's what I get.

The ten languages in *Between,* for instance, which created such a block at the time, have become a commonplace travel experience and are anyway as nothing compared to the encyclopedic, multilingual aspect of some Modernists (whose texts contain untranslated Greek, Latin, Sanskrit, Hebrew, Irish, Provençal, Chinese, etc., at a time when every educated male—but not female—reader could read only two, Greek and Latin, and probably none now). But I sat down and learned just enough Chinese to understand Pound's ideograms. In other words, these "roadblocks" (see end of chapter 5) were then automatically accepted as enriching and to be worked on, even though such practices would be totally rejected (or parodied, see second coda) if indulged in today. Not so for my merely comic and touristic use of languages in *Between,* many of which (such as exit in Polish or toilets in Bulgarian Cyrillic script) mime travel disorientation but also imply that my trilingual interpreter doesn't know everything. My light use of various sciences, too, should surely cause no problem by now. Even paleontology gets on telly.

But then, nor should my narrative technique have caused problems, since it has for some time been partly rejoined by many and should be more familiar. It derives, moreover, from another author, acknowledged, who as male got plenty of attention in France, but, as French, only prejudice in England. That prejudice is not only a period or gender problem but also one of endemic provincialism, or at least change of attitude: whereas for Moderns critics pounced with reverence on every snatch of author explanation, now, though they still pounce, it's for biographical trivia only; they ignore explanation if it's technical. This may be a good thing: a work should keep its mystery. As late as 1968 Derrida opened "La Pharmacie de Platon" with the argument that a text could only be a text if it concealed its law of composition and the rules of its game. But was not that in itself a weird French relic of Modernism?[1]

The change since Modernism, however, may also be due to loss of formal rigor and a grammatical insensitivity characteristic of transition periods in times of radical linguistic change.

In fact, the notion of difficulty has shifted from Latin and such to two domains, one easier, one harder: ethnic cultures and technology (or at least its popular use). This is a more specific version of sport and science mentioned in chapter 1. We are expected, at last, to understand many groups of people who were mere stereotypes to the Moderns. But I have yet to see a technical manual that doesn't use two unexplained "new" terms per sentence. That second, technological type of difficulty appears regarding the Internet, which (like that of administrative jargon) is riddled with the inability to make itself accessible. In other words, it is as taken for granted by its new elite as Greek and Latin references were earlier, and it is as powerful or more so (many governments would like to control it and can't). It is more easily learned by the young than by the old, chiefly because the young no longer read what the old used to. And it is taking over teaching, publishing, bookselling, criticism no doubt, finance, international trade—globalizing all that we have been doing less and less well, which it may do more and more demagogically, itsy-bitsyly, going for gold, its methods accepted and eagerly learned by the rest of us. This is not so, of course, for linguistics or narratology.

As to that radical change, I am well aware that despite my occasional computer themes, the new "virtually" oral *écriture* by word of web, is not really my idiom. Call it clickriture, perhaps. The irony of experiment may therefore turn out to be that despite all my paradoxical efforts to restore the authority or "scientific" (narratorless) neutrality of narrative *écriture*, I may have, though perhaps less than others from Joyce on, nevertheless also contributed to the final victory of speech forms, of voice over *écriture*, but without either this neutral narrative or the supposed superiority of speech (because of its "real presence"). What this new idiom is fast destroying is both that breathy orality *and* the "trace," the "authority" of the author, the authenticity of the source, the responsibility of *écriture*. This would be the way my own texts, like all texts, deconstruct themselves.[2]

The second coda is about that paradoxical use of the present tense.

೧೦

In chapter 7, I called Robbe-Grillet's (and my) use of the present tense as NS paradoxical because it is impersonal, that is, it is *like* the traditional historical past-tense NS in which no one speaks, *but* it is in the present tense (pt), which belongs to the personal speech-system. I called it "scientific" (here spt), and reminded the reader that even as nonscientists we use it in our own critical language (here cpt). But I said it was hard to use in describing action, especially as the present tense in traditional narrative is also associated with generalization (here gpt).

I also added that spt "has not been used, to my knowledge, as speakerless NS" (from chapter 7, requoted here), where "to my knowledge" allows for my being wrong. Since that lecture, and very recently, I have read a very strange novel that, in fact, does precisely that, but in a very particular and disarming manner.

This novel is called *House of Leaves* (a clear pun), by Mark Z. Danielewski, and it was published by Anchor, Transworld Publishers, and Random House Group Ltd., and printed in Great Britain by The Bath Press, Bath—indeed the trinitarian publishers look like a hoax, and one of the two long reviews I happened to read gives Doubleday as publisher, an entity not mentioned on the editorial flyleaf. Moreover, it's not "really" a novel but is "about" a film, a documentary, which is the palpitating "main story." This film is called *The Navidson Record*.

Long before we can reach it, however, this slightly wrong oddity of framework continues, hardly deserving notice, yet announcing the earliest wrong oddity (which will grow) in the main story.

First, though the contents page announces the foreword as being on page vii and the introduction on page xi, none of the preceding pages are numbered, and before we get to Arabic numbers (after the introduction which ends on page xxiii), there are five more pages in neither Roman nor Arabic numbers, then chapter 1 starts on page 3—so two pages are "lost" in the framework presentation (see the reproduced layout below).

Second, the editorial flyleaf announces the word *house* as in "full color," "2-color," "black and white" and "incomplete," which doesn't correspond to this text, where each occurrence of it is merely printed in pale gray slightly above baseline.

Third, the editorial hierarchy, emphasized by the different pages (I supply the missing page numbers in square brackets, which also illustrates the "lost" two pages), is curious:

[i]   **House of Leaves**
[ii] **Mark Danielewski's**
[iii] **House of Leaves**
      by
      Zampano
      with introduction and notes by
      Johnny Truant
      2nd Edition
      Anchor [with anchor symbol]
[. . .]
vii   **Foreword** [signed "The Editors," saying that the first edition was privately printed and did not contain chapter 21, appendixes 2 and 3 or the index]
[viii] blank

>
> [ix] "This is not for you" [epigraph in typewriting font Courier]
> [x]   blank
> xi   **Introduction** [runs to page xxiii and is signed Johnny Truant, October 31, 1998, Hollywood, Ca.]
> [1?] blank
> [2?] "Muss es sein?" [epigraph]
> [3?] blank
> [4?] **The Navidson Record**
> [5?] blank
> 3   I [Chapter and epigraph from the Beatles]

And at last the text begins.

The introduction is in Courier (typewriter font), because Johnny Truant, who works in a tattoo shop, writes in speech form (present tense mostly, past and future when needed, though sliding into the grammar and deictics of the traditional NS when using the past [my emphases]: "I still get nightmares," "During the *following* weeks," "*Then* the old man died," "From what I gather *now*," "Lude told me about this old guy who lived in his building," "It was the end of 96." But it can be a good deal more personal and colloquial, with everything called "fucking," or, for his new girlfriend, Thumper, with regard to his previous one: "She sure beat the hell out of Clara English."

This will be the tone of Johnny Truant's more and more intrusive footnotes throughout. In the introduction, he tells us about finding a vast manuscript, disorderly "reams and reams" of it, all about a film called *The Navidson Record*. At first he reads desultorily, then suddenly he loses seven hours, in the end isolating himself and nailing his windows shut (as had Zampano in life) so that not even Thumper can reach him. But, as he describes Zampano's book, he tells us that a portion of its footnotes are fictitious, indeed, that "the document [i.e., the film] at the heart of this book is fictitious," and then, in both the biographical past tense and the present tense of "critical" language (ptc):

> It's not surprising then that when it came to undermining his own work, the old man was superbly capable. False quotes or invented sources, however, all pale in comparison to his biggest joke. [. . .] Zampano writes constantly about seeing. What we see, how we see and what in turn we can't see. Over and over again in one form or another, he returns to the subject of light,

space, shape, line, color, and composition. None of which is surprising since Zampano's piece centers on a documentary film called *The Navidson Record* made by a Pulitzer-Prize winning photojournalist who must somehow capture the most difficult subject of all: the sight of darkness itself.

But, Johnny notes, there are no bulbs in the apartment, no clocks:

. . . all this language of light, film and photography, and he hadn't seen a thing since the mid-fifties.

He was as blind as a bat.

Half Zampano's books were in Braille, and he had readers and writers to help. But the introduction still sounds fairly calm and ends with Johnny Truant addressing the reader in the future tense, on what will happen to him if he gets involved:

Old shelters—television, magazines, movies—won't protect you any more [. . .] That's when you'll discover you no longer trust the very walls you always took for granted. Even the hallways you've walked a hundred times will feel longer, much longer, and the shadows, any shadow at all, will suddenly seem deeper, much much deeper.

After two more paragraphs of this he ends, as he opened: "And then the nightmares will begin."

That, of course, is exactly what happens inside *The Navidson Record*, and although we have been warned, the glacial horror of the main story becomes more and more gripping. Navidson, the photographer in question, and his wife Karin discover that their house in Virginia, moved into with their two children for closer coming together after a crisis due to Navidson's professional absences—has changed after a short trip to California for a wedding. The change seems unaccountable. Until Navidson discovers that the inside wall measures ¾-inch longer than the outside wall (the slightly wrong oddity announced by the pretext pages). Mad measurements follow and grow. Then a small storeroom behind a door turns into a corridor, which gets longer and longer. Navidson explores and almost can't get back. There's a huge hall at the end of the corridor and a spiral staircase going down. Dimensions are now vast. He sends for his brother Tom and an engineer friend in a wheelchair, Billy

Reston, as well as a man called Holloway Roberts and two others, called Jed and Wax. The last three are sent down, highly equipped with luminous markers and other technical pathfinders, but Jed and Wax get shot by Holloway, who has gone mad; one dies, one survives.

However, what I've just done is the typical blurb or review summary in the descriptive cpt. Traditionally stories are told in the past tense NS (impersonal). Here the story itself is told in spt, the "scientific," impersonal (speakerless) present tense I discussed in chapter 7: "Holloway Roberts arrives carrying a rifle [per Chekhov, if a gun appears in a fiction, it will be used]. In fact in the very first glimpse we see of him, he emerges from a truck holding a Weatherby 300" (Danielewski 2000, 80). The tone is that of *l'école du regard,* but not quite. The cpt creeps in, allowing for different time scales with four generalizing adverbs, reminding us that we are made to share the viewing of a document of the action, not the action itself, as in Robbe-Grillet, where the *regard* is more restricted, moving from moment to moment and from detail to detail. Here what we have is critical summary (my italics): "*Eventually* Jed tries again to carry Wax toward what he hopes is home. He also attempts *periodically* to signal Navidson on the radio though *never* gets a response. *Regrettably* very little footage exists from this part of the voyage; Battery levels are running low" (151).

Moreover, every *regard* is sourced, that is, the question "who speaks" is as clear as in the traditional speakerless NS, where it is always the invisible but authoritative author. Here it is not Danielewski but Zampano, who is equally self-effaced. However, he hides behind 1) the technical equipment he has invented by way of dramatized narrator (the numerous "Hi8" cameras Navidson has fixed all round the house, the personal "video-journal" entries of Will and Karen to themselves, the camcorders taken down the corridor, etc.) and 2) the endless controversy the film caused, evidenced by constant quotes from various experts (socio-psycho-techno, etc.), real and faked, and even from witnesses, including the later "Billy Reston Interview" and Navidson's "Last Interview" (both, naturally, in the past tense). Thus, although we often feel we're being told the story direct, in the present tense, what we're in fact being told is how the film is being made and how it was received, though many of the commentators later turn out never to have seen it (since, as Truant has reminded us, it doesn't exist). We have, in short, a parodic fusion of fiction, which has always depended on the techniques of documentary (chronicles, diaries etc.), and documentary, which more and more uses the techniques of fiction, a mixture now called faction.

This main story, told in spt for events or action as well as the normal gpt, and internally interrupted by critical opinion in cpt, thus has the tone of a documentary, but of impossible events. Moreover, it is constantly interrupted, in a way no documentary should be.

First (still internally), it is interrupted by a long, highly technical, digression on space and echo (with quotes and footnotes, etc.), and another digression on labyrinths.

Second (externally), it is interrupted by the footnotes, themselves complexly self-interrupting. For instance, everything in the long labyrinth footnotes is "under erasure," ~~literally crossed out~~ by Zampano, sometimes for pages, with a footnote to his footnotes by Johnny Truant calling attention to the fact. Very early on "the Editors" tell us in a smaller Roman footnote that they will print Zampano's notes in Times font and Johnny Truant's in Courier (like his introduction), and we certainly need the distinction, for the longest are Johnny Truant's. They are not only the longest but the most clashing in tone and relevance. There always is a link, however irrelevant (such as "the water-heater's on the fritz," or a "bulge of coffee arcing tragically over china" in the main story), but it is pounced on as excuse to interrupt, the way self-centered people can't listen to anyone speaking without barging in with their "me-too-for-instance-listen-to-this"; for example, in footnote 18 we read, "I got up this morning to take a shower and guess what? No fucking hot water," plus a long expansion (12), or in footnote 30, "Easily that whole bit from 'coffee arcing tragically' down to 'the mourning paper' could have been cut. You wouldn't of noticed the absence. I probably wouldn't of either. But that doesn't change the fact that I can't do it. Get rid of it, I mean" (31) and so on each time Truant works to expand on his personal problems, his boss, his girlfriends, and above all his serious attacks of out-of-time terrors that are later self-canceled as not having occurred.

And *expand* is the word. If the house expands inside and downwards in this terrifying way, so does the narrative, not only Johnny's footnotes and most others but also the main story in the spt. The chapters, which start at a low number of pages (four, ten, five, sixteen, thirty-two, three, sixteen, ten), suddenly, at chapter 9 grow to forty-five, then in chapter 10 to eighty-eight (the longest), then twenty-eight, thirty-seven, thirty-three, tailing off again until chapter 20, which has sixty-seven. Chapter 11 (the one "omitted in the first edition") has thirty, chapter 22 has three, and chapter 23 has two. These expansions and contractions echo the varying psychologies of fear, disbelief, obsession, and so on, in the events, the whole story followed by exhibits, appendixes, and a droll index of every word used, with page references, then "credits," and a last page that typographically represents an upside-down Yggdrasil (the underground tree of Norse mythology, for the house of the novel was on Ash Tree Lane), a nod to Modernist allusion but with a different mythology, bringing the book to an end on page 709. The expansions, however, differ also in appearance.

The first longer chapter (9, with forty-five pages) is the maddest and the most crowded, miming the sense of stifling apprehension and confusion of inaction in the main story, which here gets almost crushed out of print space. Indeed, nothing happens. It starts with three Latin quotes about a house of "inextricable wandering" (Virgil), all sourced and translated in footnote. The footnote's author is unnamed (i.e., it is not by "Eds" in small Roman nor by Truant, in Courier), so it must be by Zampano and is itself footnoted (as often) by Truant, who gives the secondary source of all three sources and remarks on Zampano's habit of obscuring such thefts, then launches into more than two pages of personal mishaps. This leads to the digression about labyrinths and Minotaurs, in cpt, with more than two pages under erasure. The digression includes two quotes from Derrida, one of which is translated in footnote by Truant ("Here's the English. The best I can do"), the other (from the same book) in the official translation by Alan Bass. After eleven pages of this, the main story comes at last, but a page later has a square box of print inserted in it, which is footnote 144 (on air vents and such), exactly repeated on its verso in mirror print, where there are also two vertical columns, on the left a list of architectural styles that goes on for eight pages, on the right an upside-down list of names in italics, which also goes on for eight pages, as do the boxed and self-mirrored squares. The effect is like a much-windowed Internet screen but also (since this is print) like the newspapers we read, except that this is unreadable, and the squares become half empty, then blank, then black, then larger, with the columns more spaced out, all ending in a "bibliography" (152).

The next chapter (10), which is the longest (eighty-eight pages) is long for exactly opposite, spaced-out reasons: because of innumerable quasi-blank pages, with just one or two sentences or just one word at the top, the bottom, in the middle. This spacing mimes the long silent anguish of Navidson's, Tom's, and Reston's rescue attempt, though it starts calmly and "scientifically" enough: "Using 16mm motion picture (color and

B/W) and 35mm stills, Navidson for the first time begins to capture the size and sense of the place" (154). Chapter 11 (twenty-eight pages) closes in again slightly, but it has two columns, each then split into paragraphs separated by lines of zzzzzz . . . , followed by "Tom's story" in huge (childish?) print, as spoken into his video recorder, outside his tent at the top of the spiral stairs (he wouldn't go down so Navidson had to carry the wheelchair down for Billy Reston to accompany him instead). There follow more Truant adventures in footnote, Tom again, and "A Short Analysis of Tom's Story," which is unsigned. And chapter 12, at thirty-seven pages, becomes (except for four pages of "Truancy") spaced out again to a few words a page. (Tom describes Navidson's and Reston's search for the two wounded men, bringing them back and finding that Tom is not, as ordered, at the bottom of the huge spiral staircase to help them. Instead, later, Tom throws down a rope, which is far more practical for hauling up the three bodies, one dead, one wounded, one paralyzed, on a stretcher Reston has made from their tent. Navidson finally remains alone, but loses grip of the rope, and the coin thrown down for each previous arrival to the top has taken at least fifty minutes: "I'm too muddled to do the math but it doesn't take a genius to realize I'm an impossible distance down" (305, a Zampano footnote calculates the math: the distance is 27,273 miles). The last four pages of the chapter are, on page 307 (bottom right): "The film runs out here"; on page 308 (bottom): "leaving nothing else behind but an unremarkable"; on page 309 (middle): "white"; page 310 is blank; on page 311 (middle): "screen."

This of course increases the suspense, since we won't know for some time how and whether Navidson will return.

He does, and the other very long (second longest) chapter is 20 (with sixty-seven pages), introduces a film sequence called Exploration #5, referring to Navidson's last and solitary—so, highly dangerous—attempt to find out what "really" happened. It is wholly devoted to the story. The previous chapter had no notes by Johnny Truant (who returns in force in 21), but this one has no notes at all, although again many quasi-blank pages and a new typography: sideways (after the spiral staircase or maybe a different staircase lies on its side and enters a wall), or upside down, or in angled triangles, or in five vertical lines as musical stave down the middle with notes and a tune (but *not* footnotes), and so on. The reader of this book frequently has to turn it round to read, which, with a ten-by-seven-by-two-inch paperback weighing two kilos, can be floppily awkward. The chapter ends on page 489 again with the words:

"The film runs out. / Black. / A different kind of black. / [the name of the processing lab.]"

Many of the notes are cunningly humorous; for example, on page 109, after a graphic description of what seems like clumsy sex in a long Truant note, the note is itself footnoted in the same Courier font with "So sorry," but the apology belongs, in fact, to the word *Bauplan* in the main text on labyrinths and means that he can't translate; this note itself is footnoted with "German for 'building plan'—Ed."

I don't want to spoil the reader's sense of discovery with further description and so will come to my main point, for which it was nevertheless necessary to describe certain features in sufficient detail.

The *Guardian* reviewer (15 July 2000) said that Johnny Truant is "an unlikeable feckless character" and "one narrator too many." This is true in a superficial sense. Apart from his fecklessness it is in practice impossible to read two texts simultaneously, whether in two columns (as in Perez de Ayala's *Tigre Juan,* 1929, and a no doubt unconscious B. S. Johnson imitation of Ayala in the fifties) or upper and lower (Gabriel Josipovici, *Mobius the Stripper,* 1974), or any other pattern: one automatically alternates, owing to the linearity of the medium. I tried a different kind of simultaneity in *Thru,* but perhaps it was just as difficult, for opposite reasons (see chapter 5).

Yet, on another level both more formal (stylistic) and more psychological, Johnny Truant is absolutely necessary, however irritating his constant interruptions may be. For despite its neo-surrealist framework, which starts even before the editorial flyleaf and continues throughout in the footnotes and the typography, the book is about the process of reading/fantasizing and therefore also the process of writing (expanding, retracting, crossing out, printing, etc.). Not only does Johnny Truant's editing expand lower and lower, darker and darker, as the house expands lower and lower, darker and darker, but so does Zampano's editing, or inventing, of *The Navidson Record,* and so does *The Navidson Record.* So do its footnotes and scholarly discussions. These are of course satirical, but they are also very profound in miming the constantly fed animal growth of all obsession; indeed, of all discourse. Simultaneously, the inadequacies of media, film (which we can't see) is said early on to be inadequate, while language (which we can see) is shown to be so. Indeed, the footnotes permit fairly obvious psycho-philosophical explanations of the phenomena: our inner space and our responses are individual and reflect our problems and psyches, so that each expansion is experienced and dealt with differently by the different characters. Karin, for instance, is far less credulous of the phenomena and thus can rescue her husband 27,273 miles down with astonishing simplicity; indeed, once they have escaped from it the house looks quite normal. The explanation has to be obvious because the author is also writing a popular Gothic thriller (or using the genre, very well, to illustrate the psychology of the thriller), but he wants his reader both to identify with and to understand the phenomena. The technique is that of allegory, a *Pilgrim's Progress* of the modern psyche. It is not, in other words, a Modernistically "difficult," and therefore off-putting, experiment.

I have to admit that I *was* put off first, though not by difficulty. The book seemed far too long for its slim story, even allowing for the theme of growth, which is far better told through events (e.g., the coin, or the "real" but unexplained disappearance of Holloway and later Tom). The length is chiefly due to the typography. But typography alone is seldom interesting, any more than, say, punning is: all depends on how these devices are used. So perhaps I was prejudiced. That prejudice was increased by the sheer showmanship, as my prejudice against Joyce had been. Here once again was the poet "doing his stuff," the "look-at-me" act I can never quite take, as a more "invisible" author.

Still, hoax or not, the book did finally excite me, as Joyce never did, beyond an objective recognition of his importance. It excited me, first mildly as a Gothic novel, but mostly, after my own experience as described in the preceding chapters, technically: what fascinated me was his parallel discovery (perhaps more conscious than mine was, or maybe as semiconscious) of the present tense as used paradoxically by Robbe-Grillet. For what Danielewski has done is to use the present tense in those two different ways (impersonal/personal), but to excess:

1. scientific use (impersonal)
    a) technical description of cameras, etc., including critical discussion (footnotes, comments on the film, the events, the characters. etc.) (spt and cpt)
    b) this includes generalization, which may or may not be accurate (gpt)
    c) the "paradoxical" use of this impersonal NS (unpronounced) for describing events or action, as in Robbe-Grillet (which could be called pxpt)
2. colloquial use (personal)

This belongs to the speech system, is pronouned, and can shift indifferently to other tenses of the speech system. It is found in dialogue in the main story, but mostly in Johnny Truant's long intrusive notes on his personal adventures, which have nothing to do with the main story but are triggered off by his editing of the main story. He also uses a mock cpt, as I show, but mostly he is plunged in the irrelevant personal.

Here we can clearly feel the contrast I was trying to point up in chapter 7. For this is a parody of all the innumerable first-person narratives in the present tense that have flooded us in the last decade, speech forms having won at last, but not always to the good. Johnny Truant's interventions are not badly written but they are crude, ignorant, and above all, self-indulgent.

It's as if Danielewski, alone aware of what took me so long to understand about my own efforts, had deliberately taken the different versions of the present tense, the impersonal style and the personal style, and decided to kill both in parody. But not exactly. It is still delicately used, à la Robbe-Grillet, for the main Gothic story (and that is in itself paradoxical, using "scientific" pt for Gothic, like using an architectural plan for an M. C. Escher house); but that story is almost killed by the use of cpt in comments and footnotes and scholarly digressions. Similarly, the personal use of the present tense is made quite vulgarly self-indulgent, though it is often saved by droll humor.

If that is where Robbe-Grillet's and my experiments must lead, it's sad but so be it. Perhaps not, however: parody seldom kills outright, and the thing parodied returns, refreshed. Parody, if it is parody and not simple misuse, is often necessary, nearly always amusing—but a strong "scientific" use of the pxpt should be robust enough to resist. Its past tense version, after all, lasted about three thousand years. What may not be robust enough is the personal self-indulgent use. Nothing dates like slang and colloquial speech. Inversely, a writer can be accused of being "far too conversational and even slangy" (as Forster was, incredibly),[3] yet mysteriously rise above contemporary sensibilities later. That is the mark of a great artist. After all, only time can decide what "dates."

CBR: That's the feeling of the cell, or whatever creature I'm in. The only information from the author is in the chapter headings, "x million years later." I have no idea whether a cell would be conscious of the genetic code; that, too, is a fiction. Incidentally, as my creatures slowly become human, from around chapter 9, the Code vanishes. Into their unconscious perhaps. They're much closer to the genetic code as animals or even as cells. This again is fiction. But the Code would represent what finally God became. The Code is only mentioned once again, right at the end, when the Wordmen (the chiefs and the magic men) are forecast by a traveler as interpreters of the Code. But you may have noticed that three instincts keep returning: the top-tribe or center-of-the-world instinct, already present in the nuclear cell; secondly, the upright instinct, first described with the spineless picaias (or lancelets, unnamed anyway), who stop their undulating swim to eat, in an upright stance, immobile, like sentinels, as they feed on particles that pass; thirdly, the burrowing instinct, as these same creatures burrow in the sand. For many million years our ancestors were tiny mammals, scurrying away from dinosaurs, so the burrowing instinct goes deep. This again is my fiction.

LS: One of the things I took from the Gould book[1] and made into an instant metaphor was the loose ends . . . these evolutionary trials that could have led anywhere but just happened not to. . . .

CBR: In fact I mention one, the duck-billed platypus, though I can't name it. It got stuck between a reptile and a mammal, with an advance bit of bird, a flat beak. My newly furry little mammals come across this extraordinary creature, whose young has just come out of an egg and yet is suckling, at least, the milk is pouring out all over the fur and the offspring is desperately licking all over. That's not fiction; the duck-billed platypus still exists. Is that a bit of evolution "gone wrong"? From an evolutionist's viewpoint, that would only be our teleological view of it as not leading to man or to a useful animal.

LS: It's very provocative in a literary way, the idea of loose ends, because the traditional narrative is structured from the end, the fact that you know where you're going. . . .

CBR: Teleology again. But literature is full of loose ends. As for structuring, I doubt whether every writer always knows where he's going from the start. I structure and restructure as I learn where I'm going. With this book I did have a rough idea, but many other notions occurred on the way. For instance, the paleontologist who read it for me was pleased that I had allowed for different theories about early man, because when man first appeared there may have been several species, instead of just one, and I describe different-looking stand-up creatures, who disappear and are never mentioned again. I certainly hadn't "planned" for that, but I was "paleo-plunging" as I went. Were these loose ends that didn't evolve into man, but just died out? I don't tackle that since I'm inside one female per chapter, at million-year distances.

LS: Do you think this attracts you for narratological reasons?

CBR: I try different things in each novel, so it's hard to generalize. But I love challenges. Prehistory is an unusual topic, and the few novels about it choose one period (Golding for instance), whereas I move through time in vast million-year leaps—but chronologically, so *that* at least is traditional. My type of speakerless narrative found a particularly good home here, because I'm not only inside a different creature in each chapter, I'm also limited to what they can know. I've been exploring this technique since the early sixties, so it was quite familiar to me, if to no one else, and is quite paradoxical. But in this novel it's almost like the Code speaking. It's also good for the perilous balancing trick between giving language and consciousness to creatures that have none or little and not using words for concepts they can't have. I can't even use an ordinary metaphor like "needling pain" because the bone needle wasn't invented till 30,000 years ago or so.

LS: There are a couple of different directions I want to go from this, one is about physicality. Rereading the beginning again, what's fantastically striking, well, you say, "inside the consciousness" or the mind, but it's a bodily mind; that's something you really enjoy obviously, sensation.

CBR: I'm glad you felt that. Well, I'm inside a cell, so I imagine the topology of a cell, in great detail, as I might imagine a sitting room. First, I'm in a procaryote cell (that means precenter, or without a nucleus, that is, a bacterial stick); then I express its surprise when it becomes a eucaryote cell (with a center, like all other cells)—not that I can use these modern words, I can only evoke. It's simply gobbled by another procaryote cell and therefore becomes the center of the gobbling cell—a new, nucleated cell, and feels tremendously important, because it's the center. That's fiction of course, though I did read a lot about cellular process. But then I closed the books and invented.

LS: The striking thing is the enjoyment you as a writer get out of the physicality.

CBR: Yes, I always do. I'm always called a cerebral writer, which is rather strange, because in most of my novels I'm inside somebody or other I invent as I go, just registering what they see, hear, smell, taste, feel, and sometimes it's physical, sometimes not, according to the character. Here it has to be physical.

LS: Your Helsinki lecture[2] does explain to me something I've never understood, which is why Robbe-Grillet was your point of reference rather than Sarraute, who I'd have thought was more like you in a way.

CBR: No, I was influenced at the time by her critical ideas in *L'Ère du soupçon*, which attacked certain realist conventions, but not by her novels, though I admire them. She explores what she calls *sous-conversations*, which grow and shrink like tropisms in biology. So we're closer to interior monologue, though she would have hated to hear that, and it's much more finely modulated. I don't feel that's what I'm doing, but I may be wrong.

LS: Perhaps I identified you with Sarraute for obvious reasons, because you're also a critic, as she is, and your tone is often rather like hers when you talk about literature, but actually as a writer you're not, despite her use of biological metaphors like tropisms.

CBR: No. Robbe-Grillet was the one who influenced me directly, but only in this one technical aspect of narrative, of which nobody noticed the paradoxical nature. I didn't analyze it myself until recently, for that lecture. Nor did he, incidentally; at the time he defended the present tense but not his paradoxical use of it, of which he seemed unaware. That's often how experiment works in fact, so perhaps we're nearer to evolution than I said earlier. Nor is he my only influence. I take little bits here and there. I've always acknowledged my debts—for instance, Pound and

Beckett—so I hate being saddled with others, Joyce, for example, because I've never managed to read him through. Apart from puns in one or two of my novels I have little in common with him, and even punning is free for all, it depends how aptly it's done. But influence is mysterious, and perhaps it's as Butor said somewhere, "we're all influenced by Joyce, even if we've never read him."

LS: On the modern fiction course I teach, Joyce is our indispensable set text. He was sort of God the creator for the later twentieth century.

CBR: In other words, slowly, not in his lifetime. Influence *is* mysterious. But unless analyzed or demonstrated, it can be a bit facile as critical term. I've been praised sky-high as Joycean and dismissed as sub-Joycean, without any demonstration. Both are irrelevant, biographically because I could never get through him, and in practice never had time—technically because, as I finally found out only recently, Joyce's narrative experimentation is diametrically opposed to mine, so that alone makes a huge difference. I came to Joyce very late, with continuing distaste, in the seventies, long after my first experiments, though I had earlier read the Pound-Joyce correspondence, and every letter from Joyce sounded mean and petty compared to Pound's generosity. So it started with a gut dislike.[3]

LS: What about others; what about Eliot?

CBR: Not for influence. One can admire and enjoy without absorbing. I was mad about Mallarmé at the time. Forgive me, but I think such labels can be very misleading. Even you, for instance, my most intelligent reviewer, say of me somewhere, "She is still a Structuralist, and still a Modernist."[4] It's a bit more complex. I believe I inherited the Modernist love of "difficulty," but not the need to double everything said with mythical meaning from the classics and esoteric religions. As for Structuralism, *and* Poststructuralism, I taught both, at the same time. I've used them, when relevant; I've also criticized them, and I mocked them in *Thru*. Two at least of my novels have been analyzed as Postmodern, for different reasons. But because I knew more about Structuralism than most English critics at the time, I got labeled. It's the same with influence. I was never influenced by the political and paranoiac side of Pound, only by one particular technique, that of repeating a phrase in a later and different context, which enriches its meaning. That doesn't make me an out-and-out Poundian, even if I do, or rather did, know my Pound extremely well. I admired him above all for opening up the rhythm of poetry ("To break the pentameter, that was the first heave"), and that would hardly affect my future novels.

LS: Do you think the idea of the death of God/the author means that you can enter creatures in a different way? I notice that you use the word *creatures,* here and in your Helsinki talk. It's hard to know.

CBR: It's meant to cover all life, from cell to man, but I agree, it is a bit contradictory if I allow for no Creator.

LS: Is the chain ineluctable, or is it deconstructible? Having invented God, could we go back down the chain?

CBR: What a fearful but poetic idea! Sometimes it looks as if we *are* going back, all the way to savagery and not even noble. In fact, I leave God out of this novel, though I hint at various rites after *Homo habilis,* from *Homo erectus* on. But I treat these quite casually as everyday facts, like eating, except that women are excluded. My fiction is that as long as they're hunter-gatherers, they're close enough to nature not to need *institutionalized* religion, only a kind of clan *bricolage*—though I now regret not having made more of the human specificities of rhythm and voice, that is, dancing and singing, as earliest bonding. The first traces of religion as we know it start four to five thousand years after I stop (I stop around eleven thousand years ago), and the future power of the Wordmen is glimpsed ahead by my eastern visitor, a hunter and nomad, as a probable result of the nascent sedentary life he is fleeing, brought about by the beginnings of planting and rearing, which he says will lead to landgrabbing and clan murder. His hosts can't really grasp what he says. Nothing much is known paleontologically, except that burials did begin with the Neanderthals (extinct 35,000 years ago), not before, so I felt free to invent.

LS: You don't have much trouble deciding which side you're on?

CBR: No. I tried for twenty years to believe, but my godless childhood must have laid a wrong layer, for I plunged in very cerebrally, studying theology and comparative religion, only to find that dogmas are fabricated as logical edifices based on one premise that demands pure faith, the same mechanism, incidentally, as ideologies. Make-believe is lovely, but not if it gets used to create power systems and to persecute. But I respect the genuine need for faith.

LS: Can we get around to authors and authority again?

CBR: I got involved early in the modern resentment at the author wrapping up every sentence in explanation, guiding the reader too much. Perhaps I go to the other extreme, giving no guidance at all, since my narrative is speakerless and the reader has only what goes on inside the character to go by. But there's usually a reason for it. In *Subscript,* the text is easier than, say, in *Thru,* but two nonliterary friends, while loving it, complained that they didn't know where they were. Of course they didn't. Nor did my creatures. None of our present place names existed. I enjoy that, doing everything to make people read the careful evocations carefully, but no more. Besides, we can read fairy tales without place names, and we're assailed with place pictures that all look alike.

LS: It's a different level of life?

CBR: It's more basic, yes. Even so, there's an ironic pleasure of recognition, *if* recognition occurs. I tend to reject the archly superior irony of Modernism, which is always a wink from author to reader about the weaknesses of the character. Barthes was also hard on it, in *S/Z,* after he'd declared the death of the author in the sixties.

LS: In that essay he writes about the euphoric possibility of losing your identity, your roots. Are you sharing his euphoria?

CBR: Not about the death of the author. Barthes loved to make unproved dogmatic statements, but he was often wrong. Everyone followed, of course, substituting the word *narrator,* which blurs all narrative instances. For example, reviewers often call the consciousness I'm in my "narrator," which would be particularly absurd in *Subscript.* But yes, to go back to your question about losing identity, I've been deconstructing that notion ever since *Out.* It's a twentieth-century notion, an excrescence on the "individual" being that came in with the Renaissance and then was developed by Locke. Feuds and wars have existed ever since landgrabbing, but they've become steadily more savage as people get so alienated they cling to any kind of belonging—religious, racial, political, or whatever—and call it identity. Ethnic or national identities are fabricated by parents, priests, and politicians at will, like dogmas. I enjoy not belonging, just as I'm genuinely glad that the big-time success never happened to me to give me an identity. I've done what I wanted, quietly, without much compromise, and though it's by no means perfect, I'm perfectly serene about it.

LS: More than ten years ago at a Joyce conference, Geoffrey Hartmann put a name to something in literary culture, something I'd seen happening but hadn't known how to describe: "a flight to identity." A lot of postcolonial writing is about coming to articulacy: I exist, I can speak.

CBR: "I exist" shouldn't mean "I'm seeking an identity," or "an ego-massage," but "I am content to be." I just am; I'm a cell, a fish, a human being. It's the individual being we must respect, life, all that someone is, not necessarily the identity construct. It's a good analogy with what I've always said about form and content. We can and do talk of content (as we do of identity) wrenched from form and so remain with summary and slogan, but if we can bring a being/a work alive for what it is, simultaneously trying to understand how it functions, we automatically get at the content and a good deal more besides. To get back to *Subscript*, that's also what I'm trying to say, when humans were much closer to animals, when existing through evolution was all. But here and there, if you noticed, there is a certain muted feminism; one of the women says about men, "We teach them to speak so they silence us." But such items are just slipped in, quietly, not shouted.

LS: It's a certain feminism, which is about wanting to deconstruct notions of identity, not constructing them?

CBR: Deconstruct doesn't mean destroy, but quietly show how it functions. Even for experiment I've been quiet. Incidentally, although I don't belong to any religion, the most important ones all advocate annihilating the self in favor of Nirvana, God, thy neighbor, the other, and though none of us succeed in doing that, I believe it's the only important teaching. It's just possible that women have always been slightly better at it, because they always had to follow their new clan and learn its language as a matter of course, as I show in *Subscript.*

LS: Talking of identity, the I-narrators have a bad time of it in *Textermination,* a real existential crisis.

CBR: Yes, they're having a meeting, it's a metafictional parody. The whole novel is metafictional, and there are several metalepses, that is, transgressing narrative levels. But apart from that, the actual narrative technique, unlike that of my other novels, is fairly traditional—I mean, still in an instantaneous present but a bit more author-guided, partly because the characters come from traditional narratives but also because this congress of thousands of fictional characters posed a real problem of recognition for the reader, and I didn't want to make it too hard. But I couldn't resist metalepses, like one character saying to another that the narrative they're in even uses free indirect discourse, which for me has become a mark of traditional narrative.

LS: So you think it's been replaced by the present tense, which is now everywhere?

CBR: Not exactly. The present tense has replaced the narrative sentence in the past tense, and therefore free indirect discourse has disappeared, since it's based on the narrative past. But I pose the very question of possible equivalence between the old free indirect discourse and my specific use of the present tense in that lecture [chapter 7]. It's a complex one, and I can't answer it. The present belongs to the speech system, unlike narrative sentences and sentences of free indirect discourse, which are speakerless, with a different grammar. I've been using the present tense as speakerless narrative sentence for over thirty years, and that's the paradoxical use I was referring to earlier. Of course, as part of the speech system (with a pronoun) it's not new and allows direct author intervention—as in many American Postmoderns, who started interfering with a "look-at-me" kind of tone, referring to the technique they're using, but that too goes back to Sterne, and, of course, Joyce, and back to the writing author. Like Barth defining a parenthetical instead of just using one; after the dialogue quote he adds: "long participial phrase of the breathless variety found in nineteenth-century fiction."

LS: That was wonderful, but it has made its point, and that's one of the things people say about experiment: okay, that move has been made.

CBR: Precisely; it's parody, and parody kills, for a while at least. I discussed those tricks in *Stories, Theories and Things*, I think. Experiment (in theory) proceeds less visibly. It doesn't kill; it quietly does things differently and may change things yet not even be noticed.

LS: This is partly what I was getting at when I asked about evolution. Modernism also had in it a notion that we've left that part behind now. But we keep not leaving it behind. As you say, *The Author is Dead, Long Live the Author*. Things come back—or perhaps that happens in evolution too?

CBR: Plenty of things die out, in both; some say a quarter of the animals now alive are facing extinction. Will they come back? I wonder whether that analogy can hold. I mean with cultural products there's always a person who suddenly gets inspired by, say, medieval four-level allegory and "revives" it, but for his time, as did Modernism allusively, but with only one level usually. Or Spielberg, with a fictional scientific trick, plus special effects, which unpaleologically allowed him to show men and dinosaurs together, when they're sixty million years apart.[5] There's no "reviver" in evolution. But to answer your question: I believe experimenters like me are doomed to die and be forgotten, but that something of the technique survives, or seeps through, without later users even knowing it. Look at narrative sentences in the present tense—Flaubert, who first tried them in *La Tentation de Saint Antoine*, took forty-four years to publish it, and it's not what he's remembered for, while Dujardin, who tried them later, is forgotten; then everyone mocked the style in the fifties; everyone is using it today, as you say, but not always felicitously. And never paradoxically, as a scientific Narrative Sentence without a speaker or I-pronoun. Sarraute said something of the kind when she inverted the traditional realist/formalist dichotomy, saying that experimental writers look so hard at reality they have to invent new methods to capture it, so they're the true Realists; the Formalists are the imitators who dilute those new forms, pouring a by-then familiar reality into them—and are praised as innovators. It's true that experimenters often get ignored or forgotten for the mainstream. I'm a duck-billed platypus, and hope my beak will somehow develop in new birds.

LS: You're talking like the Code now. In a sense there's no waste? I wanted to ask you about that in this novel. Is there any waste?

CBR: I've no idea, since I'm always limited to one mind, but I do hint at the question, for instance when they're grumbling that the new fur came too late, when it's too hot. All that is fiction of course; you'd have to ask an evolutionist as to the reality.

LS: And they wouldn't want to answer either? Because it's always possible that something that seemed completely pointless . . .

CBR: Yes, and the Code says, "Wait." When they complain that now they can swing from trees, the trees are disappearing, it says, "Wait and see, it might come in useful."

LS: It's an optimistic book, in that sense?

CBR: Well, no. Humans lost their swinging ability. But I'm not mimicking paleontology, just having fun with ideas, and words, and forms, and in that sense I've always been an optimistic writer.

LS: I'm interested in how else to think about experiment in a way that isn't cerebral. Is your fiction cerebral? A lot of writers teach writing, at universities, but you were a critic and a writer; were these two different things?

CBR: No, they're very close, they're both deep concentrations and language based, with different purposes: writers to write, critics to think out a problem. But critics write, and writers have to think out problems. Structuralism, of which I disapproved, did teach me to think more logically. But I hope it didn't kill the rest. One English critic, for instance, using Structuralism a bit naively, built a whole argument on a statement that the most fundamental opposition is male/female. Well, no, male/female is a contrary (both can't be true, both may be false); the most fundamental opposition is the contradictory (one must be true, one false, male/nonmale, female/nonfemale), in other words one/zero, the basis of all our computer languages: positive/negative; presence/absence; to be or not to be, *l'être et le néant*—we're back with "being" again, and any other opposition can vary with semantic investment, subjective and evaluative (the first mentioned is better), as indeed Derrida showed by deconstructing many famous oppositions. This inability to think logically, we all have it; I simply worked hard and so have it a tiny bit less than many.

LS: But already *A Grammar of Metaphor* was a very orderly book; you managed to be very orderly about this very disorderly trope.

CBR: As a bilingual child I got contrastive structures in my head very early and adored grammar. But grammar isn't logic, nor is language. I hadn't done any linguistics then. Chomsky's first book came out almost at the same time.

LS: In a way the great age of theory is also past?

CBR: Like the New Criticism, it went out of fashion, for good reasons, of self-abuse; it degenerated, and people ceased to be able to do that kind of thinking, which was for science, and now information theory. Literary people went back to simplicity—well, some have remained theoretical but cluttered, just as medieval rhetoricians and theologians did. It's as if literary people didn't want their subject "tainted" with difficult thinking. But it'll come back. It always does, in a renewed form—like everything.

November 1999

NOTES

Notes to Chapter 1

1. Example of blur: attributing a character's thought to a narrator, then including one's own critical interpretation neither could know. Example of jargon: transliterating narrative sequences into logical symbols ([X - A] XA opt Y . . . Or P1 + Q2 . . .]), which reveal nothing not already clear from the plain language descriptions given. I give no names as I'm not attacking anyone but concerned only with types of obscurity. I prefer the blur (brief inattention) to the transliteration (pretentious attention), perhaps because I'm more likely also to commit it.

2. Antoine Galland, the eighteenth-century French translator of *The Arabian Nights (Les Mille et Une Nuits)*, records the following witticism (my translation of his French): "A Persian poet ws reading a worthless gazel of his composition to the famous poet Giami, telling him that its singularity lay in the absence of the letter *elif* from every word in the piece. Giami replied, "You would make a better thing if you removed all the letters" (Galland 1999, 42).

3. And no easier in English: brilliantly translated by Gilbert Adair as *A Void*.

4. One splendid exception on one of my punctual constraints is Jean-Jacques Lecercle, who sees further into it as lipogram than I myself was capable of at the time. I render him homage in chapter 3.

5. Broadcast early fifties, BBC. This introduction, as opposed to the lectures, is written in a village and in a physical state that make it impossible for me to give accurate references to such memories, but this one struck me, and stuck. On "The Movement," it occurs to me now that this may be the first of those many critical names, typical of the second half of the century, that are in themselves empty of content (compared to, say, Classicism, Realism, Surrealism, etc.), such as Modernist, Postmodern, New, Nouveau, Nouveau nouveau, etc., on which I have commented elsewhere (1991). The content has to be redefined each time by each critic.

6. I was by then married to the Polish poet Jerzy Pietrkiewicz (later Peterkiewicz), who may have put the noun/verb distinction into my head. He was certainly interested in it, but it's hard to remember now which came first, his remark about it or my excitement at Oxford when studying Langland and *Sir Gawain*. The eventual book

was dedicated to him. My later interest in Pound, and therefore in Fenellosa's *The Chinese Written Character as a Medium for Poetry* (1951), who makes the same distinction (active/static) between verb and noun, was incorporated into the book, but not into the thesis.

7. *Poetria Nova*, in *Documentum de arte versificandi*, in *Les Arts poétiques du XIIe et du XIIIe siècle*, ed. Edmond Faral (Paris: 1924).

8. See my *Stories, Theories and Things*, where I much later take up this minor point in a short chapter called "Fiction, Figment, Feign," 1991, 157–66.

9. The Structuralist Roman Jakobson, who I was told had read my *Grammar of Metaphor* and thought highly of it, published an essay on parallel structures ("grammatical Parallelism and its Russian Facet," *Language* 42, 1966, repr. in *Questions de poétique*, 1973), without once acknowledging my earlier analysis. George Steiner told me, "But what an honor to be plagiarized by such a great man!" I laughed. This just for the record in a then still-male world.

10. All quotations are from the translation by Maria Jolas *(Tropisms and the Age of Suspicion*, 1963).The attribution to Katherine Mansfield is not in the original, only in the translation.

11. This actually happened when we (the American department at Paris VIII) invited one of them to apply his model to *The Scarlet Letter,* which we had all been teaching to first-year groups and working on in research teams. I wondered how the method would work on a James novel.

12. See references under Barthes 1967; 1968, Foucault 1969; Friedlander 1992; Kellner 1989; Ricoeur 1983, 1984, 1985, 2000; White 1973, 1978, 1987.

13. See Birch 1994, chapters 5 and 6, for a subtle but critical account of this reception.

14. This interpretation was encouraged by my fictional index cards about the patient, not part of the novel, but asked for by the publisher and printed after the title page.

15. Both *Out* and *Such* won prizes, which was encouraging, but prizes were modest and unhyped in those days, hardly attracting a comment and quickly forgotten. This ideally is how it should be: a little money to help an author but no disturbance. And indeed, that's how I treated them at the time.

16. I made the same mistake with my second novel, *The Sycamore Tree* (1958), but I had the excuse of innocence then. It was intended as a parody of glossy magazine life, but it fell into the thing parodied, a problem Bakhtin discusses, as I do much later, regarding Postmodernism (1981, 1991). This postwriting euphoria I learned to distrust, but not this time. It's always followed by a postsending conviction of the book's total awfulness (hence the importance of a publisher who reads, or pays a reader), which lasts until proofs ("oh, not so bad . . ."), then is followed by indifference. I go through this each time, though the "truth" lies scattered among those four reactions.

Notes to Chapter 2

1. Susan Rubin Suleiman, who visited me then, and heard the first chapter, can attest!

2. Its leaders are appointed not elected, and represent their country; its parliament has little power; it has no framework for foreign or defense policies. It can't even decide on its status. The latest (summer 2000) example: yet another proposal for a Federation (anathema to all pro-sovereignty conservatives), at two speeds (anathema to the lower speeds), and with a new name, The United *States* of European *Nations,* a weird mix of U.S. and U.N.O., which brings back into official blur the passions for and against the "nation-state." *C'est à désespérer.*

Notes to Chapter 3

1. The word *discourse*, so often regarded as meaningless jargon in English today, is translated from French *discours*, which normally just means "a speech" (*faire un discours*), or "a way of speaking, or of treating a topic" (*le discours politique, féministe, etc.*), and this second meaning was stretched by Genette in *Discours du récit* to mean the many ways of telling a story, *discours* vs *récit*. In English, what used to be called "direct/indirect *speech*" (from Latin *oratio recta, oratio obliqua*) became, in false imitation of French, "direct/indirect, and free indirect *discourse*," although French (and Genette) continued to call these *style* direct, indirect. And indeed it is a *style*, a convention, but the term did not make it clear that the technique refers to words spoken *or* thought by characters. I shall return to f.i.d. in more detail in chapter 7, where I shall adopt Ann Banfield's more accurate term *Represented Speech and Thought* (RST).

2. On the controversy between the traditional "two-voiced" theory (voice of character and voice of a "narrator," often invented, and Ann Banfield's more modern "one-voice" theory (the character's) see chapter 7.

3. It is often forgotten that the *nouveau roman* was at first associated with *nouveau réalisme* and phenomenology, cf. Butor: "L'invention formelle dans le roman, bien loin de s'opposer au réalisme comme l'imagine trop souvent une critique à courte vue, est la condition *sine qua non* d'un réalisme plus poussé."

4. This in itself was not "new": Ivy Compton-Burnett had attempted it in the thirties and forties, as had Henry Green. Sarraute discusses both in *L'Ère du soupçon* and decides that such a solution leads the novel into the theater, where it is bound to be inferior (without the art of actors and producer). I agree, but hope that the SF ambiance (two computer whiz kids dictating their story into a computer, quarreling about how to tell it, messages from the rock-creatures, etc.) is too far from the theater for this to be a problem; indeed, both novels are formally closer to the epistolary novel than to the theater, except for the kid slang.

5. Perec belonged to the club Oulipo (Ouvroir de Littérature Potentielle), headed by Raymond Queneau at the time, whom I greatly admired, and which relished formal tours de force of this kind. I was once invited (by a lesser member) to join, which was a huge honor, but I refused, for fear, perhaps, of being drawn into such attractive games.

Note to Chapter 4

1. *A Grammar of Metaphor* (1958), *A ZBC of Ezra Pound* (1971), *A Rhetoric of the Unreal* (1981), and *Stories, Theories and Things* (1991).

Notes to Chapter 5

1. It was not published until 1975 because the publisher's printer kept it a year then gave up, and it had to be sent to a more craftsmanly couple to set, "painstakingly," as said in the acknowledgment. I imagine this would not have occurred in this more competent computer age. [Added 2001: Yes, of course it would and does occur.]

2. Calvino 1987, 101-21.

3. I should like to point out, not just for author intention but to show the contextual limits of this triangle, that one critic, in a book of essays on me (Friedman and Martin eds. 1995, 121), reads this triangle as an allusion to the triangle ALP in *Finnegans Wake*, which is his right as reader. But then he proceeds to attribute his free association to me,

or least to the text: "If the novel begins (as it does) with Joyce's ALP triangle = Anna Livia Plurabelle and the female (birth), and ends with an inverted cross that spells EXIT THRU TEXT, then perhaps we need to read it first of all as a narrative of the journey from birth, at once a story and a symbol and an icon, an act of deference to our true beginning and our one inevitable end." We "need" to do no such thing, which reduces both my triangle and Joyce to platitude. "Story" and "icon" yes, "symbol" of our "birth and death" no, or not only. His own quote from the end (EXIT THRU TEXT) implies the story of the birth and death *of the text*, which is what I am miming and causing the reader to mime; indeed, life is treated as text in any narrative. Surely, too, the triangle is a universal enough symbol for anyone to use without necessarily owing it to a specific use in Joyce, all the less so because I also use rectangles far more, unmentioned because not in Joyce—whom, incidentally, I still hadn't read at the time, owing to a long resistance, which endures after many attempts. Explicitly, my triangle's allusiveness is contemporary only, but *if* through the typography more generally I *was* thinking of anyone, it was rather of Yeats's "I made it out of a mouthful of air" and the idea of intercepting words, dragging them down through the brain and onto the paper to form a text. Author intention may be of nil value, but then reader supposition should have the same status and be used with as much caution as only one (his) possibility, and only if it enriches.

Notes to Chapter 6

1. "Creativity and Exile," *Poetics Today* 17, nos. 3–4 (1996); later published in *Exile and Creativity: Signposts, Travelers, Outsiders, Backward Glances*, ed. Susan Rubin Suleiman (Durham, N.C.: Duke University Press, 1998).

2. Bowden 1845, 2: book 3, chapter 20.

3. *Being Geniuses Together* is the title of McAlmon 1968, quoted in Gilbert and Gubar 1989, 2:221. On the material advantages of expatriation, see Gilbert and Gubar 1989, 2:219.

4. The author was the Scottish poet James Burns Singer.

5. After that early experience I never turned to any friend, anywhere, for a leg up, nor did I ever owe a single review or success to friendship but to chance appreciation, such as my invitation to Paris. With a few treasured exceptions, male friends, in the guileful guise of admiration, have consistently been unhelpful, even harmful, but I was always able to "spring forth" in new directions. One of my most perceptive reviewers, Lorna Sage, did become a close friend after several reviews, but she is too honest to praise a book of mine if she appreciates it less than others. (Lorna died in January 2001, but I am leaving that last sentence in the present tense.)

6. For many years the department had to pass the hat for every guest professor from America.

7. This jargon is always alienating (using rare words or nonnormal meanings); for one example among countless, a reduction in taxes is called *abattement* (its normal meanings are violent: felling of a tree, killing of a man, deep depression or discouragement), and the answer to the question "does it mean 'reduction'" (or equivalents for other examples) is invariably "Non, c'est un abattement," so deeply anchored are they into their own jargon. Or, if the word is familiar, it is aggressive, for example, a person or object is *frappé par* or *échappe à l'impôt* (in English "liable/not liable"), which conjures up images of peasants pursued by all the king's men. Fraud is bred as part of a system that makes things impossible for its own citizens, rooted as it is in Napoleonic,

royal, and even medieval times. The presumption of innocence, for instance, has only just been made law and is proving very difficult to apply.

Notes to Chapter 7

1. "Personne ne parle ici; les événements semblent se raconter eux-mêmes. Le temps fondamental est l'aoriste, qui est le temps de l'événement hors de la personne d'un narrateur." It is this "nobody speaks" that may have triggered Foucault's "archeology of knowledge" as opposed to archive (*L'Archéologie du savoir*, 1969) and de Certeau's *L'Absent de l'histoire* (1973); see chapter 1 for my brief summary of parallel problems in philosophy and history.

2. Benveniste, who is as shocked as I am at a Hemingway story being translated throughout in the "historical" aorist, deals only with the indicative mood, but I imagine there are similar strictures in other moods: imperative only in Speech Mode, subjunctive in both (but the "dead" imperfect subjunctive only in Narrative Mode?).

3. Direct/indirect discourse were once called *speech*, from Latin *oratio recta, obliqua*, or in French, *style (in)direct*, etc. The "free" version did not exist in Latin (see chapter 3). The word *discourse*, already overwidely used, was meant to cover speech *and* thought, but cf. Banfield, below.

4. See Jean Ricardou, *Problèmes du nouveau roman*, 1967, pp. 33–34, for a brief analysis.

5. My translation, 1967. Robbe-Grillet's usual translator, Richard Howard, did the U.S. version and resumed all translations afterwards, but I do not have his version. In French: "Sur la droite, une forme simple plus estompée, recouverte déjà par plusieurs journées de sédiments, transparaît cependant encore; sous un certain angle, elle retrouve assez de netteté pour laisser suivre ses contours sans trop d'hésitation. C'est une sorte de croix: un corps allongé, de la dimension d'un couteau de table" (*Dans le labyrinthe*, original 1959 edition, 12–13).

6. These terms are given in French because they are variously translated: I have myself used (1981) *utterance* for *énonciation* (subjective elements) and *statement* for *énoncé*, but I have seen *utterance* used for *énoncé*.

7. Trans. Richard Howard, *Jealousy* (New York: Grove Press, 1959). Both uses of "better" seem rather awkward to me.

8. I am insisting a little on this fundamental difference because I have been compared to Joyce, either in praise or blame (e.g., "sub-Joycean" as mere unsupported label). It would be nice to be blamed or praised for what I actually do.

9. For Barthes's odd reversal of Benveniste's history/speech, see Culler 1975, 197–99.

10. See, among others, Arthur Power, *Conversations with James Joyce*, ed. C. Hart (Chicago: University of Chicago Press, 1982 [1974]).

11. This quotation comes from chapter 5 ("Ill Locutions"), of which this part of the essay is a re-thought-out version.

12. This notion of narrator as responsible for every sentence and for organization is claimed in Todorov 1966, 126, as Banfield reminds us. As a Derridean, she also briefly argues against the two-voiced theory as yielding to the privileging of voice over *écriture*. RST exists only in writing.

13. He refers to Camus (as Sarraute had) and the "stupefying presence of a world through the words of a narrator absent from himself," but using the first person. His latest novel, *La Reprise* (2001), has dropped the paradoxical present tense I discuss in

this chapter, as do most of his novels after *Dans le labyrinthe*.

14. For the "exiling" critical attitude of the time see Birch 1994. She also generously and intelligently distinguishes my writing from the *nouveau roman*, without, however, analyzing the narrative technique, calling it "the first-person-absent-narrator" (191). (There is normally no first person and no narrator; a narrator is by definition present.)

15. Robbe-Grillet also has such moments, but as I'm not sure whether he would call it "miming," I am assuming that conscious responsibility, which may, in fact, be part of my debt.

16. Philip Hughes, a painter and friend, complained that "he didn't know where he was." He's an artist who paints impressive landscapes almost geologically, without a hint of human habitation. They're intensely enjoyable without reference to the precise geographical titles he gives. These are added, outside the frame, *hors texte,* as I, the "author," am *hors texte,* except for the chapter headings, which are equivalent to his titles. He didn't seem to make the link, so I said nothing. But this is precisely what everything I've been saying on my narrative method has been about (which he hadn't read, so this isn't a criticism), and it also underlines what I said in chapter 1 about the difficulties caused by words having referents, which one ceaselessly seeks, while color and shape and sound are free of them.

Notes to Chapter 8

1. See Derrida, 1968, repr. 1972, 71–168.

2. Cf. Derrida on cybernetics, in 1967: "A supposer que la théorie de la cybernétique puisse déloger en elle [get rid of] tous les concepts métaphysiques—et jusqu'à ceux d'âme, de vie, de valeur, de choix, de mémoire—qui servaient naguère à opposer la machine à l'homme, elle devra conserver, jusqu'à ce que son appartenance historico-métaphysique se dénonce aussi, la notion d'écriture, de trace, de gramme et de graphème" ("La Fin du livre et le commencement de l'écriture," in Derrida 1967, 19). By "fin du livre" Derrida here means the end of the world as book, as command, breath, and presence of God, roughly during the eighteenth century.

3. See appendix, "An Exchange between Forster and R. C. Trevelyan" (Harmondsworth: Penguin, 1976), 163.

Notes to Chapter 9

1. Lorna must be referring to Gould 1989.

2. "The Author is Dead, Long Live the Author," repr. in a shortened version in the *Times Literary Supplement* who retitled it "Narrating without a Narrator" (31 December 1999). My own title is kept for the fuller version here as chapter 7.

3. On reflection since, I may have inherited Pound's blind attitude: for all his amazing generosity to Joyce, he just couldn't take *Finnegans Wake*. My resistance continued until very recently, when I did at last read him through, to deal with his narrative instance for chapter 7 (i.e., in recent additions to the text of the lecture).

4. *The Cambridge Guide to Women's Writing in English,* ed. Lorna Sage (Cambridge: Cambridge University Press, 1999).

5. Ray Bradbury brought them together in a story earlier, through (backwards) time-travel, but I can't find where.

REFERENCES

Note: This is not a bibliography of everything I discuss but a reference list of books I mention. I have omitted references for brief allusions to well-known and easily accessible classics such as Shelley or Pope, Aristotle, and so on.

Achebe, Chinua. 1958. *Things Fall Apart.* London: Heinemann.
Ackroyd, Peter. 1985. *Hawksmoor.* London: Hamish Hamilton.
———. 1996. *Milton in America.* London: Sinclair Stevenson.
Amis, Martin. 1991. *Time's Arrow.* London: Cape.
Andrews, E. A. 1987. *Harper's Latin Dictionary.* Originally published 1879. Repr., rev., and enlarged by Carlton T. Lewis and Charles Short. Oxford: Clarendon.
Astrachan, Sam. 1958. *An End to Dying.* London: Barrie.
Austen, Jane. 1981. *Pride and Prejudice.* Harmondsworth: Penguin. Originally published 1813.
———. 1981. *Emma.* Harmondsworth: Penguin. Originally published 1816.
Austin, J. L. 1962. *How to Do Things with Words.* William James Lectures, Harvard University. Oxford: Oxford University Press. Originally published 1952.
Bakhtin, Mikhail. 1970. *L'Oeuvre de François Rabelais et la culture populaire du moyen âge et sous la renaissance.* Paris: Gallimard. Originally published 1940.
———. 1973. *La Poétique de Dostoievski.* Paris: Seuil. Originally published 1963.
Banfield, Ann. 1982. *Unspeakable Sentences.* London: Routledge.
Barth, John. 1972. *Lost in the Funhouse.* Harmondsworth: Penguin. Originally published 1968.
Barthes, Roland. 1966. "Introduction à l'analyse du récit." In *Communications 8,* 1–7. Paris: Seuil.
———. 1967. "Le Discours de l'histoire." *Social Science Information* 6, no 4: 65-75. English translation in M. Lane, ed., *Structuralism: A Reader.* London: Cape, 1970.
———. 1968. "L'Effet du réel." *Communications* 11: 84–89. This and previous reprinted in *Le Bruissement de la langue,* pp. 153–74. Paris: Seuil.
———. 1994. "La Mort de l'auteur." In *Oeuvres Complètes,* Vol. 2. Paris: Seuil.

Originally published 1968. Trans. 1977, in *Image, Music, Text*. New York: Hill and Wang.

———. 1974. *S/Z*. Paris: Seuil. Trans. New York: Hill and Wang. Originally published 1970.

Beckett, Samuel. 1955. *Molloy*. Trans. Patrick Bowles and Samuel Beckett. New York: Grove Press. Originally published 1950.

———. 1958. *Malone Dies*. Trans. Samuel Beckett. London: Calder. Originally published 1956.

Benstock, Shari. 1986. *Women of the Left Bank: Paris 1900–1940*. Austin: University of Texas Press.

Benveniste, Emile. 1966. *Problèmes de linguistique générale*. Paris: Gallimard. Trans. Elizabeth Meek. *Problems of General Linguistics*. Coral Gables: University of Florida Press.

Birch, Sarah. 1994. *Christine Brooke-Rose and Contemporary Fiction*. Oxford: Oxford University Press.

Booth, Wayne C. 1961. *The Rhetoric of Fiction*. Chicago: University of Chicago Press.

———. 1974. *A Rhetoric of Irony*. Chicago: University of Chicago Press.

———. 1979. *Critical Understanding: The Powers and Limits of Pluralism*. Chicago: University of Chicago Press.

Bowden, J. W. 1845. *The Life and Pontificate of Gregory the Seventh*. New York: Dunham.

Brémond, Claude. 1966. "La Logique des possibles narratifs." In *Communications 8*. Paris: Seuil.

Brooke-Rose, Christine. 1957. *The Languages of Love*. London: Secker and Warburg.

———. 1958a. *The Sycamore Tree*. London: Secker and Warburg. New York: Norton.

———. 1958b. *A Grammar of Metaphor*. London: Secker and Warburg.

———. 1960. *The Dear Deceit*. London: Secker and Warburg. New York: Doubleday.

———. 1961. *The Middlemen*. London: Secker and Warburg.

———. 1964. *Out*. London: Michael Joseph.

———. 1966. *Such*. London: Michael Joseph.

———. 1968. *Between*. London: Michael Joseph.

———. 1971. *A ZBC of Ezra Pound*. London: Faber and Faber.

———. 1975. *Thru*. London: Hamish Hamilton.

———. 1981. *A Rhetoric of the Unreal*. Cambridge: Cambridge University Press.

———. 1986. *Xorandor*. Manchester: Carcanet Press.

———. 1990. *Verbivore*. Manchester: Carcanet Press.

———. 1991a. *Textermination*. Manchester: Carcanet Press. New York: New Directions.

———. 1991b. *Stories, Theories and Things*. Cambridge: Cambridge University Press.

———.1994. *Amalgamemnon*. Normal, Ill.: Dalkey Archive. Originally published 1984. Manchester: Carcanet Press.

———. 1996. *Remake*. Manchester: Carcanet Press.

———. 1998. *Next*. Manchester: Carcanet Press.

———. 1999. *Subscript*. Manchester: Carcanet Press.

Brooks, Cleanth, and Robert Penn Warren. 1959. *Understanding Fiction*. New York: Meredith.

Brunet, Eric. 1998. *La Bêtise administrative: Excès, absurdités, bavures et autres scandales*. Paris: Albin Michel.
Butor, Michel. 1960. "Le Roman comme recherche." In *Répertoire 1*. Paris: Editions de Minuit. Originally published 1955.
Calvino, Italo. 1987. *The Literature Machine*. Torino: Einaudi. London: Picador and Secker and Warburg. Originally published 1982.
Camus, Albert. 1942. *L'Étranger*. Paris: Gallimard.
Carew, Jan. 1958. *Black Midas*. London: Secker and Warburg.
Caserio, Robert. 1990. "Mobility and Masochism: Christine Brooke-Rose and J. G. Ballard." In *Why the Novel Matters: A Postmodern Perplex*. Ed. Mark Spilka and Caroline McCracken-Flesher. Bloomington: Indiana University Press.
Certeau, Michel de. 1973. *L'Absent de l'histoire*. Paris: Mame, Collection Repères, Sciences humaines et sociales.
Chomsky, Noam. 1957. *Syntactic Structures*. The Hague: Mouton.
Cixous, Hélène. 1968. "Christine Brooke-Rose: Le Langage du dépaysement." *Le Monde* 7 (12 December).
———. 1969. *Dedans*. Paris: Grasset.
Colombani, Jean-Marie. 2000. *Les Infortunes de la république*. Paris: Grasset.
Conrad, Joseph. 1911. *Under Western Eyes*. London: Dent.
———. 1913. *Chance: A Tale in Two Parts*. London: Dent.
Culler, Jonathan. 1975. *Structuralist Poetics*. London: Routledge.
Danielewski, Mark Z. 2000. *House of Leaves*. London: Anchor, Random House.
Davie, Donald. 1955. *Articulate Energy: An Inquiry into the Syntax of English Poetry*. London: Routledge & Kegan Paul.
Defoe, Daniel. 1961. *Robinson Crusoe*. New York: New American Library. Originally published 1719–22.
———. 1966. *Journal of the Plague Year*. London: Dent. Originally published 1722.
Derrida, Jacques. 1971. "An Interview with Jacques Derrida." *Literary Review* 14: 21–22.
———. 1972. "La Pharmacie de Platon." In *La Dissémination*. Paris: Seuil. Originally published 1968.
———. 1973. *La Voix et le phénomène*. Paris: Presses Universitaires de France. Trans. *Speech and Phenomenon*. Evanston, Ill.: Northwestern University Press. Originally published 1967.
———.1975. "Le Facteur de vérité." In *La Carte postale*. Paris: Flammarion. Originally published 1968. Trans. *The Postcard*. Chicago: University of Chicago Press.
———. 1976. *De la grammatologie*. Paris: Minuit. Originally published 1967. Trans. Gayatri Chakravorty Spivak. *Of Grammatology*. Baltimore, Md.: Johns Hopkins University Press.
———. 1978. "Freud et la scène de l'écriture." In *L'Écriture et la différence*. Originally published 1967. Paris: Seuil. Trans. Alan Bass. *Writing and Difference*. Chicago: University of Chicago Press.
Diderot, Denis. 1970. *Jacques le fataliste*. Paris: Garnier: Flammarion. Originally published 1780.
Doubrovsky, Serge. 1971. "Littérature: Généralifité de la phrase." In *Problèmes de l'analyse textuelle/Problems of Textual Analysis*. Ed. Pierre R. Léon et al. Paris: Didier.
Dujardin, Edouard. 1887. *Les Lauriers sont coupés*. In *La Revue indépendante*. Repr. Paris: Messein.

Duras, Marguerite. 1955. *Le Square*. Paris: Gallimard.
———. 1982. *La Maladie de la mort*. Paris: Les Editions de Minuit.
Empson, William. 1930. *Seven Types of Ambiguity*. London: Chatto and Windus.
———. 1951. *The Structure of Complex Words*. London: Chatto and Windus.
Faral, Edmond, ed. 1924. *Les Arts poétiques du XIIe et du XIIIe siècle*. Paris: É. Champion.
Fenellosa, Ernest. 1936. *The Chinese Written Character as a Medium of Poetry*. With a foreword by Ezra Pound. London: Stanley Nott. Washington, D.C.: Square Dollar Press, 1951.
Fish, Stanley. 1970. "Literature in the Reader: Affective Stylistics." *New Literary History* 2, no. 1: 123–62.
Flaubert, Gustave. 1949. *Madame Bovary, nouvelle version précédée de scenarios inédits*. J. Pommier and G. Leleu. Ed. Paris: Corti.
———. 1967. *La Tentation de Saint Antoine*. Paris: Flammarion. Originally published 1874.
Forster, E. M. 1976. *Where Angels Fear to Tread*. Ed. Oliver Stalleybrass. Harmondsworth: Penguin Classics. Originally published 1905.
———. 1990. *A Room with a View*. Ed. Oliver Stalleybrass. Harmondsworth: Penguin Classics. Originally published 1908.
Foucault, Michel. 1969. *L'Archéologie du savoir*. Paris: Gallimard. English translation *The Archeology of Knowledge*. New York: Pantheon, 1972.
Frayn, Michael. 1968. *A Very Private Life*. London: Collins.
Friedlander, S., ed. 1992. *Probing the Limits of Representation: Nazism and "The Final Solution."* Cambridge, Mass.: Harvard University Press. Originally published 1966.
Friedman, Ellen, and Miriam Fuchs. 1989. *Breaking the Sequence: Women's Experimental Fiction*. Princeton: Princeton University Press.
Friedman, Ellen, and Richard Martin, eds. 1995. *Utterly Other Discourse: The Texts of Christine Brooke-Rose*. Normal, Ill.: Dalkey Archive Press.
Frost, Robert. 1951. *Complete Poems of Robert Frost*. London: Cape.
Frye, Northrop. 1969. *Anatomy of Criticism*. Princeton: Princeton University Press. London: Atheneum. Originally published 1957.
Galland, Antoine. 1999. *Les Paroles remarquables, les bonsmots et les maximes des Orientaux*. Paris: Masionneuve et Larosse.
Genette, Gérard. 1980. *Discours du récit*. Paris: Seuil. Trans. Jane E. Lewin. *Narrative Discourse*. Ithaca: Cornell University Press. Originally published 1972.
———. 1978. *Nouveau discours du récit*. Paris: Seuil.
Gilbert, Sandra, and Susan Gubar. 1989. *No Man's Land: The Place of the Woman Writer in the Twentieth Century*. Vol. 2, *Sexchanges*. New Haven: Yale University Press.
Golding, William. 1955. *The Inheritors*. London: Faber and Faber.
Gould, Stephen Jay. 1989. *Wonderful Life: The Burgess Shale and Nature of History*. New York: W. W. Norton.
Gould, S. J., and N. Eldridge. 1977. "Punctuated Equilibria: Tempo and Mode of Evolution Reconsidered." *Paleobiology* 3: 115–51.
Greimas, A. J. 1966. *Sémantique structurale*. Paris: Larousse.
———. 1970. "Eléments d'une grammaire narrative." In *Du sens*. Paris: Seuil.
Hall, Radclyffe. 1981. *The Well of Loneliness*. New York: Avon. Originally published 1928.

Hegel, G. W. F. [N.d.] *Phänomenologie des Geistes.* Trans. Jean Hyppolite. *La Phénoménologie de l'esprit.* Paris: Aubier. Originally published 1807.
Ingarden, Roman. 1973. *O Dziele Literackim.* Trans. *The Literary Work of Art.* Evanston, Ill.: Northwestern University Press. Originally published 1931.
Iser, Wolfgang. 1974. *The Implied Reader.* Baltimore: Johns Hopkins University Press.
———. 1978. *The Act of Reading.* Baltimore: Johns Hopkins University Press.
Ishiguro, Kazuo. 1989. *The Remains of the Day.* London: Faber and Faber.
Jakobson, Roman. 1960. "Linguistics and Poetics." In *Style in Language.* Ed. Thomas Sebeok. Cambridge: Massachusetts Institute of Technology Press.
———. 1973. *Questions de poétique.* Paris: Seuil.
Johnson, Barbara. 1980. *The Critical Difference: Essays in the Contemporary Rhetoric of Reading.* Baltimore: Johns Hopkins University Press.
Joyce, James. 1968. *Ulysses.* London: Faber and Faber. Originally published 1922.
———. 1966. *Finnegans Wake.* London: Faber and Faber. Originally published 1939.
Kellner, Hans. 1989. *Language and Historical Representation: Getting the Story Crooked.* Madison: University of Wisconsin Press.
Kenner, Hugh. 1954. *The Poetry of Ezra Pound.* London: Faber and Faber. New York: New Directions.
Kristeva, Julia. 1970. *Le Texte du roman.* The Hague: Mouton.
———. 1974a. "La Femme, ce n'est jamais ça." *Tel Quel* 59: 19–24.
———. 1974b. *La Révolution du langage poétique.* Paris: Seuil.
Kundera, Milan. 1984. *The Unbearable Lightness of Being.* New York: Harper and Row.
Lacan, Jacques. 1966. "Le Séminaire sur la lettre volée." In *Ecrits.* Paris: Seuil.
Lecercle, Jean-Jacques. 1995. "Reading *Amalgamemnon.*" In Friedman and Martin, *Utterly Other Discourse.* Previously published in *Tropismes 5.* Paris: Université de Paris X et Centre National des Lettres.
Lewis, Wyndham. 1968. *Tarr.* London: Calder and Boyars. Originally published 1918.
Lubbock, Percy. 1965. *The Craft of Fiction.* London: Cape. Originally published 1921.
Martin, Richard. 1989. "Just Words on a Page: The Novels of Christine Brooke-Rose." *The Review of Contemporary Fiction* 9, no. 3: 110–23.
McAlmon, Robert. 1968. *Being Geniuses Together.* Rev. and with supplementary chapters by Kay Boyle. Garden City, N.Y.: Doubleday.
McHale, Brian. 1987. *Postmodern Fiction.* London: Methuen.
———. 1992. *Constructing Postmodernism.* London: Routledge.
Okri, Ben. 1996. *Dangerous Love.* London: Phoenix House.
Perec, Georges. 1994. *La Disparition.* Paris: Denoël. Trans. Gilbert Adair. *A Void.* London: Harvill. Originally published 1969.
———. 1972. *Les Revenentes.* Paris: Juillard.
———. 1978. *La Vie, mode d'emploi.* Paris: Hachette.
Peterkiewicz, Jerzy. 1953. *The Knotted Cord.* London: Heinemann.
———. 1955. *Loot and Loyalty.* London: Heinemann.
———. 1958. *Future to Let.* London: Heinemann.
———. 1959. *Isolation.* London: Macmillan.
———. 1961. *The Quick and the Dead.* London: Macmillan.
———. 1963. *That Angel Burning at My Left Side.* London: Macmillan.

———. 1966. *Inner Circle*. London: Macmillan.
———. 1969. *Green Flows the Bile*. London: Michael Joseph.
———. 1993. *In the Scales of Fate: An Autobiography*. London: Boyars.
Propp, Vladimir. 1965. *Morphologie du conte*. Paris. Seuil. Trans. *Morphology of the Folk Tale*. Austin: University of Texas Press. Originally published 1929.
Rabaté, Jean-Michel. 1980. "Lectures critiques de Hermann Broch, James Joyce et Ezra Pound." Unpublished thesis (Thèse d'État sons la direction de Hélène Cixous, Université de Paris-VIII).
Ricardou, Jean. 1967. *Problèmes du nouveau roman*. Paris: Seuil.
Ricoeur, Paul. 1975. *Le Métaphore vive*. Paris: Seuil, collection L'Ordre Philosophique.
———. 1983. *Temps et récit I—L'Intrigue et le récit historique*. Paris: Seuil, L'Ordre Philosophique.
———. 1984. *Temps et récit II—La Configuration dans le récit de fiction*. Paris: Seuil, L'Ordre Philosophique.
———. 1985. *Temps et récit III—Le Temps raconté*. Paris: Seuil, L'Ordre Philosophique.
———. 2000. *La Mémoire, l'histoire, l'oubli*. Paris: Seuil, L'Ordre Philosophique.
Riffaterre, Michael. 1971. *Essais de stylistique structurale*. Paris: Flammarion.
Robbe-Grillet, Alain. 1953. *Les Gommes*. Paris: Les Editions de Minuit.
———. 1955. *Le Voyeur*. Paris: Les Editions de Minuit.
———. 1959. *La Jalousie*. Originally published 1957. Paris: Les Editions de Minuit. Trans. Richard Howard. New York: Grove Press.
———. 1963. *Pour un nouveau roman*. Paris: Les Editions de Minuit. Trans. Barbara Wright. *Towards a New Novel*. London: Calder.
———. 1967. *Dans le labyrinthe*. Paris: Les Editions de Minuit. Trans. Christine Brooke-Rose. *In the Labyrinth*. London: Calder and Boyars, 1967. Originally published 1959.
———. 2001. *La Reprise*. Paris: Les Editions de Minuit.
———. 2001. *Le Voyageur*. Paris: Christian Bourgoise.
———. 1984. *Le Miroir qui revient*. Paris: Les Editions de Minuit.
Roche, Maurice. 1966. *Compact*. Paris: Seuil.
Rushdie, Salman. 1988. *The Satanic Verses*. London: Viking.
Sarraute, Nathalie. 1963. *L'Ère du soupçon*. Trans. Maria Jolas. *The Age of Suspicion*. London: Calder and Boyars. Originally published 1956.
———. 1959. *Le Planétarium*. Paris: Gallimard.
Saussure, Ferdinand de. 1969. *Cours de linguistique générale*. Ed. Charles Bally, Albert Sechehaye, and Albert Riedlinger. Paris: Payot. Originally published 1915.
Sisson, C. H. 1984. *Christopher Homm*. Manchester: Carcanet. Originally published 1965.
Spark, Muriel. 1970. *The Driver's Seat*. London: Macmillan.
———. 1974. *The Abbess of Crewe*. London: Macmillan. Repr. 1984. London: Panther Books.
Stein, Gertrude. 1970. *What Are Masterpieces?* New York: Pitman. Originally published 1940.
Steiner, George. 1972. *On Difficulty and Other Essays*. Oxford: Oxford University Press.
Suleiman, Susan Rubin. 1994. "Living Between: The Loneliness of the 'Alonestanding

Woman.'" In *Risking Who One Is*. Cambridge: Harvard University Press.
Swift, Graham. 1996. *Out of This World*. London: Picador.
———. 1998. *Last Orders*. London: Viking.
Todorov, Tzvetan. 1966. "Les Catégories du récit littéraire" In *Communications 8*. Paris: Seuil.
———. 1967. *Littérature et signification*. Paris: Larousse.
———. 1969. *Grammaire du Décameron*. The Hague: Mouton.
———. 1971. "Les Hommes récits." In *Poétique de la prose*. Paris: Seuil.
———. 1973. *Introduction à la littérature fantastique*. Paris: Seuil. Trans. Richard Howard. *The Fantastic: A Structural Approach to a Literary Genre*. Ithaca: Cornell University Press. Originally published 1970.
White, Hayden. 1973. *Metahistory: The Historic Imagination in Nineteenth-Century Europe*. Baltimore, Md.: Johns Hopkins University Press.
———. 1978. *Tropics of Discourse*. Baltimore, Md.: Johns Hopkins University Press.
———. 1987. *The Content of the Form*. Baltimore, Md.: Johns Hopkins University Press.
Wimsatt, W. K., and Monroe C. Beardsley. 1959a. "The Intentional Fallacy." Originally published 1946, *The Sewanee Review* 54. Repr. in *The Verbal Icon: Studies in the Meaning of Poetry*. Lexington: University of Kentucky Press. London: Methuen.
———. 1959b. "The Affective Fallacy." Originally published 1949, *The Sewanee Review* 57. Repr. in *The Verbal Icon*. Lexington: University of Kentucky Press. London: Methuen.

INDEX

The Abbess of Crewe (Spark), 40, 140
absence: apparent, of narrator, 58, 64, 106, 134, 146, 149–55; inscribed, 14; of last chapter in author's autobiography, 62, 122, 126; of narrator from himself, 133, 185n. 13; New Criticism's search for, 23; of "to be" as a constraint, 3–4, 17, 43–46, 49, 59; of "to have" as a constraint, 3. *See also* constraint(s); speakerlessness
L'Absent de l'histoire (de Certeau), 185n. 1
Achebe, Chinua, 115–16
Ackroyd, Peter, 132, 150–51
acrostics, 68, 70, 74, 104
Adair, Gilbert, 181n. 3
Aeschylus, 50
"affective fallacy," 29
"Affective Stylistics" (Fish), 29
A la recherche du temps perdu (Proust), 25, 148
Alice in Wonderland (Carroll), 70
alienation, 41, 63, 122, 129. *See also* exile
allegory, 167, 178
allusions: in author's wordplay, 50, 54, 94; in Modernist works, 5, 157, 173, 178
Amalgamemnon (Brooke-Rose), 17, 30–31, 46–52, 54, 59, 63, 152
ambiguity, 24, 26, 31, 40, 49, 55. *See also* blur
Amis, Kingsley, 5
Amis, Martin, 42, 43, 46

analepsis (flashback), 25, 36, 39, 140, 148
analogy, 9
An Anatomy of Criticism (Frye), 23
Anchor publishers, 159
annulment, 33–34
anti-narrative devices, 42, 66
anti-realism, 14, 41, 47, 65
aorist tense, 132, 133, 134, 150. *See also passé simple*
Apocalypse, 47
Apocalyptic poets, 5
aporia, 26
The Arabian Nights, 68, 181n. 2
L'Archéologie du savoir (Foucault), 185n. 1
archetypes, 23
Aristotle, 9, 11, 13, 28
Astrachan, Sam, 117
Auden, W. H., 111
Augustine (saint), 151
Austen, Jane, 39, 131, 143, 144–45, 147
Austin, J. L., 48, 49
author: authority, guidance, intrusion, omniscience, presence, comment, or interference of, 5, 14, 130, 134–35, 137, 140, 142, 148, 151–52, 154, 175, 177; death of, 14, 24, 28, 32, 39, 58, 142, 174, 178; and exile, 109–29; "experimental," 4–5, 10, 41, 48, 61, 156; as god, 135, 141, 174; identity of, 57–58; implied, 142; indirect discourse and, 38; intentions of, 5, 29, 30, 31,

194

INDEX • 195

32–33, 49, 155, 183n. 3; interviewing, 4, 5, 32–33, 46; as invisible, 1–19, 32, 41, 46, 48, 57–58, 109, 127, 167, 182n. 9; vs. narrator, 25, 37, 142–50, 152, 175; taboo practices for, 33. *See also* autobiography; critic(s); narration; narrator; *names of specific authors*
autobiography: author's, 19, 53–62, 117–29; elements of, in fiction, 33, 42; readers' interest in, 32; Robbe-Grillet's, 150

Bakhtin, Mikhail, 26, 153, 182n. 16
Ballard, J. G., 107
Balzac, Honoré de, 55, 66
Banfield, Ann, 136, 142, 144–50, 152, 154, 183nn. 1, 2, 185nn. 3, 12
Barnes, Djuna, 111, 113
Barth, John, 131, 177
Barthes, Roland, 80, 92, 93, 127, 175, 182n. 12; on death of author, 24, 32, 58, 142; on narration, 24, 25, 66, 131; on realism, 14, 55
Bass, Alan, 164
Bataille, Georges, 76
The Bath Press (England), 159
Baudelaire, Charles, 13, 111
Beat generation, 150
Beckett, Samuel, 50, 139, 153, 173; and exile, 111, 113, 115, 118, 127, 129; as experimental writer, 12, 23, 132, 133, 150
Beerbohm, Max, 111, 112
behaviorist novel, 139
Belgium, 125, 128–29
Benedictines, 42
Benstock, Shari, 114
Benveniste, Emile, 133–35, 145, 185n. 1
Between (Brooke-Rose), 54, 56, 57, 59, 63, 121, 122, 127, 156–57; criticism of, 33–35, 109; description of, 17, 33, 50, 58; lipogram in, 3, 17, 43–46, 49
bilingualism. *See* language(s): multiple
biographical criticism, 32, 33–35, 53, 157
Birch, Sarah, 35, 182n. 13, 186n. 14
Black Midas (Carew), 117
Bletchley Park, 125
blur, 182n. 2; example of, 181n. 1; of identity, 49; increasing acceptance of, 1–2, 10, 31; Joyce's, 133, 141; between narrator and narrative instances, 142
Booth, Wayne C., 13, 23, 29, 30, 58, 72, 142
Borges, Jorge Luis, 153
Bowles, Jane, 111
Bowles, Paul, 111
Bradbury, Ray, 186n. 5
Bradley, H. C., 13, 22
Brecht, Bertolt, 111
Brémond, l'Abbé, 12
Brémond, Claude, 24
Breton, André, 111
Brooke-Rose, Christine: as critic, 2, 5, 44, 54, 55, 121–22, 127, 172, 179; influences on, 2–3, 16, 40, 58, 137, 139, 140, 153, 172–73; interview with, 169–80; as invisible author, 1–19, 32, 41, 46, 48, 57–58, 109, 127, 167, 182n. 9; as teacher, 2, 13, 25, 27, 29, 36, 55, 58, 127, 179. *See also* narration; *titles of works by*
Brooks, Cleanth, 23
Browning, Robert, 78
Brunet, Eric, 122
Brussels (Belgium), 125, 128–29
Bunyan, John, 167
Burgess, Anthony, 111
Burke, Edmund, 118
Burns, Robert, 70
Burns Singer, James, 184n. 4
Butor, Michel, 12, 173, 183n. 3
Byron, George Gordon, Lord, 111, 112

Calvino, Italo, 111, 113, 129, 153
Cambridge University, 29
camera. *See* film
Camus, Albert, 12, 133, 134, 136, 137, 139, 185n. 13
Carew, Jan, 117
Caserio, Robert, 107
Cavalcanti, Guido, 111
Céline, Louis-Ferdinand, 12, 133, 136, 139
Cernuda, Luis, 111
Certeau, Michel de, 14, 185n. 1
Chance (Peterkiewicz), 120
chapter headings, 132, 135, 154, 170
characters (author's attempt to keep readers from identifying), 18, 29, 43, 49–50, 53, 155. *See also* consciousness; creatures; dialogue; discourse; identity(-ies); narrator; proper names; two-voiced theory (of free indirect discourse)
Charles de Valois, 111

Charles d'Orléans, 111, 112
Chaucer, Geoffrey, 6, 7, 8, 10
Chicago School, 13
The Chinese Written Character as a Medium for Poetry (Fenellosa), 181n. 6
Chomsky, Noam, 10, 59, 180
Christopher Fromm (Sisson), 42
Cixous, Hélène, 3–4
clichés, 14
close readings: author's efforts to force, 153, 175; and critics, 4, 5, 16, 30–32, 33–35; Deconstruction's emphasis on, 26; New Criticism's emphasis on, 22–23; of poetry rather than fiction, 22–23. *See also* reading
Cockney language, 18
comedy, 10, 11
Compact (Roche), 47, 127
Compton-Burnett, Ivy, 131, 183n. 4
conative function, 28, 31
conditional future tense, 39, 48, 143
Conrad, Joseph, 111, 115, 118, 120, 121, 129, 139
consciousness: author's technique of being in character's, 17, 19, 33, 43, 78, 152–55, 172, 175, 179; free indirect discourse used to express thoughts in, 36–42, 131, 135, 142–50; other novels written inside of, 137–39, 147; reflective/ non-reflective, 144, 146, 149, 152, 153, 154. *See also* author; characters; creatures; free indirect discourse; interior monologue; narrator
constative sentences, 48–49, 59, 152
constraint(s) (lipograms) (Brooke-Rose's), 16; avoidance of pronouns as, 3, 17, 43, 57, 59, 154–55, 178; avoidance of "to be" as, 3–4, 17, 43–46, 49, 59; avoidance of "to have" as, 3; benefits of using, 40, 45, 60–61, 151, 153–54; constraints within, 43, 46; content as, 36–37; defamiliarizing of familiar through, 38, 108, 121, 153–54; definition of, 2, 4; double, 44; eliminating possessive adjectives as, 57, 59; grammatical, 36–37, 43–52; invisibility of, 1–19, 45, 48, 49, 60, 104, 155; metaphoric, 17, 43, 154; as part of experimental novels, 41; restricting narration to dialogue as, 18, 43, 152–53; time reversal as, 42–43; use of future tense as, 3, 17, 46–52, 59, 152; use of present tense as, 2, 17, 40, 43, 48, 59, 130–55, 177; viewpoint as, 37–38. *See also* close readings; experiments
content (extraction; summary; themes), 9, 57, 65, 104, 133; emphasis on, in criticism of *Between*, 33; emphasis on, in teaching of literature, 20–23, 25–28, 32; vs. form, 5–17, 24–25, 35, 176
The Content of Form (White), 14
contraction and expansion, 163–64
contradiction. *See* ambiguity; contraries
contraries (contradiction), 55, 65, 66
convention(s), 6; author's attempts to refresh, 65; of dialogue in traditional novel, 36, 133, 150; free indirect discourse as dead, 38–42, 64, 148, 150, 177; of narrative sentences, 36; past tense as, in traditional novel, 36, 132, 133, 134, 135, 148, 150, 155. *See also* constraint(s)
Conversations with James Joyce/Arthur Power (ed. Hart), 185n. 10
Cours de linguistique générale (Saussure), 7
Courteline, Georges, 122
cpt. *See* critic(s): language of
The Craft of Fiction (Lubbock), 25
Crane, Stephen, 27
creative writing, 6–7, 23, 37, 64
creatures: in *Subscript*, 154–55, 169–72, 174, 176; in *Verbivore*, 18
critic(s): author as, 2, 5, 44, 54, 55, 121–22, 127, 172, 179; author's, 2, 3, 4, 5, 8, 16–17, 18, 30–32, 45, 46, 48–49, 62, 104, 106, 107, 184n. 5; on authors vs. narrators, 142–50; emphasis of, on readers, 29–30, 32, 142; job of, 25, 35; practices of, 15, 23, 26–32. *See also names of specific critics*
critical language (cpt), 158, 160, 162, 163, 168
Critical Understanding (Booth), 30
criticism. *See* biographical criticism; critic(s); Marxist criticism; New Criticism; *Nouvelle Critique*; statistical criticism
Cro-Magnon, 19
Culler, Jonathan, 185n. 9

Dangerous Love (Okri), 116
Danielewski, Mark Z., 159–68

D'Annunzio, Gabriele, 111
Dans le labyrinthe (Robbe-Grillet), 139, 141
"Dans l'oeuvre de Foucault, 'Qui parle et d'où?'" (de Certeau), 14
Dante Alighieri, 106, 111, 116
Darwin, Charles, 169
David, Donald, 8
The Dear Deceit (Brooke-Rose), 42–43
Decameron (Boccaccio), 24
declarative sentences, 152
Deconstruction, 25, 26–27, 30, 57–58, 175–76
Defence of Poetry (Shelley), 6
Defoe, Daniel, 55, 131, 132, 135
deictics, 59, 134, 135, 137, 143, 144, 160
Deleuze, Gilles, 153
Derrida, Jacques, 14, 25, 26, 65, 76, 90, 153, 157, 164, 180; on cybernetics, 186n. 2; on fixed notions of truth, 58; on more powerful interpretations, 30, 31
dialogism, 26
dialogue: Austen's use of, 39, 131; author's use of, 18, 58, 84–87, 152; in conventional narrative, 36, 133, 150; and the future tense, 48; other novels written wholly in, 131, 137, 183n. 4; Plato's dislike of, 38. *See also* discourse; interior monologue; parentheticals; Speech Mode
diaries, 61, 132
Dickens, Charles, 135
Diderot, Denis, 59, 64. *See also Jacques le Fataliste*
difficulty, 180; in author's use of constraints, 1, 48, 57, 151, 153–56; of author's works, 35, 155, 156, 166, 173; of enriching criticism, 15; Modernism's association with, 1, 141, 156–57, 167, 173; of reading, 1, 19, 129, 153. *See also* allusions; blur; close readings; constraint(s); experiments; jargon
digression, 92, 93
direct discourse. *See* discourse: direct
Discours du récit (Genette), 6, 24–25, 46–47, 183n. 1
discourse, 10, 183n. 1, 185n. 3; as contrasted with narrative sentences, 130; direct, 38, 39, 131, 143, 145, 183n. 1, 185n. 3; vs. *écriture*, 158, 185n. 12; indirect, 38, 131, 135, 142–43, 145, 183n. 1, 185n. 3; narrativized, 39; retro-, 96, 97. *See also* dialogue; free indirect discourse; Speech Mode
"Le Discours de l'histoire" (Barthes), 14
La Disparition (Perec), 3
documentaries, 55, 162–63. *See also* faction
Don Giovanni, 68
Donne, John, 5, 10, 153
Dostoyevsky, Feodor, 12, 26, 132, 136
Doubleday (publishers), 159
double reading, 139
Doubrovsky, Serge, 133
drama, 10, 23
The Driver's Seat (Spark), 40, 47
driving, 15, 22, 123–24, 127
Dujardin, Edouard, 132, 139, 178
Duras, Marguerite, 135, 136–37, 140
Durrell, Laurence, 111, 112

école de regard, 138–39, 162
Ecrits (Lacan), 58
education, 20–23, 25–28, 32
Einstein, Albert, 74
Eldridge, N., 169
Eliot, George, 153
Eliot, T. S., 3, 10, 111, 173
Emma (Austen), 144–45
emotive function, 28, 31, 32
empathy (narrator's), 146
Empson, William, 24
An End to Dying (Astrachan), 117
England, 121, 125, 127–28
énoncé/énonciation, 6, 14, 138
epics, 10, 23, 36, 38, 130
epistolary novels, 132, 183n. 4
L'Ère du soupçon (Sarraute), 11, 172
Escher, M. C., 168
Estuarian language, 19
L'Etranger (Camus), 133
Europe (in *Amalgamemnon*), 30–31. *See also* specific European countries
evolution (in *Subscript*), 19, 154–55, 169–80
exile, 109–29; author's, 121–29; involuntary vs. voluntary, 111–12, 115. *See also* alienation
exoticism, 120. *See also* otherness
expansion and contraction, 163–64
expatriates. *See* exile
experiments: author's, 2–3, 16–19, 43–52;

as genre, 41, 178; likened to evolution, 169, 172; overlooking of, 3–5, 16–17, 30–32, 46, 48; prejudice against, 150; by women vs. men, 4–5, 10, 41, 156. *See also* constraint(s); content: vs. form; difficulty; *names of specific experimental writers*
explication de texte, 14, 22
extraction. *See* content

Faber and Faber (publishers), 122
fable, 155
fabula/*sjužet*, 9, 133
faction, 55, 107–8, 163
fallacies, 29
fans (author's), 3, 17, 18, 32, 63
fantasy, 137, 153, 166
Farah, Nurruddin, 116
Faral, Edmond, 182n. 7
Fasti (Ovid), 112
fatwah, 54
Faulkner, William, 147
feminism, 25, 30, 40, 176
Fenellosa, Ernest, 182n. 6
Ferlinghetti, Lawrence, 20
fiction: behaviorist, 139; constraints in, 36–38; conventions of, 6, 36, 38–42, 130–35, 147–48, 150, 155; fictionality of, 17, 55, 63–105; levels of, 18, 54, 177; and modal logic, 49; New Criticism's inability to analyze, 22–23; Postmodern, 27; realism in, 39, 40–41, 55, 64, 65, 112–13, 183n. 3; and truth, 34, 55–57, 60, 107–8, 162–63. *See also* characters; dialogue; faction; metalepsis; narration; *nouveau roman*; science fiction; *names of specific works and authors*
f.i.d. *See* free indirect discourse
Fielding, Henry, 131, 135, 138
film, 138, 140, 159, 160–68
Finnegans Wake (Joyce), 133, 141, 183n. 3, 186n. 3
first-person narration: in author's works, 46, 57, 152–53, 177; Camus', 133, 185n. 13; and conventional fiction, 132; and narrators, 146, 152; parody of, 168; in Robbe-Grillet's autobiography, 150; and speakerless narrative sentences, 14, 135, 139–40
Fish, Stanley, 29

Fitzgerald, F. Scott, 111, 114, 129
flashbacks. *See* analepsis
Flaubert, Gustave, 132, 133, 137, 139–40, 143, 145, 147, 178
focalization, 37
form. *See* content: vs. form
Formalism and Formalists, 6, 9, 11, 13, 24, 40–41, 133, 178
Forster, E. M., 143–44, 147, 168
Foucault, Michel, 14, 58, 182n. 12, 185n. 1
Fouquelin, Antoine, 9
France, 121–29
Frayn, Michael, 47
Frazer, James George, 23
free indirect discourse, 185n. 3; author's use of, 153; criticism written in, 12; as a dead convention, 38–42, 64, 148, 150, 177; description of, 143; early French analyses of, 7, 25; thoughts in, 36–42, 38–39, 131, 135, 142–50; two-voiced theory of, 142, 144, 145–50, 183n. 2, 185n. 12. *See also* discourse; Represented Speech and Thought
Freud, Sigmund, 30, 76, 97, 104
Freudian criticism, 30
Friedlander, S., 182n. 12
Friedman, Ellen, 5, 183n. 3
Frost, Robert, 20–21, 24, 28
Frye, Northrop, 13, 23, 24
Fuchs, Miriam, 5
functions (in Jakobson's diagram of communication), 28–32
future tense, 39, 40, 134, 143, 160, 161; author's use of, as constraint, 3, 17, 46–52, 59, 152; in news, 47–48
Future to Let (Peterkiewicz), 117, 119

Galland, Antoine, 181n. 2
gender: avoidance of pronouns as avoidance of, 59; discrimination on basis of, 4–5, 10, 41, 121, 126, 156, 182n. 9; effects of author's, on reception of experimental writing, 4–5, 10, 41, 156. *See also* men; women
generalization (gpt), 158, 163, 167
genetic code, 169–70
Genette, Gérard, 2–3, 6, 24–25, 46–47; on narrators and narration, 106, 133, 139, 183n. 1
Geneva (Switzerland), 125, 128
genres, 9–10

Geoffrey of Vinsauf, 8–9, 118
"The Gift Outright" (Frost), 20–21
Gilbert, Sandra M., 184n. 3
Gissing, George, 117
Golding, William, 19, 110, 171
Gombrowicz, Witold, 111
Les Gommes (Robbe-Grillet), 132, 136, 137–39, 140–41
gothic novel, 167, 168
Gould, Stephen Jay, 169, 170, 171
gpt. *See* generalization
grammar: author's love of, 7–11, 13, 180; constraints associated with, 36–37, 43–52; generative, 10–11, 145; of narrative, 24, 28, 130–55; poetry as about, 27. *See also* constraint(s); language(s); linguistics; parentheticals; pronouns; tenses
A Grammar of Metaphor (Brooke-Rose), 8–11, 15–16, 180, 182n. 9, 183n. 1
Green, Henry, 131, 183n. 4
Green Flows the Bile (Peterkiewicz), 120
Gregory of Tours, 118
Gregory VII (Hildebrand), 110, 112
Greimas, A. J., 24, 55, 65, 66, 78, 88, 102, 104
The Guardian, 166
Gubar, Susan, 184n. 3
Guiscard, Robert, 110

Hall, Radclyffe, 111
Handel, George Friederic, 112
Hardy, Thomas, 27, 60
Hartmann, Geoffrey, 176
Hawksmoor (Ackroyd), 132
Hegel, G. W. F., 6, 40, 57
Heidegger, Martin, 14, 49, 151
Heine, Heinrich, 111, 112
Hemingway, Ernest, 111, 114, 129, 131, 139, 185n. 2
Henry VII (emperor), 110
Heppenstall, Rayner, 61
Herodotus, 30, 31, 47, 50
Hildebrand. *See* Gregory VII
Histoire de l'oeil (Bataille), 72
history, 59; vs. discourse, 6, 14, 133–34, 145
Hitler, Adolf, 118
Homer, 38, 97
Hopkins, Gerard Manley, 153
The House of Leaves (Danielewski), 159–68
Howard, Richard, 185nn. 5, 7
Hughes, Philip, 186n. 16
Hugo, Victor, 111, 112
Husserl, Edmund, 97, 151
hyperbole, 9

identity(-ies): blurring of, 49–50, 80; as a construct, 57–58, 60, 175–76; multiple, 44; narrative methods that suggest the omission of, 44; reconstruction of, 122, 129
ideograms, 157
ideological rewrites, 27, 32
idiolect, 141, 142
The Iliad (Homer), 38
"Illiterations" (Brooke-Rose), 4–5
"image," 10
imitation. *See* mimesis
imperatives, 48
imperfect tense, 133, 134, 137, 147, 150
impersonal ("scientific") sentence, 133, 134, 138–42, 149–50, 152–53, 167–68, 178. *See also* sentences: speakerless
implied author, 142
implied readers, 18, 29, 53
I-Narrator. *See* first person narration
indexes, 106, 164
indirect discourse. *See* discourse: indirect
influences (on author), 153; of Nathalie Sarraute, 13, 172; of Robbe-Grillet, 2–3, 16, 40, 58, 137, 139, 140, 153, 172–73
Ingarden, Roman, 29, 104
The Inheritors (Golding), 19
Inner Circle (Peterkiewicz), 119–20
inner speech. *See* interior monologue
innovation. *See* experiments
instability: ontological/epistemological, 46, 63; of text, 53–62; through defamiliarizing of familiar, 38, 108, 121, 153–54
"intentional fallacy," 29
interior monologue (inner speech; sousconversation), 139, 146, 148–49; Joyce's use of, 131, 132, 141, 147, 149–50; Sarraute's use of, 138, 140, 172
internet, 157
intertextuality, 106
invisibility: of author, 1–19, 32, 41, 46, 48, 57–58, 109, 127, 167, 182n. 9; of author's constraints, 1–19, 45, 48, 49,

60, 104, 155. *See also* puns
Ionesco, Eugène, 111, 115, 129
irony: of author's lipogrammic invisibility, 5; of experiment, 158; in Modernism, 175; narrator's, 144, 145–47; of suppression of talk about narrative technique, 12; as a way of reading, 147
Isaiah (Biblical figure), 111
Iser, Wolfgang, 29
Isherwood, Christopher, 111
Ishiguro, Kazuo, 111, 114
islands, 109–10, 129
isolation (of writer), 129. *See also* exile
Isolation (Peterkiewicz), 119

Jacques le Fataliste (Diderot), 59, 64, 80, 91, 98–99, 106
Jakobson, Roman, 13, 14, 28–29, 31, 32, 182n. 9
La Jalousie (Robbe-Grillet), 137, 138–39, 140, 141, 150
James, Henry, 137, 182n. 11; and exile, 111, 114, 129; on showing vs. telling, 24, 38, 131; style of, 135, 149
jargon, 2, 108, 157–58, 181n. 1, 184n. 7. *See also* blur; difficulty
John-Paul II (Karol Woytyła), 120
Johnson, B. S., 166
Johnson, Barbara, 26
Jolas, Maria, 182n. 10
Josipovici, Gabriel, 166
Journal of the Plague Year (Defoe), 55
Joyce, James: and exile, 111, 113, 114, 129; as experimental writer, 24, 113, 142, 167, 177; keys to work of, 3; narration by, 131, 132–33, 141, 142, 147–50; as possible influence on author, 173, 183n. 3, 185n. 8
Julian and Maddalo (Shelley), 110
Jung, Carl, 23

Kadaré, Ishmael, 111
Kafka, Franz, 11, 122, 125, 153
Keats, John, 111, 112
Kellner, Hans, 182n. 12
Kenner, Hugh, 8
kennings, 7
King Lear (Shakespeare), 76
Kipling, Rudyard, 135
The Knotted Cord (Peterkiewicz), 119
Korzeniowski, Apollo, 115

Kristeva, Julia, 58, 64, 127
Kundera, Milan, 111, 114, 129

Lacan, Jacques, 26, 58, 65, 78, 88, 97, 98, 107
Langland, William, 153, 181n. 6
language(s): as creating reality, 41; of creatures, 154–55, 171–72; critical (cpt), 158, 160, 162, 163, 168; and exile, 115–29; as having referents, 6, 41–42, 65, 186n. 16; ignoring of features of, 13; invasions of, 8; mimetic, 107; multiple, 17, 33–35, 43, 56, 109, 125–26, 156–57, 180; vernacular, 116. *See also* author; discourse; grammar; jargon; "look at me" tricks; narration; person; tenses; vernacular
Laporte, Roger, 139
Latin language, 116, 157–58
Les Lauriers sont coupés (Dujardin), 132
Lawrence, D. H., 111
Lecercle, Jean-Jacques, 48–49, 181n. 4
Lévi-Strauss, Claude, 13
Lewis, Wyndham, 131–32
Li Ki, 97
linguistics, 7, 10–11, 14, 24, 59–60, 78, 107, 126, 142–50, 158, 180. *See also* grammar; language; Speech Mode
lipograms. *See* constraint(s)
The Literary Work of Art (Ingarden), 29
Locke, John, 97, 175–76
London *Sunday Times*, 8
"look at me" tricks, 5, 6, 46, 106, 138, 167, 177
Loot and Loyalty (Peterkiewicz), 119
Lowry, Malcolm, 111
Lubbock, Percy, 25
Lucan, 97, 98

McAlmon, Robert, 184n. 3
McHale, Brian, 32, 46, 63
Macrobius, 118
Madame Bovary (Flaubert), 145
The Magic Mountain (Mann), 113
La Maladie de la mort (Duras), 137
Mallarmé, Stéphane, 153, 173
Malone Dies (Beckett), 50
Mann, Thomas, 111, 113, 148
Mansfield, Katherine, 12
Martin, Richard, 30–32, 34, 61, 183n. 3
Marxist criticism, 15, 30

Matthew of Vendôme, 118
Matthews, Harry, 111
Maugham, W. Somerset, 111
Melville, Herman, 37–38
Le Mémoire, l'histoire, l'oubli (Ricoeur), 14
men: experimental writing by, 4–5, 156; as friends, 184n. 5. *See also* gender; *names of specific men*
Meredith, George, 135, 141
metafiction. *See* fiction: levels of; metalepsis
Metahistory (White), 14
metalepsis, 25, 43, 153, 177. *See also* fiction: levels of
metalinguistic function, 28–29, 32
Metamorphoses (Ovid), 112
La Métaphore vive (Ricoeur), 10
metaphors: author's interest in, 7–11, 13, 16; lack of, in *Subscript*, 154; New Criticism's emphasis on, 22; Robbe-Grillet on, 16, 153; in *Such*, 16, 17, 43, 154
metonymy, 9, 11
Mickiewicz, Adam, 111, 113, 129
Miller, Henry, 111
Milton, John, 5, 29
Milton in America (Ackroyd), 151
mimesis (imitation; miming): author's allegiance to, 47–48, 150, 153, 154, 184n. 3; in *Between*, 50; in *House of Leaves*, 166; in *Thru*, 66, 88, 107; triple, 148
miming. *See* mimesis
Mimouni, Rachid, 116
mind. *See* consciousness
mirrors. *See* rectangles: in *Thru*
misuse: of author's techniques, 15–16; of free indirect discourse, 38–42, 64, 148; of present tense, 40–41, 151
Mobius the Stripper (Josipovici), 166
Moby-Dick (Melville), 37–38
modal logic, 49
modals, 48, 49
Modernism: and allusions, 5, 157, 173, 178; difficulty associated with, 1, 141, 156–57, 167, 173; irony associated with, 175; vs. Postmodernism, 46; as a term, 46, 181n. 5
Molloy (Beckett), 132, 135, 136, 139
Le Monde, 3, 4
More, Thomas, 110
Mortimer, Raymond, 8
Moses, 65

"The Movement," 5, 181n. 5
Mrs. Dalloway (Woolf), 148
Murdoch, Iris, 131
myths, 10, 23

Nabokov, Vladimir, 111, 115, 118, 129
names. *See* proper names
narration: authoritarianism of, 131; author's most-used technique of, 130–55; backwards, 42–43; conventions of, 6, 36–38, 41–42; grammar of, 24, 28, 130–55; historical/ impersonal, 133–35; modalities of, 46–48; Mode of, 133–55; structure of, 23, 171; taboo on discussing techniques of, 2–19. *See also* author; characters; constraint(s); convention(s); dialogue; discourse; fiction; grammar; interior monologue; language(s); narrator; person; sentences; speakerlessness; tenses; viewpoint
Narrative Discourse (Genette). *See Discours du récit*
Narrative Sentence. *See* sentences: narrative
narrator: as "absent from himself," 133, 185n. 13; apparent lack of, 58, 64, 106, 134, 146, 149–55; vs. author, 25, 37, 142–50, 152, 175; difficulty of determining, in *Thru*, 43, 59; as term, 136, 142; voice of, 147. *See also* author; characters; narration; person; speakerlessness; two-voiced theory (of free indirect discourse)
Nathan, Monique, 127
Neanderthals, 19
negations, 48–49
New Criticism, 6, 13, 14, 22–23, 24, 26, 27, 29, 32, 180
New Hermeneutics, 30
New Scientist, 18
Next (Brooke-Rose), 19, 153
Nietzsche, Friedrich, 27, 30
non-belonging. *See* exile
nonrealized tenses, 3, 17, 48, 59, 152. *See also* future tense
Norwid, Cyprian, 111, 112, 113, 129
Notes from the Underground (Dostoyevsky), 132, 136
le nouveau nouveau roman, 181n. 5
le nouveau roman, 16, 23–24, 40, 57–58, 132, 135, 148, 150, 153, 183n. 3,

185n. 5, 186n. 14
La Nouvelle Critique, 13, 24
novel. See fiction; titles of specific novels
NS. See sentences: narrative
numerology, 54, 62

obscurity. See blur; difficulty
The Observer, 57–58
Oedipus, 93
Okri, Ben, 116
omniscient author. See author: authority of
oratio recta, oratio obliqua, 38, 183n. 1, 185n. 3
originality. See experiments
ostranenie, 120–21
otherness, 26. See also exoticism
Oulipo (club), 183n. 5
Out (Brooke-Rose), 18, 19, 54, 121, 128, 132, 153; author's first use of lipogram in, 2, 3–4, 130; critics on, 16; description of, 16–17, 18, 19; identity in, 44, 58, 125, 175; prizes won by, 182n. 15
The Outsider (Camus), 12
Ovid, 111, 112, 119
Oxford University, 7, 22, 29, 119, 122, 181n. 6

Pan Tadeusz (Mickiewicz), 113
paradox, 5, 12, 14, 26, 40, 58; of Robbe-Grillet's use of present tense, 2, 137, 139, 142, 147, 148, 150, 151, 153, 156, 158–68, 172, 185n. 13
parentheticals, 38, 131–32, 135, 136, 140, 143, 147, 150, 152, 177
Paris VIII. See University of Vincennes
parody: in House of Leaves, 162, 166, 168; limitations of, 178, 182n. 16; of literary allusions, 157; of parentheticals, 131–32; possibility of, in Sarraute's criticism, 12; in Textermination, 177; in Thru, 108, 173; of traditional styles, 147–48
passé composé. See present perfect tense
passé simple, passé défini, 132, 134, 137, 150. See also aorist tense
PAST + NOW, 146, 149
past tense (narrative): author's avoidance of, 2, 137; in conventional narrative, 36, 132, 133, 134, 135, 148, 150, 155, 177; Duras' use of, 137; in free indirect discourse, 38, 143, 147, 148; in House of Leaves, 160; impersonality of, 133–34, 138, 158; Joyce's use of, 141; and Robbe-Grillet, 12, 151
Paul et Virginie (St. Pierre), 110
Perec, Georges, 3, 46
Perez de Ayala, Ramón, 166
performatives, 48
person, 38–39. See also first-person narration; third-person narration
Peterkiewicz, Jerzy, 33, 117–21, 122, 125, 126, 128, 181n. 6
Petrarch, 111, 112
Phaedrus (Plato), 26, 97
"La Pharmacie de Platon" (Derrida), 157
phatic function, 28–29, 32
The Phenomenology of Mind (Hegel), 6
philology, 7
physicality (sensation), 171–72
Pilgrim's Progress (Bunyan), 167
Pinget, Robert, 23
Le Planétarium (Sarraute), 132, 136, 137
Plato, 9, 26, 38, 56, 131
pluperfect tense, 36, 39, 134, 140, 143, 148
Poe, Edgar Allan, 26
poetic function, 28, 29, 31
Poetics (Aristotle), 9
poetry, 5–8, 13–16, 20–23, 26–29, 53, 151, 174. See also names of specific poets
point of view. See viewpoint
polemic, 26
polysémie, 24
Pope, Alexander, 5, 6
possessives, 21, 57, 59
Postcolonialism, 40, 111, 115, 116–17, 118, 176
Postmodernism, 32, 46, 129, 150, 182n. 16; author's works identified as, 63, 173; "look at me" tricks of, 5, 6, 46, 106, 138, 167, 177; as term, 25–26, 27, 181n. 5. See also self-reflexivity
Poststructuralism, 25, 55, 173. See also Deconstruction; Structuralism
Pound, Ezra, 10, 78, 153; author's work on, 121–22, 156, 157, 172, 173–74, 182n. 6, 183n. 1; and exile, 111, 112
Pour un nouveau roman (Robbe-Grillet), 11, 132
Power, Arthur, 185n. 10
present perfect tense (passé composé), 12, 133, 134, 150, 151
present tense (pt): author's use of, as con-

straint, 2, 17, 40, 43, 48, 59, 149–52, 177; Beckett's use of, 132, 135, 136; *d'écriture*, 133, 158; historic, 132, 138, 152; as "living present," 14; misuse of, 40–41, 151; narrative, 2, 12, 14, 40, 130–55, 177; nonexistence of, 151; paradoxical use of, 2, 12, 40, 58, 137, 139, 142, 147, 148, 150, 151, 153, 156, 158–68, 172, 178, 185n. 13; Robbe-Grillet's use of, 12, 132, 136, 137–39, 137–42, 140, 141, 147, 148–50, 156, 157, 158, 167, 168, 172; Sarraute's use of, as critic, 12; scientific, 138–42, 149–50, 151, 158, 159–68, 178; triple, 151

Pride and Prejudice (Austen), 39, 144

The Princess of Clèves (La Fayette), 12

Problèmes du nouveau roman (Ricardou), 185n. 4

prolepsis, 25, 40

pronouns, 61, 141, 147, 150–51; author's avoidance of, as constraint, 3, 17, 43, 57, 59, 154–55, 178; Robbe-Grillet's avoidance of, 138–39, 167–68

proper names: fictional, in autobiographical novels, 57; lack of narrator's, 43, 58; multiple, for same character, 49–50; in *Thru*, 64, 78, 79–82, 106; use of, when pronouns are avoided, 59–60

Propp, Vladimir, 24

Protagoras, 81

Proust, Marcel, 11, 25, 27, 47, 133, 134, 139, 148

provincialism, 117, 157

Psalms (Bible), 110

pseudofuture, 47–48

psychoanalytic theory, 15

pt. *See* present tense

publishers, 8, 42, 62, 122, 128, 129, 155, 159, 183n. 1. *See also names of specific publishers*

puns, 54, 60–61, 68, 113, 173

The Purloined Letter (Poe), 26

"Quand vous serez bien vieille, au coin du feu" (Ronsard), 27

Quarterly West, 65

Queneau, Raymond, 183n. 5

questions (interrogatives), 48

The Quick and the Dead (Peterkiewicz), 119

Rabaté, Jean-Michel, 141

Rabelais, François, 26

Rachewiltz, Mary de, 122

racism, 16–17, 58, 124–25, 128

Random House Group (publishers), 159

readers, 131, 138, 148, 153; critical emphasis on, 29–30, 32, 142; implied, 18, 29, 53; irony as provided by, 147. *See also* close readings; critic(s); fans; reading

reading: capacity for, 8, 53, 129; difficulty of, 1, 19, 129, 153; double, 139; irony as way of, 147; mis-, 106; process of, 166. *See also* close readings

realism: anti-, 14, 41, 47, 65; vs. Formalism, 6, 9, 11, 13, 40–41, 178; in the novel, 39, 40–41, 55, 64, 65, 112–13, 183n. 3; and the past tense, 36, 132, 133, 134, 135, 148, 150, 151, 155

rectangles: of contraries and contradictions, 55, 65, 66; semiotic, 24; in *Thru*, 65–74, 76, 78, 80, 88, 92, 102, 104, 183n. 3

The Red Badge of Courage (Crane), 27

referential function, 28, 29, 30, 31, 32

reflexive pronouns. *See* pronouns

religion, 174–75, 176

The Remains of the Day (Ishiguro), 114

Remake (Brooke-Rose), 19, 53–62, 109, 121, 122, 126

rememoration, 56, 57, 60

representation: of consciousness, 153, 154–55; of language, 41; of narrative structure, 55; of sentences in free indirect discourse, 145; vs. truth, 14; of women, 58. *See also* Represented Speech and Thought

Represented Speech and Thought (RST), 145–50, 183n. 1, 185n. 12. *See also* free indirect discourse

La Reprise (Robbe-Grillet), 185n. 13

The Republic (Plato), 38

Les Revenentes (Perec), 46

reviewers. *See* critic(s)

Rezeptionsgeschichte, 30

rhetoric, 25

Rhetoric (Aristotle), 9, 13

The Rhetoric of Fiction (Booth), 13, 23, 58, 72, 142

A Rhetoric of the Unreal (Brooke-Rose), 107, 121–22, 183n. 1

Ricardou, Jean, 185n. 4

Richards, I. A., 6
Ricoeur, Paul, 11, 14, 148, 182n. 12
Riffaterre, Michael, 29
rituals, 23
Robbe-Grillet, Alain, 133, 162; as experimental writer, 23, 132, 151; failure of, to discuss his narrative techniques, 12, 148, 172; and free indirect discourse, 148, 149–50; influence of, on author, 2–3, 16, 40, 58, 137, 139, 140, 153, 172–73; use of present tense by, 136, 137–39, 140, 141, 147, 148–50, 156, 157, 158, 167, 168, 172
Robinson Crusoe (Defoe), 55, 132
Roche, Maurice, 47, 127, 153
Roche, Violante, 127
romance, 7, 13, 23, 38, 130
Romantic poets, 27, 113
Ronsard, Pierre de, 27
A Room with a View (Forster), 143–44
Rousseau, Jean-Jacques, 27
RST. *See* Represented Speech and Thought
Rushdie, Salman, 54, 111, 114, 116
Russell, Bertrand, 146

Sage, Lorna, 123, 169–80, 184n. 5
Sarraute, Nathalie, 152, 182n. 10, 185n. 13; on dialogue in the novel, 131, 149, 183n. 4; on discussing technical aspects of writing, 6, 11–12; as experimental writer, 23, 132, 133; as influence on author, 13, 172; on Realism and Formalism, 40–41, 178; use of present tense by, 136, 137, 138, 140
Sartre, Jean-Paul, 146
The Satanic Verses (Rushdie), 54, 114
Saussure, Ferdinand de, 7
The Scarlet Letter (Hawthorne), 182n. 11
School of Slavonic Studies (London), 126
Schwitters, Kurt, 111
science: author's use of, 157; impersonal sentences like those in, 133, 134, 138–42, 149–50, 152–53, 167–68, 178; Structuralism as, of literature, 2, 23, 24, 37, 55. *See also* evolution; science fiction
science fiction, 110, 183n. 4; author's writing of, 16–18, 43; free indirect discourse in, 39, 148; tenses used in, 47, 153
Secker and Warburg (publishers), 8

self-reflexivity, 63–105
semantics, 81, 146–47
Semprún, Jorge, 111
Senhouse, Roger, 8
sentences: constative (declarative), 48–49, 59, 152; impersonal "scientific," 133, 134, 138–42, 149–50, 152–53, 167–68, 178; narrative (NS), 14, 36–37, 38, 130–55, 158–68, 178; speakerless, 14, 135–55, 156, 158–68, 177, 178; unspeakable, 147. *See also* grammar; language(s); narration; *specific tenses*
Le Seuil (publishers), 127
Seven Types of Ambiguity (Empson), 24
Shakespeare, William, 5, 6, 10, 13, 22, 27, 76
Shelley, Percy Bysshe, 6, 110, 111, 112
"showing one's stuff," 5, 6, 46, 106, 138, 167, 177
Simon, Claude, 139
simultaneity, 2, 166
Sir Gawain and the Green Knight, 181n. 6
Sisson, C. H., 42, 43
sjužet/fabula, 9, 133
Snow, C. P., 150
Socrates, 81
Solzhenitsyn, Aleksandr, 111, 113, 129
Sordello (Browning), 78
sous-conversation. *See* interior monologue
Soyinka, Wole, 116
Spark, Muriel, 40, 42, 47, 61, 111, 140
speakerlessness: of historical past tense, 134; narrative, 134–42, 145, 171, 175; of present tense, 135–55; in sentences, 14, 135–55, 156, 158–68, 177, 178
speech. *See* discourse; Speech Mode
Speech Mode, 2, 14, 130–58, 160–68, 177. *See also* dialogue; discourse
Sphinx, 93
Spielberg, Steven, 178
spt. *See* present tense: scientific
Le Square (Duras), 135, 136–37
Staël, Madame de, 111, 112
Stalin, Joseph, 118
statistical criticism, 15–16
Stein, Gertrude, 111, 113–14, 132
Steinbeck, John, 12
Steiner, George, 4, 182n. 9
Sterne, Laurence, 131, 135, 138, 153, 177
Stevens, Wallace, 96
Stories, Theories and Things (Brooke-

Rose), 5, 147, 178, 182n. 8, 183n. 1
Structuralism, 7, 11, 13, 24, 28, 142, 145; author's teaching of, 13, 25, 55, 173, 179; emphasis of, on narrative structure, 24–25; as extraction, 15; on narrating and speaking, 131, 134; as "science" of literature, 2, 23, 24, 37, 55. *See also* Poststructuralism
The Structure of Complex Words (Empson), 24
style (stylistics), 7, 29, 45, 135, 151, 183n. 1, 185n. 3
style indirect libre. *See* free indirect discourse
subjunctive, 48
Subscript (Brooke-Rose), 16, 19, 62, 154, 169–80
Such (Brooke-Rose), 3–4, 16, 17, 43, 54, 58, 182n. 15
Suleiman, Susan Rubin, 33–35, 109, 182n. 1, 184n. 1
summary. *See* content
Swift, Jonathan, 110, 118, 131, 135
Switzerland, 125, 128
The Sycamore Tree (Brooke-Rose), 182n. 16
synecdoche, 9, 11
Syntactic Structures (Chomsky), 10
syntax, 40, 146–47. *See also* grammar; language(s); sentences
S/Z (Barthes), 66, 175

Tarr (Lewis), 131–32
techne, 6, 51
technique, 6, 7. *See also* narration
tenses, 13, 38–39, 134, 143. *See also names of specific tenses*
La Tentation de Saint Antoine (Flaubert), 132, 137, 178
Textermination (Brooke-Rose), 18, 29, 43, 53–54, 111, 153, 155, 177
Thackeray, William M., 135
That Angel Burning at My Left Side (Peterkiewicz), 119
themes: of exile, 112–15. *See also* content
Thibault de Champagne, 111, 112
Things Fall Apart (Achebe), 116
third-person narration, 56, 57, 134, 135, 137, 148
Thomas, Dylan, 5, 8
Thoth, 78, 79

Thru (Brooke-Rose), 54, 109, 126, 128, 153, 166, 173; constraints in, 43, 127, 175; description of, 17, 59; self-reflexivity in, 63–105
Tigre Juan (Perez de Ayala), 166
time: narrator's position to, 47, 58, 59; reversal of, in *Dear Deceit*, 42. *See also* tenses
Time's Arrow (M. Amis), 42, 46
The Times Literary Supplement, 44, 63, 117–18, 122, 130n
"to be" verbs. *See* constraint(s): avoidance of "to be" as
Todorov, Tzvetan, 23, 24, 25, 68, 127, 131, 185n. 12
"to have" verbs, 3
tragedy, 10, 11, 13
Transworld Publishers, 159
travel, 44, 58, 156–57. *See also* exile
Treasure Island (Stevenson), 110
Trevelyan, Raleigh, 128
triangles, 67, 78, 102–3, 183n. 3
Tristia (Ovid), 112
Trollope, Anthony, 135
Tropics of Discourse (White), 14
Troylus and Criseyde (Chaucer), 8
two-voiced theory (of free indirect discourse), 142, 144, 145–50, 183n. 2, 185n. 12
typography: in *House of Leaves*, 160, 161–68; of *Thru*, 17, 43, 55, 63–105, 127, 183n. 1, 184n. 3
Tzara, Tristan, 111

Ulysses (Joyce), 131, 132, 141, 149–50
The Unbearable Lightness of Being (Kundera), 114
Understanding Fiction (Brooks and Warren), 23
Under Western Eyes (Conrad), 115
The Unicorn (Murdoch), 131
unity (organic), 23, 26
University of East Anglia, 64
University of St. Andrews, 118, 122
University of Vincennes (Paris VIII), 4, 29, 122, 123, 126, 182n. 11
unspeakable sentences, 147
Unspeakable Sentences (Banfield), 145–47
Utterly Other Discourse: The Texts of Christine Brooke-Rose (Friedman and Martin), 183n. 3

"The Vanishing Author" (Brooke-Rose), 58
Verbivore (Brooke-Rose), 17, 18, 43, 54
vernacular language, 116, 157–58
Veronica (saint), 88
A Very Private Life (Frayn), 47
La Vie, mode d'emploi (Perec), 46
viewpoint(s): confusion of, with narrative instance, 25; and evaluation, 145, 146; in *Moby-Dick*, 37–38; multiple, 153; outside, 135; timing of shifting of, 72
Vincennes, University of. *See* University of Vincennes
Virgil, 164
Voltaire, 111, 112
Voyage au bout de le nuit (Céline), 133, 136
Le Voyageur (Robbe-Grillet), 12
Le Voyeur (Robbe-Grillet), 137

Warren, Robert Penn, 23
The Waste Land (Eliot), 3
Waugh, Evelyn, 131
Wharton, Edith, 111, 114
What Are Masterpieces? (Stein), 113–14
What Maisie Knew (James), 149

"When to the sessions of sweet silent thought" (Shakespeare), 27
White, Hayden, 14, 182n. 12
Wilde, Oscar, 55, 111
Wimsatt, W. K., 29
women: experimental writing by, 4–5, 10, 41, 156; selflessless of, 176–77. *See also* gender; *names of specific women*
Woolf, Virginia, 57, 131, 135, 137, 143, 147, 148, 156
words. *See* acrostics; language(s); "look at me" tricks'; metaphors; puns; typography
Woytyła, Karol (Pope John-Paul II), 120

xenophobia, 124–25, 128
Xorandor (Brooke-Rose), 17–18, 31, 43, 54, 153

Yale school of Deconstruction, 26–27
Yeats, William Butler, 27, 111, 118, 184n. 3
Zauberberg (Mann), 148
A ZBC of Ezra Pound (Brooke-Rose), 183n. 1
Zweig, Stefan, 111

THE THEORY AND INTERPRETATION OF NARRATIVE SERIES

James Phelan and Peter J. Rabinowitz, Editors

Because the series editors believe that the most significant work in narrative studies today contributes both to our knowledge of specific narratives and to our understanding of narrative in general, studies in the series typically offer interpretations of individual narratives and address significant theoretical issues underlying those interpretations. The series does not privilege any one critical perspective but is open to work from any strong theoretical position.

- *Misreading Jane Eyre: A Postformalist Paradigm*
  JEROME BEATY

- *Matters of Fact: Reading Nonfiction over the Edge*
  DANIEL W. LEHMAN

- *Breaking the Frame: Metalepsis and the Construction of the Subject*
  DEBRA MALINA

- *Framing Anna Karenina: Tolstoy, the Woman Question, and the Victorian Novel*
  AMY MANDELKER

- *Narrative as Rhetoric: Technique, Audiences, Ethics, Ideology*
  JAMES PHELAN

- *Understanding Narrative*
  Edited by JAMES PHELAN AND PETER J. RABINOWITZ

- *Before Reading: Narrative Conventions and the Politics of Interpretation*
  PETER J. RABINOWITZ

- *Narrative Dynamics: Essays on Time, Plot, Closure, and Frames*
  Edited by BRIAN E. RICHARDSON

- *The Progress of Romance: Literary Historiography and the Gothic Novel*
  DAVID H. RICHTER

- *A Glance beyond Doubt: Narration, Representation, Subjectivity*
  SHLOMITH RIMMON-KENAN

- *Psychological Politics of the American Dream: The Commodification of Subjectivity in Twentieth-Century American Literature*
  LOIS TYSON

- *Ordinary Pleasures: Couples, Conversation, and Comedy*
  KAY YOUNG